REALIZING
RATIONAL
EXUBERANCE
An Appreciation of the Mundell-Huang Da Lectures

REALIZING
RATIONAL
EXUBERANCE
An Appreciation of the Mundell-Huang Da Lectures

**China Financial Policy
Research Center**

World Scientific

NEW JERSEY · LONDON · SINGAPORE · BEIJING · SHANGHAI · HONG KONG · TAIPEI · CHENNAI

Published by

World Scientific Publishing Co. Pte. Ltd.

5 Toh Tuck Link, Singapore 596224

USA office: 27 Warren Street, Suite 401-402, Hackensack, NJ 07601

UK office: 57 Shelton Street, Covent Garden, London WC2H 9HE

Library of Congress Cataloging-in-Publication Data
Realizing rational exuberance : an appreciation of the Mundell-Huang Da lectures / edited by China
Financial Policy Research Center, Renmin University of China.
   p. cm.
   Includes bibliographical references and index.
   ISBN 978-9814295321
   1. Economics. 2. Economics--China. I. Zhongguo cai zheng jin rong zheng ce yan jiu zhong xin.
   HB171.R3795 2013
   330--dc23

                                                      2012031331

British Library Cataloguing-in-Publication Data
A catalogue record for this book is available from the British Library.

In-house Editor: Alisha Nguyen

Typeset by Stallion Press
Email: enquiries@stallionpress.com

Printed in Singapore.

I am delighted to come back to the Renmin University and participate in the opening ceremony of *Mundell–Huang Da Lectures on Economics*. It is a great honor for me that the sponsor China Financial Policy Research Center named the series of academic lectures after me and Professor Huang Da. I have always paid close attention to China's situation and China's higher education. Today I also had an in-depth discussion with the chancellor Ji Baocheng on cooperation in education and I hope that we could make some achievements in a few years.

A significant event in the last century is the integration of China into the world economic system. People shall share a common concept and make joint efforts to link Chinese economy with world economy. China's entry to the WTO is of great significance to both China and the whole world, it is also a favorable condition for China to accelerate its economic growth. I believe that China can have quick economic development after its entry to the WTO.

Robert A. Mundell

The current development of China and the world all demands for the enhancement of talents cultivation. Professor Mundell mentioned that the advantage of China lies in talents. Without doubt, we should have quality requirements for talents, what we need are talents with high qualities. Concerning the current development situation of China, I feel that the talents we need most are able to freely move and roam between the two cultural platforms of the East and the West, including our economic scholars.

Professor Mundell gave lessons at the Ford Foundation training program of the Renmin University of China in 1996. Since then, he believed that he should do something for the construction of economics and cultivation of talents in China and he has worked hard toward this objective. I hope that this lecture can help us grasp some basic theories and frontier issues, catch up with the situation and make our contribution to the development of China and the world.

Huang Da

An Open Speech

Ji Baocheng

President of Renmin University of China

Honorable guests, dear friends,

First of all, I would like to congratulate China Financial Policy Research Center of Renmin University on the successful launch of Mundell–Huangda Lectures! Meanwhile, please allow me to extend a warm welcome to Professor Mundell on behalf of my university.

As the "father of Euro," Professor Mundell has made epoch-making achievements in the theories of optimum currency areas and coordination of macroeconomic policies in an open economy. For these accomplishments, he won the Nobel Prize for economics in 1999. On the other hand, Professor Huang, a famous expert in economics and finance in China, has also made pioneering contributions to the theoretical study of commodity price, macro-control and money supply, comprehensive balance of macroeconomy and capital markets. Thus, I believe that the lectures that are named after the two professors and run by China Financial Policy Research Center must be one of the world's leading academic lectures with a high-level starting point and superior quality.

Currently, Renmin University is striving to become a world-class university with humanities and social sciences as its key disciplines. Communication and cooperation will help the university become an integral part of the international academic community. Recent years have witnessed the school's efforts to communicate and cooperate with overseas high education institutions, research institutions as well as academic organizations. Mundell–Huangda Lectures will invite renowned foreign economists to deliver speeches in this university, which will certainly enhance the school's academic level, expand its academic influence at home and abroad, promote its communication with other countries, let the famous foreign scholars know us better and facilitate the long-term development of subjects such as finance and cameralistics.

From the very beginning of its establishment, China Financial Policy Research Center of Renmin University has been aiming at becoming a base for international academic communication that is internationally influential. This center has hosted several significant international academic exchanges like China International Finance Forum, High-Level Forum on the Forefront of Modern Economics, etc. With the globalization of the world economy and China's entrance into WTO, China will participate in the world economy on a larger scale, a broader field and a higher level; and this requires that our economic study must be in line with the international norms. Mundell–Huangda Lectures are the center's new attempt in academic communication. Lectures of the top economists will bring in the latest economic research findings for Renmin University and the Chinese academic sector. This will not only promote the development of China's economic study, but also further enhance the international fame of the center.

Finally, I earnestly hope that Mundell–Huangda Lectures would become an important brand in economics and finance for Renmin University, and an academic activity that can sketch the frontline of economics, guide policy making and exercise importance influence at home and abroad.

A Speech for the Launch Ceremony of "Mundell–Huang Da Lectures"

Robert A. Mundell

I feel very glad to come back to Renmin University, and to take part in the launching ceremony. It is a great honor that the lecture series organized by China Financial Policy Research Center would be named after Professor Huang and me. I have always been caring about China and its higher education. Even today I have just discussed the matter of educational cooperation with President Ji and we hope that we could really do something in a few years.

China's entrance into WTO is a hallmark for the 20th century and the growth of China's economy is a miracle for the world. Since its opening up to the outside world in 1978, capital and resources began to flow into China, which had played a significant role in boosting Chinese economy. Thanks to the opening up policy, many areas have made rapid and remarkable achievements, especially Beijing and Shanghai.

The US economy showed signs of slackening even before 9-11. After quite a long time of rapid growth, the US economy suffered a tardy increase. Because of 9-11, our economy will undergo a recession for a certain period in the future and even negative growth. Besides, undoubtedly, 9-11 makes the situation worse. I estimate that the recession will touch its bottom in one or two years. However, I am not pessimistic about the future of the US economy. After coming to its knees, the economy will recover slowly.

The slowdown of the world economy also gives China great pressure and urges this country to speed up its economic restructuring. I know that in 1978, the state-owned enterprises made as much as 80% of contribution to the country's economic growth while the private sector accounted for only 20%. But through twenty years of reform, the portion of state-owned enterprises reduces to 30% whereas the share of the private sector goes up to 70%. Meanwhile, one should see that the economic recession also provides China with an opportunity: on one hand, it forces China to develop itself hard, especially to nurture private economy by policy support; on the other hand, 9-11 has triggered a flow of international capital toward China for security's sake, which will also promote Chinese economy.

Now let's come back to the issue of education I mentioned at the beginning of my speech. Human resource is China's greatest wealth, so focus should be devoted on human resource development so as to improve economic efficiency. Education is surely an important facet in the exploitation of human capital. China's large population and economic volume has constructed a good platform for economic development and efficient division of labor. We should all have the common notion to integrate the economy of China, the country with the world's largest population, into the global trend.

China's entrance into WTO is significant not only for this particular country, but also for the whole world, and this event will serve a more rapid economic development for China.

A Speech for the Launch Ceremony of "Mundell–Huang Da Lectures"

Huang Da

The current development of the world and China requires that we intensify our effort in producing talented people. As Professor Mundell put it, human resource is China's advantage. Of course, this advantage does not only lie in quantity; China surely has an unparalleled population. Talented people must have certain quality and what we need is highly qualified talents. In view of China's present situation, we feel that what we need most is talents who can freely range on and cross between the culture platforms of both the East and the West, economists included.

Do we have such kind of people already? In early or mid 1980s, a group of people went to study abroad, the excellent part of whom have ridden into Western economists' clubs. Yet there are still some people who came back and served their motherland in various means. In recent years, our self-produced talented people also went abroad to make investigation or pursue further education. They broadened their horizon and mastered the dynamics of the world's academic study. One could say that in this way, we have produced a number of talents who can freely cross between the barriers of the East and the West, but the problem is that such talents are scarce in quantity. People studying abroad may be highly specialized in Western economics and finance, but they do not know much about the situation xii Realizing Rational Exuberance: An Appreciation

of China, and it takes time for them to tap into the economic pulse of their motherland. Similarly, people studying in China often fail to grasp the essence of Western theories, for the time they stay abroad is quite short. Therefore, the ideal talents are still in need and we still have a long way to go.

There are various means to produce such talents and different people have different proposals, for example, President Ji and Professor Mundell are thinking of educational cooperation. Now that I am just a professor and the honorable director of China Financial Policy Research Center, my mind is purely stuffed with teaching. I think it is important that China Financial Policy Research Center should do something for information exchange of cutting-edge topics in economics. The domestic academic sector often fails to catch up with the important trends abroad. We need to be timely informed of what questions have emerged on the economic frontline and where the focus of attention is. As the research base of Chinese financial and cameralistic policy, this center ought to shoulder this task and this is why, upon discussion, the professors here proposed to organize such lectures. The lectures will be conducted by foreign experts who have a good mastery of the foremost development in a certain economic field. Meanwhile, considering that the lectures may lack attraction if they are just named after Chinese scholars, we think of inviting a foreign celebrity and name the lectures also after him. Unders such consideration, we turned to Professor Mundell who has been keeping close touch with us and is enthusiastic for this cause. Professor Mundell once taught in the Ford Fund training program of Renmin University in 1996 and since then, he has been working for the construction of China's economics. This time, we had Professor Mundell here and the lectures are named after Professor Mundell and me. So far I have been introducing our overall design for the lectures. I hope these lectures would help us grasp the basic theories and latest development of economics and keep up with the newest trend, and make contributions to the development of the world and China.

Contents

Chapter 1

Globalization and the RMB Exchange Rate

Robert A. Mundell

Biography

Since 1974, **Robert A. Mundell** (born 1932) has been Professor of Economics at Columbia University, New York. He has been an adviser to a number of international agencies and organizations including the United Nations, the IMF, the World Bank, the European Commission, and several governments in Latin America and Europe, the Federal Reserve Board, the US Treasury and the Government of Canada.

In 1970, he was a consultant to the Monetary Committee of the European Economic Commission, and in 1972–1973 a member of its study group on Economic and Monetary Union in Europe. He was a member of the Bellagio–Princeton Study Group on International Monetary Reform from 1964 to 1978, and Chairman of the Santa Colomba Conferences on International Monetary Reform between 1971 and 1987.

The author of numerous works and articles on economic theory of international economics, he prepared one of the first plans for a common currency in Europe and is known as the father of the theory of optimum currency areas. He received the Nobel Memorial Prize in Economic Science in 1999.

He formulated what became a standard international macroeconomics model, was a pioneer of the theory of the monetary and fiscal policy mix, the theory of inflation and interest, the monetary approach to the balance of payments, and the co-founder of supply-side economics. He has also written extensively on the history of the international monetary system and played a significant role in the founding of the euro. He has also written extensively on the "transition" economies and in 1997 co-founded the Zagreb Journal of Economics.

Speech

Thank you very much. It's always a great pleasure for me to be here at Renmin University and to receive enlightenment on this occasion of the opening of these lecture series. I remembered the very founding of my association in Spring 1995 when I was here and spent a wonderful time and made many new friends. And I have been able to come back to this place and I think of it having a lot of old friends and a kind of home in China.

I am going to talk on the subject of "Globalization and the RMB Exchange Rate." This thing, this accurate name, RMB has become world famous if China had a plan to establish a brand on its currency and it has done it in the most spectacular way possible over the past years. Because every conference I have been in act in European, in the US and of course in Asia, all want to hear about the RMB, the famous RMB, which a year ago, most people outside of the Asia did not know anything about. So it has established a brand now. It's world famous. I will talk about a few things connected with globalization and changes in the world economy, and so on the exchange rates in China, Asian money and things like that.

The key trend I want to touch on is globalization. First of all, that's one item in the subject mattered I have on. The globalization comes about whenever becomes possible, because trade is the natural inclination of mankind. Man is a trading animal, and trades whatever they can and whenever they gain from trade, and keeps on, and stops only when there are barriers.

Imposed by China's transportation costs, communication costs, migration costs, or political boundaries that forbid trade between areas and blocks, so whenever there is a breakout that breaks down these blocks, there is an expansion of movement to globalization.

Of course, there is a kind of globalization in the last part of 19th century before World War I and then World War I established a whole period of great blocks and so did World War II. We had a long period after the wars in Europe of 1914–1945. After that, there was the Cold War that separates the world into the First World, the Second World, and the Third World and that inhibited globalization. So the big thrust for globalization today results from the breakdown, the end of the Cold War around 1990. And since then we have been in the phase of globalization, which is being combined very much with something else that is new. There was actually a positive side of the Cold War, the Internet and the information technology revolution along with computers technology that is made greatly shorten the amount of time it takes to move anywhere; time it takes for ideas to travel and communication. The IT revolution is going on, the biggest explosion, the tremendous explosion in the last part of 1990s, 1995 to 2000; you had what people were calling the new economy with a growth rate doubled in the US. In a long time, the growth rate in the US was 2.5%, in the last 5 years, 1995 to 2000, it doubled to 5%. People thought that it was going to grow on forever. But what it did that doubling of the growth rate enormously so much with the normal expansion of the wage growth, led to tremendous explosion of profits and expected profits. That is what is called the big increase in the capital values and the stock markets. Enormous capital values increased in the 1990s and went up too high and the investment in these areas went far too much over capacity and overshooting in the areas, and I think it has came down with the collapse and we will have the global slowdown which were now. But the IT revolution is going on persistently all through this slow down of productivity, gains and cost reduction has been made in every aspect of economic life in firms, households, institutions, and government. Then we come out of the global slowdown and with a higher level of productivity than we were into it.

And we are going to continue the experience. I mentioned that the US local motives that people used to call it for the world economy. I mentioned the US because the US economy accounts for 23% of the world economy. And what happens to the US affects the rest of the world in a big way. People used to say that when the US caught a cold, the rest of the world got pneumonia. That is an extreme form. But the fact is that over the last 20 years, the US economy has been performing very well exceptionally in temporal years. We had 20 years since 1982 of expanding growth. And first in 1980s, the secret of that success was the supply-side revolution, the enormous tax reductions, in the US the revolution fueled up the US economy, made it the most efficient in the world. Capital imports fed the growing expansion, and then the low tax rate, particularly the income tax was cut from 70% to 28% during the Reagan period. It was easy and profitable to set up new firms, and that's what created the Silicon Valley, building on the computer revolution and the development of information technology and the Internet. So the second decade of 1990s, just says, the start of 1990s, was the Reagan's tax cuts and supply-side revolution, in the 1990s, it was the IT revolution. Back to back decades very powerful made the US pull the rest of the world. In this way, how did they pull it, well, they pull it partly to the huge US current account deficit, which make the rest of the world could lend to the US all buy dollars and achieve surpluses. The rest of the world now has a 500-billion-dollar surplus against the US, which can take out achieves partly by buying capital assets in the US or dollars simply. Now with its slow down, the question is that if the local motives is not going to work and if it does not work as well, what is going to be pulling ahead the world economy, what else is going to need, what other countries are going to pitch in and take up the slack here. That is a big issue.

The first issue of the rise of China, you have heard something about that country, is the advent of the Euro. The Euro was an enormous revolution because never before in history had 12 countries including 3 or 4 very big and very important countries, formal world powers, great world powers, like France, Germany and Italy, never before had a group of countries voluntarily scraped the national currencies and exchange them for a super currency called middle currency and they did this had created demonstration effect. While the rest of the world was having flexible exchange rate pushed on them, Europe is going to the opposite direction to not just fixed exchange rate, which is the beginning process, but actual elimination of exchange rates, which is a part of the oaths of fixed exchange rate and form a single currency.

Then the next thing I mention is the OCA islands of stability. What is OCA? OCA is the Optimum Currency Area that recently started. Because the Euro Area has created demonstration effect to the rest of the world, the rest of the world is now going to say, if big countries like France and Germany, big economies like France and Germany, Germany is the third largest economy in the world, can scraped their own currency for a bigger currency, what about our smaller countries who are worth shaped. Do not say any even bigger regional groups as we said before, that everywhere and every continent sets new currency rearrangements in the world.

Look at the world economy in the 1970s when the world had fixed exchange rates system. It is based on anchor largely on the US dollar, because of the importance of the US in the world system and the US economy. But when the dollar restricted to gold, the price of gold had been set in 1934 as 35 dollars an ounce. 35 years later, in 1970s, all prices of everything else had gone up; they doubled or tripled by 1970. But the price of gold stayed constant. What do you think happened? When one price is fixed, suppressed the other prices, there is an excess demand for it. everybody want gold because it is undervalued, then the European countries took gold out and the US had lost a lot of gold. in 1971 it said enough is enough, stopped dollars for gold. And the gold became inconvertible, and the world broke up into flexible exchange rate. Never got back to it. There was no agreement to go under flexible exchange rate, there was just the fact that there was no mechanism for doing it. When the dollar was no longer convertible into gold, I do not want to go into details why that is, but when the US took its currency off gold, no other countries were using gold. The other countries took their currencies off to dollar and floated them. There was no way you can go back it under the way the system was arranged. So they tried to find a way, a formula for 4 years. 60 officials from the group of committee of 20, an instrument of the leading countries, each with 3 represented them. So they made 60 people worked solemnly for 4 years trying to find a formula to get back to the fixed exchange rate system. You see that they want to do is the one thing that is obvious to anybody with a first-year course of economics, gold, the excess demand for gold because the price has been surprised raised the price of gold in annual restore system. But the US did not want to do it for political reasons. A lot of them were connected with the fact that the South Africa has big resources of gold and who had a system of government that nobody liked. The second biggest producer of gold was the Soviet Union, the enemy in the Cold War. And third, the US had been telling all its partners hanging on the gold that hold on to the dollars, do not exchange the dollars to gold, which might break up the system. "We are not gonna change the price of gold," they had been saying that. They got trapped by that message untill the solution did not work. They tried to create a special drawing rights. They once created the (SDR) special drawing rights in 1968 to try to save the system. But that got to have a gold guarantee to go. That scraped and did not work out itself, to make the thing move into flexible exchange rate. That became the second momentum to IMF. The first momentum is to create the SDR which is supposed to be a reverse currency in the 1970s that really failed. The second momentum was to admit the possibility of flexible exchange rate as the new system. I make that point because a lot of people do not understand that the movement to flexible exchange rate was not a planned movement of authorities, but just the opposite, the desperation movement because they could not find the formula for getting back to the international monetary system of fixed change rate. There was no love for flexible exchange rate in any countries. There were only a few academics that had been favored. But now, the whole tide has changed and the general view of the IMF has been centered of flexible exchange rate and pushed the flexible exchange rate with the same enthusiasm that it ridiculed the flexible exchange rate 1950s to 1960s. You only have to read their annul report to show the truth of that saying. Well, look at currency areas when the world broke up into separate currency areas. There are about 200 countries in the world which means nearly 200 currencies in the world all floating against one another. Imagine how ridiculous it would be if you had 200 currencies independently floating against one another. What chaos would it be? What would you make decided pricing who could do the calculation, how many exchange rate would there be? Totally taking into account cross exchange rate, the number of exchange rate if n is the number of currencies in the world, then the number of exchange rate is $\frac{1}{2} \times n \times (n - 1)$ So if n is 200, then the number of cross exchange rate is 19,900. What chaos that would be? Well, fortunately, the movement to flexible exchange rate beaking it up did not lead to that chaos. Because, automatically, the currency that already been known to be the most important currency is dollar, took over as *de facto* a global currency. And that meant there was no chaos in the system so coherent because that everybody's most important exchange rate, with very few exceptions, was the dollar exchange rate. So here is what we have now with the exchange rate, the world we look at now does not have 200 countries-currency areas with all the same size. This system is a kind of Oligopoly, competition among the few. And the circle there represents monetary mass. And that amount of proportion to GDP. So the monetary mass of the US, the GDP of the US is about 11 trillion dollars. Of the Euro Area, is about 8 trillion. The Japanese Yen area is about 4.5–5 trillion. The Britain itself is about 1.5 trillion and the China is about 1.3–1.4 trillion. So in China it is more rapidly growing. So if we look at the exchange rate, we see inside each of these zones, the dollar zone, the euro zone, the yen zone, price stability. These are zones of price stability. There is no inflation in the dollar zone, the euro zone, or the yen area. The yen area is especially having a bit of deflation. There is no inflation, in China or in Britain or any of these big currency areas. But between these areas, there is anomalous instability. That is a great puzzle and also a great problem of the exchange rate, dysfunctional exchange rate instability.

Just look at the exchange rate instability that caused the so-called Asian Crisis. It was the fluctuations with dollar/yen exchange rate. In

April 1995, the dollar had bottomed against the yen, 78 yen/dollar was the bottom in April 1995. At that time, I read some articles and some Chinese economists suggested: "We should give up using the dollar and holding the dollar as our reserves, we should hold the yen." I thought that was a very good idea. But do not do it when the yen is at its high price, the highest price possible and the dollar was at the lowest price. So 3 years later in June 1998, the dollar was 158 yen. From 78 yen to 158 yen, almost a doubling of the dollar price against the yen, big sweeping fall in the value of the yen against the dollar which was the basic cause of the Asian Crisis. With its low exchange rate, it choked off FDI from Japan into countries like Taiwan, Malaysia and Indonesia and Korea and that would cause the shock of the Asian Crisis. Overall, look at the dollar/yen exchange rate, Japan itself suffered by this instability, because in 1985, the dollar was 250 yen then in September 1985 at the time the Plaza Accord took place it went down to 239 yen. But from 239 yen in September 1985 to April 1995, ten years later, the dollar dropped to 78 yen. That was the yen tripled in value against dollar in that period. You take any currency in the world, and triple its value against the other currencies, the mainstream as the US of the world economy which the dollar was and what is going to happen. Balance sheets of all major firms are going to crumple; losses are going to be made; and banking system is going to be settled with non-performing loans. That is the cause and reason that the banking system, maybe 40% of GDP in non-performing loans. This is a tragic because of an unstable exchange rate. If you want to see how unrealistic that was, the dollar/yen exchange rate, the yen/dollar exchange rate was absolutely fixed from 1948 until 1970. It was fixed for 32 years from 1948 to 1970 at 360 and that was the great heyday of Japanese economic growth from 1955 to 1970, one 16-years of 9% growth. So this is a Japan's great economic success during the period of the fixed exchange rate. But it handled its exchange rate policy not entirely Japan's fault because Japan was pushed into this policy by the US. The new phrase came into being — "Japan-bashing." "Japan-bashing" was the basic policy of the US in the 1980s. It was derived by some people and praised by others. Whatever the case was, it made great problem.

What it means is that we have any way to save the exchange rate. I could talk the same thing about the instability of the dollar/mark exchange rate. In 1975, the mark being the third most important currency in the world before the euro came into being, before it was replaced by the euro. In 1975, the dollar was 3.5 Deutsche mark (DEM). 5 years later, the dollar had dropped in half to 1.7DEM. Five years later, the dollar doubled again, back to 3.45DEM. 7 years later, in 1992, the dollar dropped to all time low of 1.34DEM. And then till the end of the decade with this strong dollar, the dollar went up to something like 2.2DEM. And now there is no DEM anymore, but dollar/euro rate has been very unstable. So the unstable exchange rate among the most important currencies in the world is a major source of distress in the world economy and it is a major problem for the world and a major threat to global prosperity. I think we have to look how this system evolving, it has a logic of the tones, international monetary system evolves in ways that are partly predictable. We can predict some, and look at some scenarios. Look, moving ahead 2020, China has become much bigger, and Europe has got bigger because they are adding the three Britain, Denmark and Sweden. They are probably going to join in 3 or 4 years and I would make that prediction and the accessing countries are going to come into it. This maybe in 5 years they will come into the Euro Zone. Poland is really thinking of going into the Euro Zone in 2007. And with two more accessing countries at least maybe 5 more accessing countries will be entering the Euro Zone. So this is going to be a big block.

China's achievement since 1978, I talked about the rise of China, is important. The 25-years of 9% growth at all time record, export from less than 1% to 5% of world export, stable price level and exchange rate over the past 7 years, anyway, since about 1995, foreign direct investment over 60 billion, more than half of the FDI in the world economy as a whole. Strong trade surplus, foreign exchange reserve over 350 billion, soaring manufacture capacity, the indexes of GDP and exports, 8.5 times GDP expansion, 33.4 times export expansion in this period. Problems for China, I will just list some as I want to go to them now, the non-performing loans in the banking system, lost-making state-owned enterprises, they need to improve the education system. In China, there are 680,000 schools but there are 7 million teachers. e-learning will be the natural thing that increase that activity and China would lead forward ahead of its education system if it introduces and makes investment in e-learning in the public schools. With great poverty in the interior and growing unemployment, 200 to 300 million roll under employment. Partly is a cause of the poverty but not only that corruption, inefficiency of local administrations, inconvertible RMB and the famous again and international pressure on the RMB.

Several arguments were made about why China should change. One argument was made by Japan that China was exporting deflation. Japanese Minister of Finance made that argument at the Paris Summit last February that stated the whole processes are deflation. But deflation is a non-monetary phenomenon. Imports from China count for only 1% of Japan's GDP. China's price level has been stable and Japan has a floating exchange rate. Any country with a floating exchange rate using inflation targeting that set the term of inflation does not import inflation from abroad. A country with a fixed exchange rate is a country that can import inflation or export inflation. But under a floating exchange rate, seldom is there the connection between inflation. Any country in the world can have hyperinflation with floating exchange rate. Any many of them do. So countries like Japan with flexible exchange rate determine their own price level by their monetary policy.

China is not the fault of inflation in Japan. And it could not a theory be exporting deflation to fellow members of the same currency area? But is China exporting deflation to the US? No. Actually, in the late 1990s, the US was exporting deflation to China and to all other countries around the world that kept their currencies fixed to dollar. China had in 98', 99', 00' and 01', a little bit, very slight deflation but so did Panama, which chooses the dollar. So did the Gulf countries like Saudi Arabia, which were fixed to the dollar. So it is a universal phenomenon of countries fixed to the dollar that the US if anything is exporting deflation. You could tie that up with the IT revolution. Because the IT revolution increased greatly the productivity of the US industries that were traded goods or internationally goods industries. Productivity in export/import industry soared over that period. Economic theorists know that when a country has a very rapid growth in its international goods industries, it has to experience a change in increase and improvement in its real exchange rate. What that means is that the prices of international goods have to fall relatively to the price of its domestic goods. And the way that it would occur with a fixed exchange rate would be, 5% net improvement every year needed in the real exchange rate. Then the US price level went up, domestic goods prices went up by 5% while trade goods price stayed constant. That would do it and that would not cause any problems. But the US price level went up by 79.2%. So the rest of the difference has to be taken out in the appreciation of the dollar, which imposes deflation on those countries that I mentioned. So it all fits the theory what was happening. Anyway, China is not exporting deflation to Japan or to the world.

But it does not mean that Japan and the other countries that have been complaining includes of course the US do not have a problem. The problem with China is the competitive pressure. This has a great impact on the rivals in terms of trade, of countries that are producing the same products as China is. If China's productivity in exporting products goes up, a lot of this inevitably is going to replace to some exchange that export of countries that produce the same products. And that is the process that often happens in the industry world. More efficient economies replace those that are not so efficient as it were before. And that even includes the countries that have in general much higher levels of productivity. It does not mean their industries are going to be replaced, but it means they are not going to expand at the same rate and that may have some impact on job creation.

So the recent basic problem and there is a model that fits into the problem. If any of you buy the volumes of my books, the 6 volumes of my book. The first volume of it, the first three chapters discusses the classical model of international trade. And it works beautifully to explain the effects of output expansion in the export industry in one country and how that affects the wealth of the rest in the world. Normally in the trade models we think that growth in one country exchanges the benefits to the rest of the world as well as to itself.

Because normal growth in the export industry in one country will result in falling in price level of the export products and will improve the terms of trade. And that will mean a gift to the rest to the world. And that is certainly true what China has been doing. China's export productivity changes have lowered the price and improved the terms of trade of the rest of the world. But there is a group of countries and there is we say individual country that produces those same goods as China is exporting, do not get any improvement. Their terms of trade go down and they do not know anything to compensate for that. If you compare the advantage, you are going to be a buyer of China's products. You are going to gain a lot from China's increasing importance in the world economy. But if you are a seller of products that China is now exporting a lot, you are going to be a loser in this game. There are a few countries that will be losers in this. So they have to wake up and do something else. I say in Chapters 1, 2 and 3 of the first volume you may have the model explaining all that.

Let's look at those facts now about US's and China's trade balances. As I put down in 1987's for comparison with something 15 years ago. Looking at the recent figures you see that the surpluses of China have been central but very consistent, very constant of this period. Trade surpluses are what we are talking about but not services. And the US has been increasingly in the debtor position which is deficit position. Now we look further, the first slide gives imports. The basic conclusion of the table is that China is the only country during the global slowdown to increase its import substantially. China's import in the past 2 years, among 2002, increased by more than all the G7 countries put together, and more than the rest of the world put together. So look at the tables of the US, the import went down a little bit but so low in the year 2000. Of those 2 years, US's import went down 57 billion, Japan's went down 43 billion, Taiwan's went down 29 billion, the non-China world — all those countries except China put together minus 84 billion, but China's went up by plus 70 billion. So China has made a big addition to holding the line and preventing the down term from becoming worse than it would have been. Substantial appreciation would be in RMB that people are talking about knowing the dollar goes down to something like 5, but

40% change, a very big change that would delay convertibility. This is the first time in international history that a country with an inconvertible currency has been asked to appreciate it. Previously, IMF, for 50 years has been preaching to countries with inconvertible currencies to devalue and get rid of the exchange rate control you do not really need. Now it is a turn around because time has come to China that an inconvertible currency on capital account. And this would just put up for long, long time and the experiment is convertibility. It would quickly aggregate deflation in China. When China devaluated in 1994, the dollar was raised from 5.5RMB to 8.28RMB. With that change, increase in the price of dollar, the devaluation created a big price bite. And in 1994 and 1995 together, the price level in China rose in those two years by 41%. And that was unusual and that indicated that the devaluation was either excessive or was even an unnecessary at that time. But anyway, whatever the case, the devaluation was, in terms of competitive, was completely eliminated by the increase in the price level that followed immediately the after. But if China appreciates it now, the reverse process will be devastating because with deflation in the price of international goods, it will cause devastating deflation in the rural sectors and in farms. Farm prices will drop like a stone and commodity prices will drop and it would be a devastating experience for China. The poorest part of China is the interior. It would worsen the budget deficit and aggregate the burden of non-performing loans. The non-performing loans can be solved and is easily manageable. All China need to do is to establish good credit rating system and just do not allow commercial banks to lend money to state-owned enterprises that have bad credit ratings. Of course fire the heads of banks if they give loans to state-owned enterprises with bad credit ratings. You have to allow credit rating system to get really started in order to act as a goal keeper. And the credit rating system should be allowed to be independent of the government. That would be a step to solve your problem. And then to get the non-performing loans out of the books of the banks that have forbidden the bank from increasing anymore, and you could have an increase in treasury debt will take over those loans and that treasury debt is under 8% of GDP now and it would not do any harm to increase that to 30%. And that would probably cover enough of the non-performing loans. Anyway, it would increase losses of the SOEs and inefficient companies. Appreciation is not bad. You might end up getting that appreciation will make it harder for exporters to compete, but the most efficient exporters would stay in business and even might be a little bit in some sense better off, because the inefficient exporters who get into this of low exchange rate would not be knocked out of the market and made them a more monopolize position. But by and large this would be a devastating bad thing. Lead to a weak RMB and subsequent depreciation, and will disenable lots of trades in Southeast Asia.

So should China appreciate? The answer is no. It is not going to solve. It will be very harmful to China and it will be harmful to Southeast Asia. It will not solve the problem with the US's current account, which is probably a systemic problem rising from the role of the dollar in the world economy. As you all know, the US had current account deficit and trade deficit since 1975 and it got bigger in 1980s and the US was still a net creditor. And now in 1990s, the US has become a net debtor. 1989 was the turning point. From World War I, 1915 to 1989, the US was a net creditor in the world economy. From 1915 to 1970, the US had trade surplus. Now for the past 30 years, trade deficits. This is the problem of the US, is not a problem that China can solve. Even if China did everything, it forgot itself, whatever it was going to do, it would not solve the basic problem of the US, which was raised from the defective among our international monetary system.

Well, should float? I said devaluation would be a bad idea. First of all, nobody should ever suggest a country to float; to have they got a fixed exchange rate float. Because the fixed exchange rate is a monetary rule, it gives the country an anchor for monitoring stability. Since the past several years, China has been getting an inflation rate more or less comparable to that of the US within 2 or 3% of that in the US. If China follows automatic monetary policy as it is doing today, this year for the first time, it is really following almost an automatic monetary policy when it is buying foreign exchange reserves as long as that be monitored in the increased money base in China. And that means the expansion in credit. But the relevant question is not whether a country should flex or fix its exchange rate that I call a "oxymoron." It is that whether a country should have one monetary rule or different kinds of monetary rule or the "three monetary rules" that people talk about. We could have gold pricing or others but these are the ones people talk about. The exchange rate targeting, which is actually China has been doing, plays successfully; the inflation targeting, which the US does, which the European Union does and Britain does. And money supply targeting does not work any more; nobody believes in it anymore. Even Milton Friedman has renounced that he gave too much emphasis to that policy he does not believe. There is an interview that he had on the *Financial Times* in which he made that very explicit. So exchange rate target or inflation target? The US does inflation targeting because the US has no option to do exchange rate targeting. The US is the biggest economy in the world and the big countries cannot fix to little countries. The US cannot get any monetary stability by fixing to the Mexican peso or to the Canadian dollar or the Chinese RMB. Even if all that happened; it took its fixing seriously, it would disabled these foreign countries. It would not do anything to give it stability. The US has no option but nearly every country in the world has an option. And Britain is doing its monetary targeting — inflation targeting and they have big debates on it. But Britain is not doing well in its inflation targeting. It is getting a low rate of inflation, it has been successful in that, but it systematically has higher interest rate than the neighbors on the continent and than the US. And maybe it is true that countries do inflation targeting, if you are not the US itself, you have to end up with a higher interest rate or otherwise beneath. Well, these cases against floating for China, and that means with inflation targeting in China would first of all, creates fluctuating returns on FDI. People should realize what happened on Ireland through 1999 being so super successful in the European community because it has got FDI, even though it is a very small country, it has got a lot of FDI where as Britain and Scotland combined in the UK did not get it and it kept going away from Britain because Britain stay out of the EU. You think what would happen to house prices in Beijing, not in the certain position to buy house, but for bigger industrial buildings, if they can be priced in RMB, but if the RMB starts to fluctuate up and down with US dollar, and very quickly you will see all house prices will use the dollar as the basic unit of account. And if they have to be paid for in RMB, they should be paid for. But they need to be converted at the existing exchange rate. That is what is happening to all our life in America. All those currencies that are too small to have any genuine money of their own use prices in USD. That is the dollarization process based on the unit account function of money which is the most important function of money. China would lose its anchor for monetary policy I think you have big disputes geographically and otherwise should expand or contract different philosophies. Maybe after 50 years discussing and studying you might become really get-to-know what works and what does not work in China, but the process of experimentation would be a big mistake. Making monetary policy will become a political football as it often is in some other countries. But China is more complicated than other countries. Being a regional country that vast and large, having most people in the world, very big differences between the regional prosperity and it would be a very bad idea. China has done better since 1997. The price more stable than any other countries fixing the exchange rate, than any major country did by inflation targeting. And that accounts for all the countries in the Euro area, Mexico, Chili, Brazil, the UK, the US and Russia.

Consequencies of I have already mentioned that 40% of devaluation. Going beyond that now, to other issues that should Japan, China sponsor an Asian currency. I think that is worth thinking about particularly if China is totally pegged to the US. The US no longer wants it to fix its currency to the US dollar. I do not see why the US would want to do that, but if they did then it will be our argument for China that do we have to float against to the US dollars. But it would not mean that the RMB could fix to the Euro is an alternative, or it could fix maybe with Japan, or APEC, an Asian currency. I have brought some thought that if Japan and China could work together, they could create an Asian currency area. But to begin the process, it would be better to use a common anchor such as the US dollar. And to do that, it would have to stabilize of Japan exchange rate against the dollar, which recently Japan has been seem to be stabilizing to the dollar. For 2 years, the exchange rate was between 115 and 125, and I thought they were targeting 120 as a kind of central rate, until the US started to pressure Japan to appreciate its currency. Because not being so much they can get China to appreciate, Japan's move to say that China should appreciate back for it, so now the America says the Japanese yen should appreciate against the dollar. Remember a lot of this is driven by politics. In the US there is an election year coming up so people do all kinds of things because of politics. But would not APEC currency not be easier thing? APEC includes the US, Japan, China, and also Russia. And that would be very interesting to see that area if they had an APEC currency, because an APEC currency area, if the US were interested in, probably may not be easy. It would be worse because it would be an difficult organization problem with Japan and China, I do not see either why on some important issues. Maybe it is hard to organize anything on the currency area. Of course in the long run, I've often thought of what 3 years ago I was arguing, and I still think it would be a good idea to dollarize, Hong Kong's dollarize. I am not an advocator of dollarization. But Hong Kong would get special benefit from it. First of all, it will be easy. Hong Kong is getting about 140 billion dollars of foreign exchange reserves. All we need to do is to take the total money supply of Hong Kong. It is only about 15 billion dollars. Take 15 of those foreign exchange reserves buy up with Hong Kong dollars and burned them up or put them in the museum. The dollariz is a very easy thing to do, you then would not need any longer, even the Hong Kong monetary authority, and you have interest rate automatically the same as area in the US. There would not be any premium and there would be no speculation against Hong Kong dollar, which is now to be the US dollar. So I think it would be like making Hong Kong a little bit like Panama. I think it is a great step and it will be a very useful thing for China to have a strong step to be an anchor of stability for the Asian currency area and APEC currency area.

Of course in the long run, I think we need to have to work for a global currency, Paul Volcker asked the question, "does the global economy need a global currency?" Our answer is that the global economy needs a global currency. Paul Volcker is our Greenspan's predecessors, Chairman of the Fed, who stopped the big inflation in the US in the late 1970s. Would an Asian dollar be useful? A single currency is not practical, we are not talking an Asian but a single currency. Europe could do a single currency, because the EU is at the beginning process of what is becoming a federal state. Europe is not near that the level of political integration area, so we are talking about the fixed exchange rate zone and then a multiple currency monetary union. To get to an Asian monetary area, all the countries should have to agree on what the criterion for monetary stability was. It could be fixed to the dollar. I think that will be the easiest, or could be an inflation target. I do not think that would be so easy. We need a common measure of inflation, and national price index is not enough. We need a common price index that every body uses. Then lock exchange rate, have a common monetary authority and policy and then divide up to Seigniorage.

These are the five steps that the European Monetary Union took when they formed the Euro area. Exactly these five steps, this was a kind of the prototype kind of the monetary union that Asia could have. It would not be the Euro area with only Euros there, but the Euro area as it was before, the national currencies were replaced by the other. If there was a perfect monetary union, exchange rates were locked, there was no speculation back and forth between countries, so it worked. The Asian currency would have a pattern that would look something like this, much bigger area, the Asian area would be comparable to the Euro area. Not yet, it is as big as the dollar area, but it will probably be by then. To get that currency stabilization agreement with Japan, China, Korea, and ASEAN countries, Asian monetary system, common anchor, create an Asian dollar.

Instead of the Asian currency area, if you go to the APEC currency area idea, this must be a much more comprehensive thing, but sometimes a wider unit, a bigger association, is easier politically to manage than smaller association. In 1944, the major countries set up the IMF. This was the fixed exchange rate monetary union for the world economy. And there were exceptions to it, but it was nevertheless a fixed exchange rate monetary union for the world economy.

And it worked very well, much better than the subsequent singular authorities. So a wider area, is easier sometimes politically to make and certainly help people. In 1945 as it did, you have got a leader within the US at that time. Also in the APEC arrangement, if the US wanted this too, and the US would also be the role of a leader. The US leadership were take the edge off competitively relations between Japan and China. Politically, this thing will work very well.

Anyway, make cases for global currency, global currency would involve what everything inside, and every currency would be convertible to global currency. I would have the top 3 currency areas in the world would inside stabilize their own common currency and use that as their basic one. A platform that we must build, could invent a tool, a kind of combination, maybe the major currency, a basket of those. And every member of the IMF, or member of the new authority, would have a share with it, perhaps in proportion to the quotas of countries in the IMF for example at present time. Global currency should be long to every country in the world. In the long run, in fact I would like to see it happen. It may take a while to do it, but it usually bring them about something like this which politically at the moment doesn't seem to excite people too much. What would bring me about would be a kind of crisis in the international monetary system. A crisis has brought on for example by a major dollar crisis. If you did not have the euro, the dollar, and the yen in the world economy, what kind of world it would be like, what would the exchange rate system be like. I bet anything, that you have countries coming together and deciding to use something common an external unit for the world economy, you have the world currency, but what blocks it is the fact that the big currency areas are getting in the way of it and they tend to dislike the idea of that kind of national arrangement.

To conclusion, in nearby year, China keeps the RMB exchange rate fixed, Japan stabilize the yen, which they would have to fight with the US over that. Asia explore currency stabilization, establish monetary fund and keep options open to collaborate or integrate a future world currency.

Thank you!

Review

Chen Yu-lu

Chen Yu-lu was born in November, 1966 in Hebei Province. He is Professor in the School of Finance, Renmin University of China. He has a Ph.D. in Economics, and is a Ph.D. supervisor. He has been a Senior Fellow of Eisenhower Foundation, and a Fulbright scholar at the University of Columbia. He is now Vice President of Renmin University of China. He is also Deputy Director of the Chinese International Finance Society, and Deputy Secretary-General and Executive Director of Chinese Monetary Society. He was listed in the "New-Century National Experts" Project commissioned by the Ministry of Personnel in 2004, and is receiving a special government subsidy from the State Council. He was awarded the "College Young Teacher's Prize" by the Ministry of Education, and also awarded for supervising the Excellent Doctoral Dissertation.

Professor Chen Yulu worked as a lecturer in the Department of Finance, Renmin University of China, from January 1989 to June 1992. He was Deputy Director and Lecturer from July 1992 to January 1993, Deputy Director and Associate Professor from February 1993 to April 1997, Vice Dean and Professor from May 1997 to January 2002, and Dean from January 2002 to May 2005. In November 2011, he became President of Renmin University of China.

Professor Chen's academic interests are monetary and financial theory, international finance, corporate finance and fixed-income financial instruments. His research is mainly on financial theory and policy in an open economy, as well as the global capital market. His recent publications include 14 academic books and translations, and dozens of research papers. The major academic awards he has been granted include: First and Second Awards for Research Achievements of Universities, First Prize for Excellent Scientific Research in Philosophy and Social Sciences in Beijing, the Eighth An Zijie International Trade Prize, and many other awards granted by the Beijing Municipal Government, the Ministry of Education, and the State.

Master's Wisdom in RMB Controversy

No one can doubt Robert A. Mundell is the prince of economics. We can read his analysis of monetary and fiscal policy under different exchange rate regimes and his theory of optimum currency areas in virtually all textbooks on international economics or international finance. His prediction of common currency in Europe is a negation of all doubts on practicability of social science. Professor Mundell has received over fifty Honorary Professorships and Doctorates, but always strives for the truth with calmness and preciseness. Especially, we are all deeply moved by his serious concerns about China's economic development.

Professor Mundell's lecture on globalization and RMB exchange rate illustrates the trend of global economic integration and technology progress. Based on the analysis of foreign exchange regime of China, he gives many valuable suggestions about the position of RMB in Asia monetary system.

It is well-known that the issue of trade deficit had a pernicious influence on stability of employment, prices and economic growth in some Western countries. Faced with criticism from voters, politic bureaucrats use RMB as a scapegoat. They claim China output deflation to global market by RMB depreciation. Since the end of 2002, this situation has become more serious. International forum such as G7 and the headline of many popular newspapers view RMB appreciation as a marvellous antidote to the global imbalance.

In fact, RMB exchange regime reform has started since 1994. However, dragged by Asia financial crisis, the pace was subsequently slowing down. Facing with such situation, where should RMB go?

When the crunch came, Professor Mundell's social responsibility and academic courage was admired by us. He pointed out that China cannot output inflation or deflation to developed countries. On the one hand, import from China is only a small part of GDP of developed countries and price level is very stable in China. On the other hand, US dollar and Japanese yen can float freely. In other words, America and Japan can decide their domestic price level with monetary policy operation. Therefore, neither undervaluation or overvaluation of RMB has a trivial influence on western countries.

Professor Mundell did not approve of rapid appreciation of RMB. His viewpoint is that RMB appreciation will cause domestic inflation pressure, reduce FDI, and worsen budget deficis. Deteriorating economic situation will block the progress of monetary and financial reform. Furthermore, RMB appreciation does nothing about global economic problems, such as trade imbalance, liquidity excess and powerless economic developing.

Since America is the main trade partner of China, RMB appreciation may seemingly reduce import from China to America. Professor Mundell went right to the heart of the matter. He pointed out the problem of America is over borrowing, which RMB can do nothing to help.

Professor Mundell's warnings remind us to keep calm in the RMB controversy. RMB should cautiously avoid syndrome of conflicted virtue and find a correct way of exchange regime reform.

Professor Mundell is a strong advocate of fixed exchange rate system. In this speech, he was opposed to floating RMB just as in the past. He believes that floating exchange rate means unstable currency, which can be considered a symptom of economic and social instability. I do not approve his argument. Fixed exchange rate can encourage international trade and absorb foreign capital during initial stage of economic developing. However, fixed exchange rate is losing ground as acceleration of GDP growth. On the one hand, independence of central bank in monetary policy operation will be threatened by ragid exchange rate. We can take the present economic situation as an example. Current monetary policy faced with double pressure, including mitigating the inflation pressure caused by excess liquidity and RMB appreciation pressure caused by foreign trade surplus. On the other hand, ragid exchange rate may aggravate market expectation, which will discourage economic stability. Prior to 2002, despite strict controls over the capital account, capital flight was popular driven by the expectation of RMB would depreciate. In 2002, the balance of net errors and omissions was a positive number for the first time, which means speculation capital inflow and reflects market expectation on RMB appreciation.

Therefore, my viewpoint is the goal of RMB exchange regime reform should strengthen flexibility of currency, improve efficiency of monetary policy and stabilize expectation in capital market.

Professor Mundell's speech reminds us the importance of balanced reform route. As Professor Mundell says, many potential problems have not been solved in our economic infrastructure, such as imperfect commercial banking and financial market system, absent entrepreneurship, slowpaced educational business, etc. Therefore, stabilize price system is very important. Gradual reform on RMB exchange regime can stabilize market expectation and safeguard financial security. Radical appreciation may mean unexpected reversion of idle money, which will cause the financial and economic unrest.

Compare to other works by Professor Mundell, his speech is very short. But by listening to it, we can learn the master's perseverance in research and professional ethics, which are most valuable for young scholars.

Chapter 2

The Issues on China's Macroeconomy Strategy Under Current International Situation

Robert A. Mundell

Speech

Thank you very much for your spectacular introduction. It is a great honor for me to see you here. It is always very pleasant to be in Renmin University since my first visit in 1995 and this time, I see some new buildings in Ren Da. It's my first time to come to Minde hall and the Huang Da–Mundell lectures, all of which makes me very happy. Thank you, Professor Huang Da. Thank you, Ren Da. It is my honor to receive the reward of Chang Jiang Scholars. I hope that my effort in the future can enhance the education of Renmin University. My theme today is "China's Microeconomic Policy in the Changing World." Before that, I would like to tell you a piece of good news, that is, not far ago, my colleague Edmund Phelps won the 2006 Economic Nobel Prize. I suppose that some of you here may have heard of him. In 2005, he was already a nominee of the Nobel Prize. He has given an excellent speech, but failed to won the prize that year. It was a pity. But he made it this year. I believe he would like to be the Honorary Professor of Ren Da and come here as often as possible. Just like me.

Now, I want to say something about the Nobel Prize. In its earliest stage, the Nobel Prize was only awarded to the achievements in five fields that were physics, chemistry, medicine and physiology, literature and peace. It was founded by Alfred Nobel, the inventor of dynamite, probably because he felt guilty for the enormous pains brought by his invention. Many people may find it weird that there is no prize for maths. In fact, there is a story about that. It was said that one of the best mathematicians was having an affair with Nobel's wife. Alfred Nobel did not establish a prize in mathematics on purpose in case of that man would win it. But someone believed it was just a rumor. Nobel Prize was first conferred in 1901. In 2001, my wife Valerie and I joined other Nobel Prize winners in the 100-year anniversary of Nobel Prize. Here I would like to list some prominent physicists in the scientific history: Roentgen, M. Lorenz, Marie Curie, Lord Rayleigh, Albert Michelson, Max Planck, Albert Einstein, Niels Henrik David Bohr, Werner Karl Heisenberg, Paul

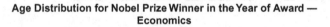

Age Distribution for Nobel Prize Winner in the Year of Award — Economics

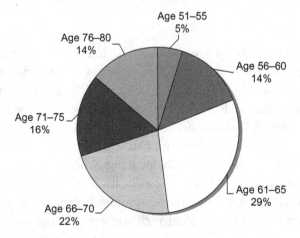

Adrien Maurice Dirac, and Enrico Fermi. In 1969, Sveriges Riksbank (Sweden's central bank) established a prize in economic sciences in memory of Alfred Nobel, which made the Nobel Prize cover 6 fields. The cash reward of the Nobel Prize in total is 14 million US dollars. From 1901 until now, there are 776 Nobel Prize winners, among whom 33 are female. The youngest winner is only 25 years old, who shared his Nobel Prize in physics with his father in 1914 and the oldest one is 88 years old. 4 winners refused to accept the prize.

When it comes to the age distribution for Nobel Prize winners, age 61–65 occupies the largest proportion, and age 66–70 the second. 57 economists have won the Nobel Prize for economics since 1969. Now the number is 58, including Phelps. 20 of the winners won the prize by themselves, and the other 37 shared the honor with others. The first Nobel Prize in economics was awarded jointly to Ragnar Frisch from Norway and Jan Tinbergen from Netherlands. Both of them are econometricians.

Type of Award (Solo or Shared)

Solo winners account for 36% and shared winners account for 64%. At most, three people can share one Nobel Prize.

The following Nobel Prize was awarded to Paul Samuelson in 1970, who was the first solo winner of economics. Next, Hicks and Arrow shared the Nobel Prize. Both of them are theorists. Friedman won the Nobel Prize in 1976. I did it in 1999. Last year it was shared by Robert Aumann from Israel, Tom Schelling and Phelps from America. This is a picture of Phelps before he won the prize, and this one afterwards. The Nobel Prize in economics was awarded for their contributions in strategy game and defense strategy. The Nobel Prize winner in 2006 was one of my colleagues, whose decisive explanation over the period balance between long-term and short-term was considered worthy of the prize by the judging panels. We will talk about this later. The following graph describes the distribution of the nationality of Nobel Prize winners.

Please look at the blue area in the graph. It represents the proportion of America, which is 67%, accounting for 2/3. The second is the

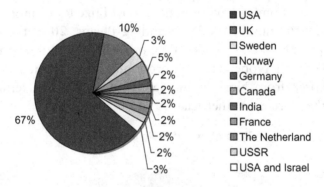

Distribution of the Nationality of Nobel Prize Winner at the Time of Award

proportion of England, which is 10%. The following is the proportion of Norway, which is 5%. This graph includes the nationality of all Nobel winners. Most of the winners were German and few were American, before 1944, namely, before the Second World War. But the situation changed completely after the war, for most of the European scientists immigrated to America, which turned to be the advantage of human capital of America.

Phelps is the sixth among the American Nobel Prize winners. It means that all the prizes are awarded to Americans except the Nobel Prize for Literature and Peace, both of which have not been announced yet. It does not mean that the Swedish prefer American winners. They are neutral as always. The Swedish Academy of Science considered that the work by Phelps had deepened our understanding in connection between the long-term and short-term effects of economic policies. He was one of the first economists who set up the "Golden Age" model on development, which links the best savings with the profit levels. In the mid of 1920s, Phelps criticized the Philips Curve together with Friedman. He puts forward such a fact that inflation will lead to anticipation of inflation in the future, which then reduces the efficiency of reducing inflation as a stabilization policy. He demonstrateds how the low inflation leads to law inflation anticipation, and its influence on the decision-making of company and government leaders. Phelps also develops the analysis of the importance of human capital in the business and corporation world. The human capital or the workers themselves, helps in extending new technology and economic growth. You may ask whether there is someone who is supposed to win the Nobel Prize but was not awarded. Here I have a name list. One must win the Nobel Prize when he or she is alive, because the Nobel Prize can only be awarded to living people. One may die before receiving the prize. My colleague Vickery was awarded the Nobel Prize in October, 1997. We held a celebration party for him at Columbia University. But two days later, he died during his drive to Boston at midnight. He only enjoyed the prize for two days. One of his colleague and his wife brought the Nobel Prize back. So he could not have won the Nobel Prize if he had died 2 or 3 days earlier. The name list I mentioned includes Sir Frank, Count Ludwig Hamilton, John von Neumann, Oskar Morgenstern, Roy Harrod, Joan Robinson, Lloyd Metzler, Harry Johnson, Jacob Viner, Robert Triffin, Lionel Robbins, Harold Hotelling, and Nicholas Kaldor. All of them should have won the prize but were not awarded. Why? Because the Nobel Prize for economics is different from others. It did not start until 1969. There are many people who can win the prize, but it can be awarded to three people at most every year. There are occasions that it cannot be awarded to three winners at the same time and the above situation happened. Economics is a wealthy science of leading position, for it has the general equilibrium theory, which can be widely used in every place. The thought of economic theories has been reflected in all living and nonliving branches of science. Economics calls for economical, which is essential in every area. Economics is closely connected with the whole functioning mode of economy, which is called macroeconomics. Monetary and fiscal policies, as well as exchange rate policy, are important instruments of macro economics. My major works covers these fields. For example, I built an international mode on monetary theory, which is named "Mundell–Flemming

Model." Economics has different schools and they have different policy applications. Every policy standpoint is related to a certain school of economics, because different economists call for different policies. Although they may share the same economy, they will disagree in income distribution and the efficiency of policy, or they are different in logic. Therefore, although these economists from different schools, who are also observers, may be prejudiced, the most important thing is to expound their values. Joseph Schumpeter once said that there were only two kinds of economics; one is "good economics" and the other "bad economics." I agree with him, really. Logically speaking, he is right, but not practical. You can see many schools such as Keynesian Economics, Neoclassical Economics, Marxist Economics, and New Keynesian Economics. In a word, they are many schools because people have different views and they build different economic models. Keynes once said that the improvement in economics is to improve economic models. We keep building new economic models to make economics better. Sometimes people will not change their views because they may believe that their own are always right, or because they too stubborn, or because they are too old. The great physical scientist Planck said, "Science advances, funeral by funeral." What did he mean by that? The old people do not like changing their ideas. They will not take new thoughts immediately. After their death, young people with new ideas go on. It is like what happens in the animal world, as animals seldom change their thoughts in all their lives.

Now we come to the RMB problem. The theme of my speech today includes the currencies in the world economy, especially concerned with Asia and other countries that are related to the RMB policy in China. During the recent visit of Chinese President Hu Jintao to America, one of the topics for discussion put forward by George Bush is the undervaluing of RMB. Should China transfer its monetary policy from fixed to dollars to free float? We will start from the following graph that describes the present world currency system and see how it will evolve in the future decades.

This graph describes the energy distribution of each currency, which is more or less the same with the proportion of its GDP. The amount is very important. The money supply has to correspond to its GDP. The top 5 are dollar, euro, Japanese yen, RMB and pound. The biggest area is dollar, representing its GDP of 13 trillion dollars, the second one euro, 10 trillion, the third one Japanese yen, 4.5 trillion, the forth one RMB, 2.4 trillion, and the fifth one pound, 2.2 trillion. Other countries are far from these.

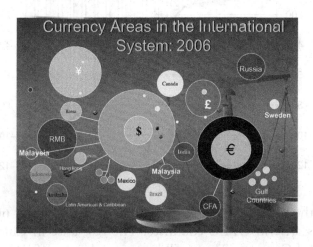

In the past few years people are always complaining about the balance problem of trade in China. Asian currencies are demanded to appreciate again and again at every summit of Seven Countries. In the Committee shall meet of IMF, held from August 22–23, 2006, IMF declared a new task, which is to lobby each country for rectification of the "globe imbalances," the meaning of which is still unknown to us. However, as IMF member, Rodrigo Prieto said, to reduce the "imbalances," the world requires coordinated action now. Thus, in theory, America has transferred the pressure for RMB appreciation to IMF. The following graph shows US deficits in Current Account.

US Deficits (US$)

In 1990, there was, in the main, no deficits. Then it decreased to 800 billion dollars in 2005. There was also some debt before 1990, but the debt afterwards was much more. What are the "imbalances"? No doubt that America has deficits of 800 billions, which is more than GDP in Korea, and the number is still increasing. Meanwhile, there are corresponding surpluses of the same amount in other places

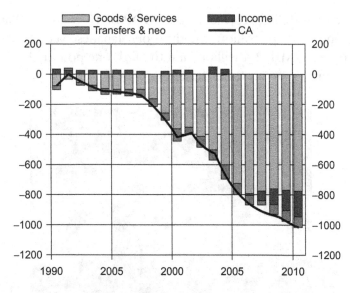

around the world. Owing to the rise in oil price, about 60% of the surpluses arise in OPEC countries. The rest arise in China, Japan, Russia and Germany. There will be no surplus or deficit considering the world as a whole. If the deficit rises in America, there must be surpluses correspondingly in other places around the world. If thve deficit in America is to be rectified, the surpluses in other places around the world must do the same. Look at the following graph.

Current Account Imbalances

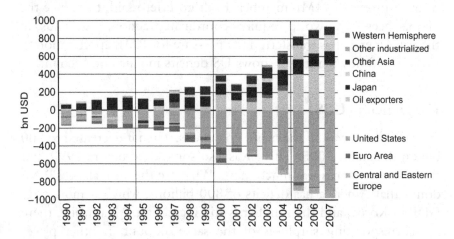

The lower is deficits and the upper is surpluses. America is represented in purple and OPEC in yellow, which accounts for a great proportion owing to the high oil price. The following dark blue represents Japan, and light blue China. The latter is more than the former. All these indicate "imbalances." But we doubt about the existence of balance. Is it oversupplied, or over demanded?

The following graph describes the surpluses in OPEC countries.

Oil Exporters' Surpluses

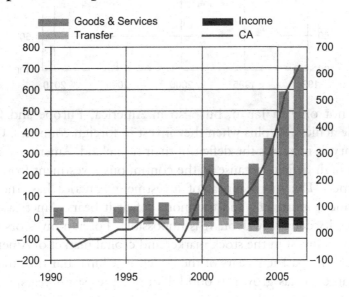

The surpluses in Japan are showed in the following graph.

Japan's Surpluses

Japan has been in surplus for a long time. We can see from the graph that the surplus was started from 1990, but actually, it was started in the 1970s, remaining 25–26 years. Now the surplus in Japan is 100 million US dollars per year, but that was because there was no savings glut exceeding investment. This covered a great proportion, as the population of Japan has registered negative growth, with less and less young people and more and more old ones. As the average age increases, people are saving up for retirement. But they

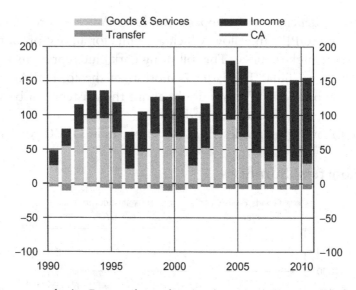

do it not only in Japan, but also in America, Europe and China. People achieve surplus when they invest in foreign countries. On the contrary, it increases the deficit of their homeland. America is in deficit, in high deficit, because of the continuous investment from other countries. The more appeal of investment America has, the more investment it attracts, and the more deficit it bears. America cannot balance its deficit by debt. It is impossible. Foreign investors would inevitably invest in the stock market and capital market of America. It was just the past few years of the deficit in China, but the amount is very large. It has grown to 600 billion for the past 4 years, which is the largest around the world and has the potential to grow fast. The global imbalances means huge deficit in the Current Account to America, while to Japan, Germany, OPEC countries, and China, it means surpluses. As long as dollar is used as an international currency, the deficit of America is a worldwide natural state. America functions as the word central bank, which provides dollars and assets in dollar to other places in the proportion of demand according to its own standard. If the change in exchange rate can balance the payment, IMF will exert press on Saudi Arabia and other Gulf states for an appreciation in the value of the currencies of Iran, Venezuela, Norway, Iraq, Nigeria and Canada. But no official can propose such a policy officially. The high oil price unveils a real condition of the real trade phenomena. It is not affected by the nominal monetary variables at all, such as exchange rate. The OPEC countries at the Middle East peg their currencies on dollars. Japan has been in chronic surplus for nearly half a century. The surplus is always well over 100 billion dollars. After the Plaza Accord, Japanese yen was forced to appreciate three times to dollars. But the appreciation destroyed the Japanese economy, with the stagnation of economic growth and no decrease of the surplus in the Current Account. I do not think the appreciation of RMB is a way to solve the problems in China, learning from the experience of Japan. The surplus in Japan now is a result of the life cycle, since the two generations have different saving models, which is related to the ageing of population. After the deflation over about 10 years in Japan, it is known to IMF that the savings over investment in Japan would not make Japanese yen appreciate. The Group of Seven meeting forced "Asian" currencies to appreciate, with the exception of Japan. As a country with emerging markets, Russia needs much more savings than it has achieved. Germany, which now joins the Euro Area, has no currency to appreciate. Germany has surpluses, indeed, but no currency. As a result, China is brought forward. The surpluses in China in recent years only takes less than 20% of the American deficit, but it is the only country that received criticism.

What did America function in the process of deficit? In the whole process of achieving its status of superpower, America has experienced four stages in the balance of payments as follows. The first stage was roughly before 1900, when America was a young nation in debt and deficit. With foreign investment, becoming in debt and surplus, America joined the First World War. America transformed from a debtor nation to a creditor nation during the war. In the 60 years from 1915 to 1975, America remained a creditor nation with surpluses. Form 1975 to present, America is in deficit, with the exception of the depression in 1990. It remained creditor nation with deficit from 1975 to 1989, and debtor nation with deficit after 1989. This order is nothing unusual. These stages are constant with the classical division of "Balance of Payments Stages" by Elliott Keynes, the sagacious applied economist in the mid-19th century. According to the above classification, Keynes respectively named debtor deficit, debtor surplus, creditor surplus and creditor deficit as immature debtor, mature debtor, immature creditor and mature creditor. Ironically, the wealthiest countries around the world have started a new cycle. The revolution of suppliers in the 1980s sparked a new-style infancy or vitality.

Let us see the following graph.

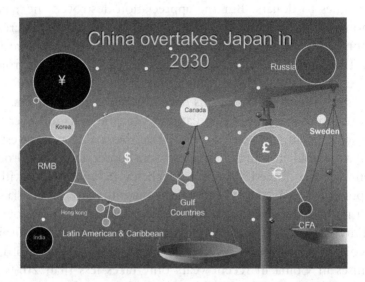

China is the fastest growing country, with the speed of 9%, even 10%. The average speed is 9%. China may overtake Japan in GDP before 2030, or even early in 2020. In 2060, it may overtake Europe.

However, the deficit in America has nothing to do with China. In the long term, China has no connection with American economic movement. As Greenspan said last year, the change in the trade surplus of China would only remove to that of other exporting countries and it would have no effect on American deficit. It is very dangerous for the decision makers to start adjusting the imbalances when the reason is unclear. The classical danger is "mending an unbroken system." For example, in the 1960s, America balanced its deficit in payments through the connection of gold loss in America and the balance of dollars overseas. It is hard to believe that other nations around the world are not expecting the balance of payments in dollar. The graph describes the relative change between European currencies and dollars from 1971.

The prices of European currencies are showed in dollars. Look at the graph. The dollars is falling while the European currencies are rising. This is the inflation in America. The trend remained till 1990, when the IT revolution first occurred in America and the economic growth rate doubled to 5%. At that time, the fixed exchange rate policy of RMB to dollars was adopted. The deflation of RMB arose at the same time. In the 1970s, it was a consensus of IMF that flexible exchange rates would solve any problem in the payments. But things went contrary to their wishes. Under the flexible exchange rates, the balance of dollars rose sharply to a new high, form tens of billion in the 1960s to 4 trillion, probably 4.5 trillion now, among which China took 1 trillion, Japan 1 trillion and Europe 50 million. But none of the international system managers has taken some time to find out that the global system has changed. For example, the Euro–dollar market holds 1 billion dollars. These changes were caused by global currency, as well as the prosperity of American economy after the revolution of suppliers in the 1980s. The efforts forcing RMB to appreciate rapidly will be unprecedented in the monetary history. As I said, RMB is inconvertible. In the aftermath of war, America refused to appreciate its convertible currency in shortage of dollar. So the bankers and economists were still talking about dollar gap while the market had been in dollar glut for long. After the Plaza Accord, Japanese was forced to appreciate. It appreciated thrice from 1985 to 1995. But it did not change the surplus in Japan, which was even more than that in China in recent years. It destroyed the economic growth in Japan. Non-performing loans and improper monetary and fiscal policies, which did not match the economy, restrained the financial system in Japan. However, American economy is distinct a lot with Japanese and Chinese economy. In the 1950s, America and Switzerland are the only countries with free convertible currencies around the world, while others have exchange control. Similarly, when Germany was forced to appreciate its currency in the 1960s and Japan in the 1980s, their currencies were convertible. No country can be forced to appreciate its currency when it is unconvertible. Is RMB undervalued? No research has approved it yet. What is certain is which test to be used is still unknown. Without the intervention of People's Bank of China, RMB will appreciate. But what will happen without the exchange control in China? The answer is obvious. If the currency exchange control in China is relaxed, RMB will depreciate rather than appreciate. The result will be disastrous if RMB appreciate and it is convertible. IMF has completely changed its forcing position on the floating rate policy of RMB, because this policy will delay the convertibility of RMB. In the history of IMF, some country, whose currency was unconvertible, was forced to relax its currency exchange control, and then followed with currency depreciation. Is there any example recently? The answer is yes, such as China in 1994. In support of IMF, China pushed toward convertibility in Current Account and depreciated RMB from the exchange rate of 5.5 to 8.7. It was called floating rate, while it did not float actually, which delighted IMF. After the financial crisis in Southeast Asia in 1997, China refused to take the suggestion of depreciating RMB by IMF. This exchange rate remained at 8.28 until 2005. Surely it was still called floating rate, but it just never floated. China established a new system in July, 2005 under the constant pressure from "international authorities." The change was to let dollars depreciate step by step, that is, to let RMB appreciate 2%. Now the exchange rate is a little over 7.9, but there is no evidence that the exchange rate will change faster, which will be a mistake. The following graphs describe respectively the exchange rate of RMB to dollar, Euro and Japanese yen from 2005.

The appreciation will damage China's economy. It will decrease the price of agricultural products, which will make the frailest part of China poorer. It will also increase unemployment, which will aggravate the non-performing loans of banks. China will lose foreign direst invest, and then the drive of economic growth. It will destroy the longitudinal construction of the stably growing Asia economy, in which China was the assembly center. It will provoke the crash in real state sector. It will decrease the growth rate of Chinese economy, which may drop to the lower level of that from 1989 to 1990. The result will be great depression around the world, or economic recession in China or Asia, which will destroy the world economic growth and have incalculable consequences to American economy and world trade. With the fixed exchange rate policy from 1997 to 2005, China had done better than seven western countries in stabilizing prices. There is no better record. The system to take inflation as a present goal is difficult to be adopted in China, and it will make no improvement in macroeconomic policy. It was an improvement for China to

RMB/Dollar Exchange Rate

——RMB/US$

RMB/Euro Exchange Rate

——RMB/Eur

adopt the policy of fluctuating rate. Look at the cases of other countries. Europe adopted the system to take inflation as a present goal after the birth of euro. The exchange rate of euro to dollar is 1.18 in 1999. It dropped by 40% to the low level of 0.82 in the following two years. Then it appreciated by 70% close to 1.4. If it is the same case with RMB to dollars, the situation of 40% down and then 70% up will be destructive to China. It will influence the financial operation and the real state sector in China. The prices will be dollarized like that in Latin America and other places around the world.

The fixed exchange rate to dollar has mixed the influence of American economy into Chinese economy. China cannot ignore reasonable connections with other regions around the world. China can't be pushed out of the dollar area by America. It is the bottom-line. China has to decide whether to balance the payments or to face with the pressure of appreciation. In my opinion, the cost of balancing payments is far away from that of appreciation, although the former has to resist the temptation of continuingly increasing foreign exchange reserve by billions of dollar per week. I am not talking about converting RMB to be completely convertible, but about relaxing the RMB exchange control in general. It will allow companies to exchange more foreign currencies for necessary investment and international travel. China should lessen the restrictions and control on importing at the same time, and also adopt similar policies to increase import and capital export. The foreign exchange reserve of China reaches 1 trillion US dollars, generally more than any other country. As a result, China can take the risk of change in foreign exchange policy. Tianjin, in the charge of mayor Dai Xianglong, is trying out the convertibility of foreign currencies. We should pay close attention to this admirable attempt. When the search for Asian currency began, we should follow the exchange rates in Asia countries. It is not a step forward for China to take the managed floating rate system. If China can balance its payments under the present exchange rate and make continuing progress in the economic reform in the following two years, its policy will be recognized.

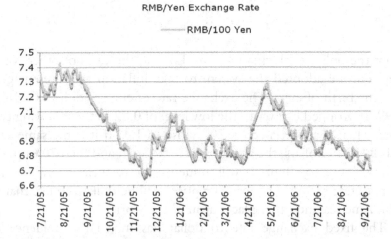

RMB/Yen Exchange Rate

RMB/100 Yen

Review

Wang Chuanlun

Wang Chuanlun is Professor of Public Finance at School of Finance, Renmin University of China. He is a senior specialist in public finance. He received his B.A. in Law at National Southwest United University of China in 1942 and his B.Sc. in Economics at Tsinghua Univesity in 1948. He also obtained M.Sc. in Economics at the University of Glasgow where he also worked as a research fellow. Professor Wang also worked as a research fellow at the Wilson College, Princeton University. Professor Wang was the member of the executive board at Chinese Monetary Society, Chinese Finance Society and Chinese International Finance Society, and a consultant for the International Taxation Institute of China.

Professor Wang Chuanlun's main research interest lies in financial theory and he is one of the lead persons who introduced western financial theory into China. His publications include *Public Finance of Capitalism* (1981), *The Development of Western Finance* (1991), *Money in Theory of Finance* (1994), *International Revenue* (1995), *Modern Western Finance and Economics Theory* (1995), *The Economics of Money, Banking and Financial Market* (1998).

Professor Mundell has been an old friend to Chinese economic circle. Over the past ten-odd years, he made many speeches in Renmin University, elaborating on important economic issues and introducing foreign economic circles, which were warmly welcomed by RUC teachers and students. Today, he has given us a speech about China's macro economic strategy and how China can respond to the pressure for RMB appreciation both in short term and long term. Professor Mundell has talked about it on many occasions. There are three points in his analysis worthy of deep consideration.

First of all, he gave us some background knowledge about the pressure China is faced with RMB appreciation. According to the balance of payments, neither surplus nor deficit exists while considering the world as a whole. When there is deficit in America, there must be some surplus in other countries. Deficit in American Current Account is about 800 to 100 billion dollars per year. Correspondingly, there must be the same amount of surplus in the Current Account of petroleum exporting countries, China, Japan, Russia, Germany and so on. America has to reduce its deficit while pushing down the surplus in Chinese Current Account; if not, it will increase the surpluses in other countries besides China; as a result, the total deficit in American Current Account will stay the same. It does not improve matters of balance of payments for American Current Account just by pressing the Chinese government to appreciate RMB.

Secondly, from the perspective of monetary factor, professor Mundell analyzed the reasons why RMB should not appreciate. As the "international currency," US dollar or assets in US dollar may be sold to investors from other countries by American monetary authorities. There lies one of the reasons of the long-term huge deficit of America. Foreign investors needs to hold dollars and assets in dollar, however, it is neither costless nor always satisfactory. Without the privileged status of dollars, it is not possible for America to be the country with the highest debt and the highest deficit in Current Account at the same time. Then, can this privileged status of dollars remain for a long time? What measures can American government take to keep this situation? One thing is for sure, that is, the value of currency must remain stable. It has been proved by history that any currency cannot maintain its special status without stability, no matter it is dollars or other currencies.

Thirdly, he talked about the decisive role of real economy. This graph has been used several times by Professor Mundell to indicate the scale of each currency zone. As shown in the graph, the energy of each currency is more or less relevant to the GDP of that country. Historically, the international status of each currency grows and declines with its national strength. What happened in America has proved this. With the development of new technology in America during the 1990s, its economic growth rate, has been increased to reinforce the status of dollars. It works the same in China. Without the economic growth during the recent 20 years, there would not be so much surpluses in Chinese Current Account, and the status of RMB would not be reinforced. As a result, the pressure for RMB appreciation would not appear. The currency regime, free float or float with intervention, and the adjusting range of exchange rate have some effect on the balance of payments, but they are of less importance than real economic factors. More attention should be paid to the real economic conditions in the external macro economic strategy of a country, such as productivity capacity, production efficiency, employment, change in investment and consumption, trade scale and so on.

The theme of Professor Mundell's speech today is the exchange rate problems of RMB. After the analysis of above three points, he proposed the following advice with his wide perspective and deep insight. The Chinese government does not have to attach too much importance to the RMB appreciation pressure from America. The basic system should not be changed to let the exchange rate of RMB float freely. Strategically, the real economy should be regulated to affect Chinese balance of payments, so as to reduce the surplus in Current Account and balance the payments on the whole. However, some restrictions on the exchange of RMB could be properly lessened from the foreign exchange management. I believe that Professor Mundell's advice is reliable.

In his speech, Professor Mundell talked about the Nobel Prize and introduced Professor Phelps, his colleague, who was also Nobel Prize winner in Economics. until 2007, there are over 60 Nobel Prize winners since 1969 when the Nobel Prize for Economics was first founded. Chinese economic circle pays close attention to this prize.

It is natural for this attention to be paid for. Most of the winners are influential around the world. Some of them are representatives from some foreign schools of economics. They keep building different models, which are used to explain how the economic activities function. Their theories influence the economic policies of some countries, and their real economy in one way or another. Our concern on the Nobel Prize in Economics will help to grasp the change of economic trend around the world and to understand the development of real economy.

However, as Professor Mundell said in his speech, most of the economists, including the Nobel Prize winners, belong to certain schools of economics. With varying policy viewpoints, their logical explanations also differ and biased perspective may be come into being. Believing in their own ideas, they neither change their views nor accept new ideas. Mundell did not support to distinguish "good economists" from "bad economists." But he pointed out that the most important thing at present is to expound the values. Different schools of economics and different economists have different values. Clearly expounding the values of different economists will lay a solid foundation for understanding their theories and ideas. Based on this, we can benefit from their theories and ideas whether we agree or not, accept or refuse.

Chapter 3

Growth: Does China's Economy Keep on High-Speed Growth in 20 Years From Now on?

Michael Spence

Biography

Michael Spence's research interests focus on the study of economic growth and development, dynamic competition and the economics of information.

Michael Spence is a senior fellow at the Hoover Institution and Philip H. Knight Professor Emeritus of Management in the Graduate School of Business, Stanford University. He is Chairman of an independent Commission on Growth and Development, created in 2006 and focused on growth and poverty reduction in developing countries.

In 2001, he was awarded the Nobel Memorial Prize in Economic Sciences for his contributions to the analysis of markets with asymmetric information. He received the John Bates Clark Medal of the American Economic Association awarded to economists under 40.

He served as Philip H. Knight Professor and Dean of the Stanford Business School from 1990 to 1999. As dean, he oversaw the finances, organization, and educational policies of the school. He taught at Stanford as Associate Professor of Economics from 1973 to 1975.

From 1975 to 1990, he served as Professor of Economics and Business Administration at Harvard University, holding a joint appointment in its Business School and the Faculty of Arts and Sciences. In 1983, he was named Chairman of the Economics Department and George Gund Professor of Economics and Business Administration. Spence was awarded the John Kenneth Galbraith Prize for excellence in teaching in 1978 and the John Bates Clark Medal in 1981 for a "significant contribution to economic thought and knowledge."

From 1984 to 1990, Spence served as the Dean of the Faculty of Arts and Sciences at Harvard, overseeing Harvard College, the Graduate School of Arts and Sciences, and the Division of Continuing Education.

From 1977 to 1979, he was a member of the Economics Advisory Panel of the National Science Foundation and in 1979 served as a member of the Sloan Foundation Economics Advisory Committee. At various times, he has served as a member of the editorial boards of *American Economics Review, Bell Journal of Economics, Journal of Economic Theory, and Public Policy*. Among his many honors, Spence was elected a fellow of the American Academy of Arts and Sciences in 1983 and was awarded the David A Wells Prize for outstanding doctoral dissertation at Harvard University in 1972.

He has served as member of the boards of directors of General Mills, Siebel Systems, Nike, and Exult, and a number of private companies. From 1991 to 1997, he was Chairman of the National Research Council Board on Science, Technology, and Economic Policy.

He is a member of the American Economic Association and a fellow of the American Academy of Arts and Sciences and the Econometric Society.

Speech

Thank you very much, I am delighted to be here, it is an honor to be part of this important gathering. So I would like to talk today a bit about this subject of human capital and education and, to some extent, information and communication technology, all in reference to the question of whether China can sustain this very high growth rates for another twenty years.

Tomorrow I am going to talk in greater depth about the impact of network-based information technology on the informational structure of market in the contest of global economy. So today I will be a little lean on that subject. It is something that I am very interested in.

But it is not a subject that excessively done in the matter of time we have available today.

So let us first talk about what it means to grow 8 or 9% for twenty years, and what challenges are there that generated by very high growth rates. 8 to 9% of growth rates means that essentially the per capita income will double every decade. Or in the twenty year period, they will quadruple.

This is very likely to produce stresses, major stresses in the economy and major challenges the they do not find in the economies like the US's, or the European economies, since they grow much more slowly.

There is a tendency to think about high growth rates like this in the contest of macro economy considerations which is of course important, but I am going to focus on the micro economic issues that raise in industries and regions, and things like that.

The historical performance of China's economy will help us to understand a little about what we are talking about. If you take the period of 1978 to approximately the present, the poverty reduction in China is really very impressive.

If you use the standard of 1 dollar a day or 365 dollars a year, then the poverty rate in percentage term from almost 30% to approximately 2% in the Chinese economy. If you use the standard of 2 dollars a day then the reduction is from 74% to 18%, which is even more impressive.

So the general issue here is income distribution. The rural population in the same period went from 82% of the total population down to 62% and this trend will continue, if the growth rates are as high as we are talking about.

Urban incomes in 1978 were 3.5 times the level of rural areas. And they declined rapidly because of the agricultural reform after 1978 to 1.5 times, hovered that level. And now on the way back up and currently at the level of 2 times the level of rural incomes.

The growth rate has been high in all the regions, but they have been the highest in the central areas and in the southeast than the most of northwest, so they have been different. The average is 8.9%.

But the starting point is different as well. So there are significant income differentials.

So the first big challenge is really the challenge of making sure that the income differentials don't get so high to produce dissolutionment on the part of significant fractions of the population and stress in the political and politically economic processes. And there are closely related issues of managing this transition from the rural to the urban economy. That transition is characteristic of all industrial revolutions that we have seen or have faced in the Europe today.

Next challenge that I would like to flag is in high growth mode, income and wages rise very rapidly, which is a good thing. But this causes fairly rapid change in relative competitive positions in various industries in this country in the global economy.

This means if you get blow at the microeconomic level, actually look at the economy, the structure of the economy, the portfolio economic activities in industries, in all countries that are growing rapidly, the evolution of that portfolio, the mix, changes rapidly as well.

To the beginning example, a company called Nike, makes shoes and clothes and first manufactured, believe it or not, in Japan. And then when Japan's economic development prices them out of the market, and so moved to South Korea and Taiwan, and they no longer manufacture there either and manufactured most their footwear at least in China and Vietnam.

So in the relatively short period, 35 years, there have been two major shifts in the location of labor intensive, high quality manufacturing activity because of the speed of development of the countries in which the manufacture originally occurred.

My colleague at Stanford, Paul Roamer is well-known for his studying of growth and influence of technology, he has also generated some interesting data, on the rates of growth in various industrial revolutions.

So in the UK, which is the first to industrial revolution, they grew at real terms 1% a year, the US and the European countries, grew 2%. South Korea, you know, 5 plus, sometimes higher than that, South

Korea, well above that. China is running at 9%. You can as fairly easy to see that this process is accelerating.

So in the UK, in a single working life time, it was very unlikely that your industry will disappear. But in a country that is growing at 7–10%, it is likely that the economic activity that many of the citizens are engaged in will move somewhere else, sometime, maybe more than once, in the course of their life time. This is huge challenge because it causes great anxiety among individuals, because of their uncertainty associated with those transitions.

So to summarize, this is very big challenge that there are only two ways to meet it. One is to let the natural protection extinct ring, to some extent, and slow the process down, which has the consequence of slowing growth down. Or one can invest in a variety of kinds of intangible assets that make these transitions easier to people, economic social safety nets, education and training and re-training programs, and other measures that increase the flexibility that the economy has and the people have.

So an example of flexibility is probably the most important the safety bill in the economy's labor mobility. We have that in the US. You are increasingly get one of the challenges for the Europeans is in a region or a country, when the economic activity falls off, it is not as easy for them to move to where the jobs are being created, or located.

The next challenge I want to identify has to do with the global economy. Domestic demand in China, unlike 15 or 20 years ago, was now quite large, and therefore interesting. To some extent, the domestic demand will fail growth in the domestic market, but not as the rate we have been seeing. The export component of the economy is still tremendously important; therefore, China is heavily dependent on the global economy involving successfully with the appropriate government structures, and the appropriate behavior on the part of leading the economies in the world.

China has, as everybody in this room knows, increasing important role in the global economy, just one index of that, I heard recently, the foreign ministry of Korea explain to a group in LA that the export from South Korea to China will exceed the export to the US this year.

So what the challenge here is that in addition to everything else has to be done, China's growth requires increasing openness, it involves involvement with understanding, the global economy and other players in it, other countries and regions. And it requires investment in everything, from generally education, to language training, to accomplish these challenges.

All high growth in environment generates bottles in lots of different areas. Human capital, shortage of manager, shortage of people with particular expertise, shortage of people with relevant political expertise, infrastructure, and ships can get into ports and so on. To some extent, a market system that you have and are involving, starting in 1978, helps solve out these bottles by essentially dealing with through the information generated by price signals. But the market system does not solve all these problems. And particularly the ones involve government activity, regulation and intervention, or investment, and it takes a great deal of skill of the type has been displayed of management this economy for the past 25 years to navigate through these bottles. If they are not dealt with effectively, then they can significantly slow down the growth rates by producing whole batch of imbalances, which purses longer than they should, on the microeconomic level.

I guess it is fairly obvious to everybody in this room, but it is important. The financial markets are crucial to the efficient use of capital and savings in the economy. These market at present are immature in a number of dimensions, including information, the main point I want to make is that the work that Jo, George and I and the whole of other people did 30 plus years ago makes it pretty clear that the market has its information asymmetry, that as large as they are in financial market in everywhere require, we absolutely require, appropriate regulation, and that regulation and the set of exposure laws have to be built up around the development of these financial markets for them to function effectively. It is a major commitment of resources of human capital to get this done.

This is the subject I promise will not talk about excessively, so let me just make a few remarks and expand them tomorrow. Building the information technology infrastructure and in parallel capacity to use it effectively is critical to the ability to sustain these kinds of growth rates in the global economy.

The integration of the global market and global supply chain that whole process is simply built on top of this kind of technology and the transaction causes reducing capabilities. It is the key also, to achieving the advanced economies, such as the one I was living in, key to achieving productivity gains in the private and public sectors.

If you look at the US productivity data, you will discover that in the last 5 or 6 years, our productivity gains have been abnormally high by the standard of post-war period. And that increase corresponds almost exactly with the making available of a high speed, always on, standardized protocol called network. Then that reason that network is important and causes the productivity gains in the way that other kinds of information technology did not is that it is the network that allow you to coordinate economic activity over vast geographical territory relying on the fact that time is irrelevant in the information era and distance did not matter.

If you look back over this list of challenges, maintaining reasonable income equity in the economy, managing the world migration maintains millions of people adapting to a rapidly shifting industrial mix with all threatening aspects that has to real understanding of integration into the global economy in all terms of human recourse, overcoming bottle in human capital, infrastructure and in private sector, wise and measured policy transition in the complex path from a planned to a social market economy and deploying information and communication technology infrastructure and capacity to use it.

Your reaction to these activities is probably as same as mine; they are formidable challenges, but this is not impossible to deal with them. The one thing I think that they have in common is not one of them can be met successfully absent a large even massive investment in education and human capital. In scientific language education may not be sufficient condition for meeting these challenges and therefore achieving the growth rates that the country hopes to achieve. But it is certainly a necessary condition.

Education and investing in human capital is the largest asset in the balance sheet of any country including in the US, it is going to be the largest element in the vector of investment China will make over the next 20 years by a lot, and I mean it will dwarf next years' competitor. And it needs to be made at all levels. Extending the schoolings of the 12 years, including vocational education, retaining and re-education programs that help people to manage the transitions, higher education for the people who have manage the economy or the under prices, managed education, science and engineering so the technological side of the economy develops, public policy and public management and language training, are all important.

So the question we started with that can China grow for the next 20 years at 9%, I think the answer is yes, but it can be a big challenge. There are no instrumentable obstacles, and it will not be easy. And I hope I convince you by outlining what there challenges are, suggesting that education is the critical ingredient that in fact that is the case. Essentially what these challenges have in common is the creation in the economy and in its people, the ability to understand and adapt to very rapid changes in the structure of the economy. I guess the reason that I have been a lot optimistic is our outside observers of the past performance in terms of achieving and meeting these challenges since 1978 has been excellent so I do not see any particular reason, notwithstanding there are doubt that will not be met in the next 20 years.

I cannot wait to get to the end and finalize what I have said, thank you very much.

Review

Xiaoguang Chen

Xiaoguang Chen is the lecturer of School of Finance at Renmin University of China. He graduated and obtained the Ph.D. in economics from Guanghua School of Management at Peking University in July 2005. His papers were published in several top journals in China, such as *Economic Research Journal and Economics Quarterly*. One of his papers was awarded the Gregory Chow Best Paper Award in 2005 and his Ph.D. dissertation won the CICC Best Dissertation in Economics and Finance of China in 2007. His current research interests include human capital, labor market, taxes and economic growth.

Professor Michael Spence, together with George Akerlof and Jesoph Stiglitz, won the Nobel Prize in Economics due to their original contributions in the field of asymmetric information. In his speech recently delivered in China, Professor Spence tried to answer the question that whether China is able to continue its rapid growth in the next 20 years. Since Professor Spence's previous research did not care much about China's economy, in his speech, he tried to make the analysis within a relatively abstract framework. Nevertheless, his sharp economics intuition and deep insight on the Chinese economy helps him accurately grasp several, if not all, factors that determine economic growth of China in the future.

At the beginning of his speech, Professor Spence discusses the achievement of China with respect to the poverty reduction resulted from the rapid economic growth, which in turn, as he believes, will trigger a couple of outcomes that may affect China's economic growth in the future. First, rural–urban income gap and the inequality between the east and the west region have become prominent as the economy grows. Because of the frequent labor mobility, Professor Michael Spence thinks China's government needs to properly manage the labor mobility from rural areas to urban areas. Second, due to the economic structural change and industry upgrading, the workers have to switch between jobs more frequently than ever. To keep the labor market more flexible in response to the economic structural change, education and on-the-job training should be put as priority. Of course, the flexibility of the economy lies in a free and open labor market. Professor Spence, therefore, attaches much importance to the free mobility of labor force.

Besides, Professor Spence also emphasizes the importance of financial market to the economic growth in China. Due to his own preference, he analyzes this problem from the perspective of the surveillance on the financial market, which he thinks is able to solve the problem of asymmetric information. In addition, new information technology should be used to improve the ability to deal with the information issues.

After analyzing several factors that determine the economic growth in China, Professor Spence summarizes these factors. He thinks that education is a necessary condition for economic growth. He even proposes the specific suggestion that the length of compulsory education should be increased to 12 years, and the vocational training, re-training and higher education should be underscored. By doing so, China is then able to achieve the fast economic growth in the next 20 years. He also believes that China can achieve the annual growth rate at 9% in the next 20 years, but will face some challenges. And the investment in education is the most important factor to overcome these challenges.

Theoretically, to predict the economic growth in the future, we need to know about the power house and sources of economic growth in the long run.

The endogeneous growth theory in the past 20 years tells us that technological growth and human capital accumulation are the driving forces of long-run economic growth. Technological progress is the creation and utilization of the new knowledge. And human capital accumulation refers to the assimilation of existing knowledge and skill improvement. Due to the decreasing return to physical capital, the economy will converge to the steady state which is determined by the technological level and human capital level. In the short-run, the economic growth can be driven by the physical capital accumulation. While in the long-run, the economy, without technological progress and human capital accumulation, will be stagnant. In the past 30 years, the economic growth in China was mainly driven by the investment in physical capital and the foreign direct investment. For China, to promote the education level of the labor force in a more practical strategy compared to the research and development. There are at least two reasons. First, the technological level in most of the industries of China is still far behind the world technological frontier, which implies that it is more profitable for Chinese companies to learn and assimilate the advanced technology from their counterparts in other countries. The speed of learning foreign technology, however, is determined by the education level. Second, the efficiency of the utilization of the existing equipment and machinery can still be improved with better educated workers.

In fact, the importance of education does not only rely on the mechanism mentioned above. If the aggregate economy is divided into three sectors: agriculture, manufacture, and service, then the economic growth can also be driven by the re-allocation of labor force among these sectors. Due to the labor productivity differences in these three sectors, the total labor productivity of the economy as a whole can be improved due to the movement of labor force from less productive sector to the more productive sector, even though the labor productivity does not change in any of these sectors alone. For most of developing countries, the economic growth is driven by the shifting of workers from agriculture sector to the manufacture and service sector, and by the concurrent migration of labor force from rural areas to urban areas. For example, the percentage of labor force that is in the rural areas dropped from 82% in 1978 to 57% in 2005. To predict China's economic growth in the future, the analysis should be rest on the economic structural change. In the past, migrant workers generally went to the manufacturing and service sectors which do not have very high skill requirement. As the rise in the labor cost and the weakening of competitiveness of China's labor-intensive sector in the world market, the process of economic structural change will be dampened if the education level of the labor force is not improved.

When it comes to the financial market, Professor Spence discusses it from the perspective of information. Actually, the financial market is important to the human capital accumulation. Compared to the physical capital accumulation, the investment in human capital is a very long process. Private investment in education, especially the higher education, is generally funded by bank loans. In an economy with huge income inequality, it is extremely difficult for the poor to get the loan if the economy does not have a sound and healthy financial market. Thus the income inequality continues to exist and obstruct the economic growth.

In summary, Professor Spence puts forward several factors that demine the long run economic growth in China, such as human capital accumulation and structural change. Actually, these factors are the general driving force in the developing countries. Therefore, although the rapid growth of China during the past 30 years is regarded as "miracle" by some researchers, China's experience is not surprising at all if we look into it through the lens of the standard economic growth and development theory.

Chapter 4

Employment, Inflation and Continuable Economic Growth

Edmund Phelps

Biography

Edmund S. Phelps is the 2006 Nobel Memorial Prize Winner in Economic Sciences. He received his B.A. from Amherst College in 1955 and his Ph.D. from Yale in 1959. After working at Yale University and University of Pennsylvania, Phelps started working at Columbia University in 1971 and has been the McVickar Professor of Political Economy at Columbia University since 1982. Phelps was the former Vice President of American Economic Association. He was also a senior advisor of Brookings Panel on Economic Activity and a consultant of Research Department of the International Monetary Fund.

Phelps's research focused mainly on neo-classical growth theory, following the seminal work of Solow. He is best known for his work on economic growth at Yale University's Cowles Foundation in the 1960s. This includes the idea of the Golden

Rule savings rate, which is about how much money should be spent and how much should be saved for the future. Some of his best work is on microeconomics of full employment and how prices affect wages. Part of this work is about the natural rate of unemployment.

Speech

Ladies and gentlemen, I am very glad to attend this meeting. I am always excited to talk about the Chinese economy and the connection between China and other countries around the world. China is now in an unprecedented condition. The present excellent economic situation in China could not have come about without the distinctive economic policy of the past two decades. China is fortunate to have industrious people and the ardent wish of its government for prosperity and development, which has made the country very attractive to foreign investors. This phenomenon sparked a remarkable increase in investment within the Chinese economy, and also in the employment and productivity development in China.

First of all, I would like to briefly introduce the connection between investment and employment, but I will not introduce the methods I have been using in detail. I must emphasize one point: defining such a method of analysis without the consideration of monetary policy does not mean that it is not important. In my opinion, the domestic economy in America is giving up some of its historical advantage in competition. Originally, American workers were the only beneficiaries of new American technologies, which brought the wage of American workers to a new height. Owing to investments and technologies transferring to China, Chinese workers can now also share these benefits. As a result of the adverse development in the terms of trade, the wage of American workers is shrinking on this account while the wage of Chinese workers is increasing, owing to increasing productivity. There is not much competitive advantage left to be transferred from American or European companies in the future. Under such circumstances, China must adjust itself to the next stage of economic development — that is to say, China should take stronger measures to promote better economic institutions and greater capabilities in the development of science and technology if China hopes to catch up with the high technology of America and Europe. The situation China is faced with is similar to the situation of post-war Europe, from 1950 to 1975, and Europe successfully managed that period. If China hopes to manage such a period as well, it has to reach the general level of Europe in the 1950s or 1960s, including extremely complicated capacity of management, a new level of research and development, and further development of proprietary technology. China is now in transition, which may bring all kinds of new problems to western European countries. China is setting up new financial institutions to provide financing help for well-functioning enterprises and financing support for commercial views. As America has such new financial institutions, so will China.

In addition, I would like to talk about the influence of foreign economic activities on Chinese employment. Europe has been in a long-term recession for the past ten, or even twenty years. In the past three and half years, America increased its level of investment sharply, but we cannot say it has reached its normal commercial level. The commercial activities in America are in recession now. The host just mentioned two proportions. One is the present activity ratio in America; that is, the proportion of employees in the total workers, which is below 1993 levels. Another is the participation ratio in America, that is, the proportion of labor force in the total population, which is below 1988 levels. According to the theories of the Keynesian school of economics, the economic depression in Europe and the newly arisen small-scale recession in America will have a negative effect on the overall effective demand in China. If China decreases its interest rate to avoid the nominal appreciation of exchange rate, deflation, and economic depression, the economic depression in Europe and the newly arisen economic recession in America will be unfavorable for investment activities, since investment development in China is greatly promoted by the low interest rate in America and Europe. As I said before, such development of investment activities would promote wage increases, as well as employment, especially in some new industries and commercial fields. Therefore, it is obvious that if the economy in America and Europe revives, China will face difficulties in its future economic development:

the revival will increase the interest rate, or real interest rate around the world, which will consequently decrease the effective demand.

I would also like to talk about economic overheating and excessive investment so as to help us solve these two problems. Over the past two years, the monetary policy in America has not been neutral. It has resulted in a much lower real interest rate than normal, in which the economy is developed in balance. According to new theories in the 1960s, monetary policy that is not neutral will promote rapidly an increase in employment. The effectiveness can be seen sooner than other policies. Now the employment in China is also likely to increase rapidly, since it is easy to get capital support, owing to the low interest rate in America. The exchange rate of RMB is fixed to dollars. If Greenspan decreases the interest rate, China has to adapt its interest rate to America's. Some people think that the fact will contradict with my prediction, as we do not see the inflation growing in America, nor in China. But I think that negative affairs, such as company scandals, or situation intervention in the Middle East, will reduce the effect of deflation or inflation increase. According to my experience and observation in the 1960s, it takes a long time for people to recognize such real inflation caused by un-neutral monetary policy, and even longer to understand it. This is an interesting phenomenon; in my opinion, such cases are caused by the low interest rate in America, which makes it easy to get capital support and then results in excessive investment. According to my own standard theory, monetary policy should be applied to stabilize the real interest rate and take it as a way to boost the whole effective demand. It is also very effective for fiscal policy — we have to see the other side. The inflation is a result of investment enthusiasm, not fiscal policy. The enthusiasm speeds up the development of investment, which is supposed to rise later or fail to rise. In this way, no problems will occur in a closed economy. As economists say, in the case of closed economy, the interest rate will decrease enough to make the investment increase enough to restore employment. But in an open economy, especially China's, which doesn't take a great part in the world economy, the real interest rate cannot be too much lower than the world interest rate, which is greatly determined by the real interest rates in America and Europe. That is to say, the rapidly increasing capital stock arising in advance can't be counteracted by decreasing the real interest rate. We have realized the importance of the problem in capital stock increasing. Excessive investment increases the capital stock, and finally results in inevitable negative effect on employment. The negative effect will more or less counteract the expansionary effect of related policy.

Lastly, the present capital stock in China is excessive and the production activity is increasing rapidly, so superfluous capital stock will be used to build factories or purchase equipments. This means that the problems resulting from an overheated economy or excessive investment are only short-term problems for Chinese government and will not have a negative effect if counteracted in two or three years. Those are the short-term problems; now we come to China's long-term problems. Ultimately, China must solve the problem of bad investments, which should not be funded or should not be carried out as scheduled. The low efficiency of the investment decision in China requires a solution: China must further reform its financial system and financial structure.

Review

Zhang Chengsi

Zhang Chengsi is Professor of Finance at Renmin University of China. Professor Zhang obtained his Ph.D. from the University of Manchester. He is a member of Royal Economic Society, a member of Econometric Society, and an anonymous referee for a number of international journals. Professor Zhang's research interests are monetary policy, inflation dynamics, and financial time series analysis. He publishes two monographs: *Financial Econometrics* and *Inflation Dynamics and Monetary Policy in Practice.* His recent publications appear in *Journal of Money, Credit and Banking, Oxford Bulletin of Economics and Statistics, The World Economy, Empirical Economics, China and World Economy,* and *Frontiers of Economics in China.* Professor Zhang was an invited keynote speaker at the international conference, "The Impact of International Liquidity on China and the Trend in the Future," jointly organized by the State Administration of Foreign Exchange of China and the World Bank in October 2007.

Edmund Phelps is regarded as the most influential figure in the modern economics. As one of the most famous macroeconomists, Phelps made great contributions to the area of inflation, unemployment, and economic growth. His contributions help people to deeply understand the relationship between inflation, unemployment, and expectations, and the relationship between short- and long-run effects of macroeconomic policy.

In particular, Phelps plays a leading role in exploring micro-foundation of macroeconomics, which pays the way for creating the micro-founded macroeconomic models. The recently developed dynamic models of real output, inflation expectations, and inflation, in particular the New Keynesian Phillips Curve of Rational Expectations, are in the spirit of his academic contributions[1]. Because of these fundamental contributions, Phelps wins the 2006 Nobel Prize in Economics.

During the most recent decade, China is witnessing marked economic growth. In the same time, both the internal and external economic conditions are changing. Phelp's speech, therefore, not only provides insightful knowledge for Chinese economists to understand the relationship between unemployment, inflation, and sustainable economic growth, but also promotes us to think more deeply about the future route of China's economic development, amidst the institutional and financial revolutions.

In his speech, Phelps discussed the opportunities and challenges that China is faced with, in terms of the driving forces of economic development, new paradigm of the world economy, interest rate policy and economic overheat, and capital stock over accumulation in China. He underscored the interactions among China's economic policy, financial revolution, and short- and long-term economic development.

In his speech, Phelps appreciated the remarkable achievements in China economic development over the past 20 years, and provided positive comments on the importance of the macroeconomic policy in China on the economic development. Indeed, since the opening-up, China's macroeconomic policy of attracting foreign capital and encouraging investment has played an indispensable role in sustaining stable and fast economic growth in China. During this process, China benefits from the advanced technology and Chinese workers' wage also increase considerably. Therefore, Phelps believes that China has increased its technology advantage during this process,

---

[1] See Zhang, Osborn, and Kim (2009). The New Keynesian Phillips curve: From sticky inflation to sticky prices. *Journal of Money, Credit and Banking*, 40(4), 667–699, for more details about the NKPC models.

which is one of the most important driving forces for China' economic development.

However, we must acknowledge that the benefits China got from the foreign capital investment is not the only driving factor of China's economic growth. Albeit some statistical figures show that Foreign Direct Investment (FDI) contributes substantively to China' economic growth, particularly the spillover effect of technology, the innovation capability in China has been improved significantly over the recent years due to the relevant macroeconomic policy implementations. The products made in China also gain more competitive power in the world market. In addition, market expectations are well-anchored over the present era of high economic growth in China. The positive expectations reinforce the good trend of economic growth in China. The combination of these factors, I believe, is the real driving force for sustainable economic growth in China.

Phelps' view is not inconsistent with my comments. Nonetheless, I should emphasize that we need to think more about the "new" round economic growth, raised by Phelps. That said, we may not be able to further obtain competitive advantage of developed countries at present and in the near future. Meanwhile, China is faced with a tough objective of constructing modern financial markets. Therefore, it is important for China to develop technological innovation by ourselves and train professional talents with modern finance knowledge.

Phelps also discussed a multi-country macroeconomic model of open economy. By using this model, he pointed out that the ongoing recession in the Europe and the US may induce negative impact on China's economic development. From the point of effective demand, however, China may also encounter difficult situation if the Western economies start to recover and attracts international investment moving from China to these countries.

We should note that the world economic condition is still under changing. In particular, the negative impact of the US subprime crisis on the US economy may be more evident a few quarters later. Despite the recent drop of the federal funds rate, the future development of the US economy is unclear. Moreover, the impact of this crisis on other countries across the world may manifest soon, albeit we are not sure about the degree of the negative impact of the crisis. What is clear, however, the interest rate adjustments will affect investment activities.

Another important question that Phelps raised in his speech is the relationship between interest rate policy and economic overdevelopment. In this regard, he mentioned the important theory of Keynesian School, namely the non-neutral monetary policy of interest rate adjustment. Phelps believed that the interest rate policy in the US over the recent years has been non-neutral low interest rate policy. This low interest rate policy is by no means surprising because inflation in the US has been low and stable since 2000. As an illustration, Figure 1 depicts year-on-year growth rates of Consumer Price Index (CPI) series of both the US and China over 1999M01 to 2007M08. We can see that CPI inflation in the US is slightly higher than that in China during 1999–2006, but the difference is not very striking. It is worth of noting that inflation in China after 2007 has been higher than that in the US. Based on the Purchasing Power Parity, this inflation differential should predict damped expectations on RMB appreciation. Of course, this is not the key point that discussed in Phelps' speech. But we should understand that the dynamic change in the

Figure 1.   CPI inflation Series of China and the US: 1999M1–2007M8

inflation differentials will eventually influence monetary authorities' strategy in determining interest rates.

Finally, Phelps discussed the over accumulation of capital stock in China. This is also a focus of the present debate on China economy both in China and abroad. Phelps believed that the economic overheat caused by the high capital accumulation in China is only a short-run problem. What China should concern about is to distinguish categories of different capital stocks. In particular, China should curb unhealthy investment and improve investment efficiency. Phelps' suggestion is right. The key question is how we can identify and revoke unhealthy investment and optimize capital stock. In my view, short-term international capital, driven by international yield spread, is now sneezing into China through various legal channels. Therefore, it is urgent for China to increase regulations on international capital movements. To achieve internal and external balances, China must make use of both interest rate policy and exchange policy.

Overall, the illumination of Phelps's speech is more important than the content of the speech. Faced with new paradigm of the world economic development, Chinese economists should realize that our historical task is tougher than any time in the history. We should explore useful ideas from the world-renowned economists and use scientific methods and rational thoughts to find suitable way for China economic development. The Mundell–Huang lectures are important contributions toward this direction.

Chapter 5

Will Renminbi Become the Third Power Currency of the World?

Ronald I. Mckinnon

Biography

Ronald I. McKinnon received his B.A. from University of Alberta in 1956 and his Ph.D. from University of Minnesota in 1961. He has taught at Economics Department, Stanford University and served as William D. Eberle Professor of International Economics ever since 1984. His teaching and research interests include international trade and finance, economic development, East Asian economies, money and banking, and alternative international monetary systems, etc. McKinnon began giving advises in monetary policy and economic and financial development to International Monetary Fund, World Bank, the Asian Development Bank and governments of developing countries in 1965. He has been serving as the monetary policy consultant to Hong Kong Monetary Authority from 1999 up to now. He is also editor for *The Economist, Financial Times,* and *The Wall Street Journal.*

Professor McKinnon is an applied economist whose primary accomplishments are in economic development and international economics. He is well recognized as founder and authority in financial deepening and financial liberalization. McKinnon's research has been more than welcome by monetary authorities of the developing countries around the world and built up very good reputation.

Speech

Let me say how delighted I am to be here at the Renmin University talking to students. I am not used to be on television at the same time. So please forgive me if I stumble.

China has succeeded in overcoming financial repression by keeping a stable price level, making it attractive for people to build up their financial assets — bank accounts. But they are now faced with the problem of "conflicted virtue", which is different and also very difficult to translate. "Conflicted virtue" is a dilemma faced by the high saving East Asian countries collectively. Not just China, but all these East Asian countries are high savers. America is a very low saver. And the Asian countries lend to America, but they build up dollar claims, which is very difficult to deal with. So right now this problem of "conflicted virtue" is common to the East Asian counties as a whole, particularly because they become more and more integrated in foreign trade.

We can see is that exports as a share of total trade of East Asian countries have been rising more quickly within Asia than exports to the outside world (see Figure 1). By 2002 the East Asian exports, leveled half, were to other East Asian countries, while exports to the rest of the world had fallen in relative importance. The position of the US in the East Asian trade does remain fairly stable, has not changed a great deal. I should remind you that although the relative exports to the rest of world have been declining, measured as a percent of total exports, the absolute growth of Asian economies has been so high that absolute exports are still increasing to Europe, as any European will tell you.

We see the similar story on the import side that East Asian imports from each other are now approaching 60% of their total trade. And China is a particularly important importer from the rest of East Asia. China imports huge quantities of goods and services from other East Asian economies, but then exports to the US. So the China's bilateral trade surplus with the US is very large. So, at Christmas time last December when my family was assembled and my grandchildren were opening their presents, every kind of gifts you can imagine, almost all were made in China.

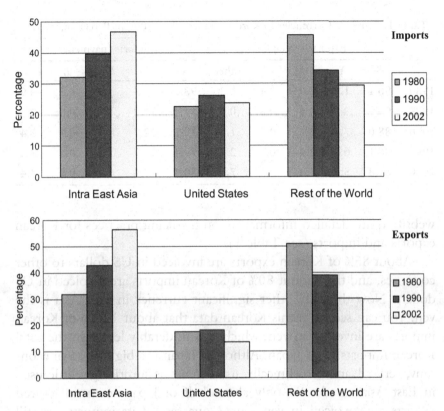

Figure 1. The Rise of Intra Regional Trade in East Asia*, 1980–2002 (Share of Total)
* East Asia: China, Hong Kong, Indonesia, Japan, Korea, Malaysia, Philippines, Singapore, Taiwan, and Thailand

China has become very visible in the American politics, particularly economy of the trade surplus. But really this surplus is the East Asian surplus, because other East Asian countries are behind China exporting to it.

Now what is unusual about the integrated East Asian economies is that it does use outside money as the principal money for invoicing foreign trade and dominating capital flows — the US dollar. Now it turns out to be very difficult to get comprehensive data on how goods are invoiced in foreign trade for most countries. And by good luck, one of my research associates managed to find on the Bank of Korea's

Table 1.   Invoice Currencies in Korean Trade, 1980–2000 in Percentage Terms

	Exports (receipts)					Imports (payments)				
	$	¥	DM	£	other	$	¥	DM	£	other
1980	96.1	1.2	2.0	0.4	0.3	93.2	3.7	1.7	0.5	0.9
1985	94.7	3.7	0.6	0.3	0.7	82.4	12.3	2	0.5	2.8
1990	88.0	7.8	2.1	0.5	1.7	79.1	12.7	4.1	0.9	3.4
1995	88.1	6.5	2.4	0.8	2.2	79.4	12.7	3.8	0.7	3.4
2000	84.8	5.4	1.8	0.7	7.3	80.4	12.4	1.9	0.8	4.4

website quite detailed information on invoicing practices for Korean exports and imports (see Table 1).

About 85% of Korean exports are invoiced in US dollars to other countries, and then about 80% of Korean imports are invoiced in US dollars. Now the only other significant currency in East Asia is the yen. You can see from this Korean data that about 12.4% of Korean imports are invoiced in yen, which is considerably less than the total Korean imports from Japan. Although Japan is a big industrial economy, very advanced technically, its currency is surprisingly little used in East Asian trade. So only about half of Japanese manufactured exports are invoiced in yen, but 3 quarters of its imports are still invoiced in dollars. So the yen is only used when that trade is directly with Japan, as with the Korean example here. Otherwise, everything else is dollar based. And when China trades with Singapore, they don't invoice in RMB or Singapore dollar, it's the US dollar. Or, when Thailand trades with Malaysia, they do not use the baht or the ringgit, but they use the US dollar.

Now it's not surprising given this dollar dominance for historical reasons. Just happens to be a fact of life. It is not surprising that most of these East Asian countries try to peg their currencies to the dollar, as you can see in this slide (see Table 2 and Figure 2).

We have the pre-crisis period before 1997. We see the measure of volatility of the daily exchange rate against the dollar of each of these East Asian economies. Of course China is pretty well fixed at 8.28 yuan to the dollar, but the others show very little volatility in

Table 2. Standard Deviations of Daily Exchange Rate Fluctuations Against the Dollar

	Pre-crisis	Crisis	Post-crisis	2003
Chinese Yuan	0.03	0.01	0.00	0.00
Hong Kong Dollar	0.02	0.03	0.00	0.00
Indonesian Rupiah	0.17	4.43	1.15	0.42
Korean Won	0.22	2.35	0.44	0.51
Malaysian Ringgit	0.25	1.53	0.01	0.00
Philippine Peso	0.37	1.31	0.53	0.27
Singapore Dollar	0.20	0.75	0.27	0.36
New Taiwan Dollar	0.19	0.50	0.21	0.15
Thai Baht	0.21	1.55	0.39	0.26
Japanese Yen	0.67	1.00	0.64	0.53
Deutsche Mark	0.60	0.58	0.66	0.63
Swiss Franc	0.69	0.66	0.71	0.72

Data source: Datastream. Percent changes. Pre-crisis = 02/01/94–05/30/97, crisis = 06/01/97–12/31/98, post-crisis = 01/01/99–12/31/03, 2003 = 01/01/03–12/31/03.

their movements against the dollar. The biggest exception in East Asia is the Japanese yen. The yen has fluctuated wildly over the last 30 years, while the other East Asian countries try to keep the range of variation against the dollar fairly narrow.

Now when the crisis came for Malaysia, Korea, Indonesia, Thailand and Philippines, they lost control. So the exchange rate fluctuations against the dollar became very large. It is really only China and Hong Kong together that kept their exchange rate stable during the great crisis. The IMF blamed much of the East Asia Crisis on the fact that smaller East Asian economies were pegging to the dollar, softly pegging to the dollar, and claimed that this attracted too much foreign capital into these economies. So the IMF sternly warned the East Asia Crisis economies do not go back to pegging the dollar. And much to everybody's surprise, particularly IMF's surprise, they have gone back to soft dollar pegging now 2003–2004, much like they did before the crisis.

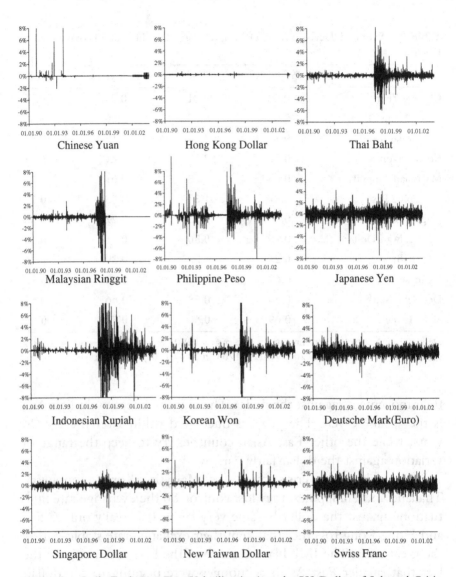

Figure 2. Daily Exchange Rate Volatility Against the US Dollar of Selected Crisis and Non-Crisis Currencies

The biggest exception is Japan, for the yen–dollar rate continues to fluctuate. We see that the daily fluctuations of the yen against the dollar are consistently very high. But for the other East Asian countries, they only have high daily fluctuations when they are in crisis, like the 1997–1998 Crisis. So now besides China, the Malaysian ringgit is also pegged to the dollar without any variation –3.8 ringgits to the dollar.

It turns out it is a general principal that the floating exchange rates among the industrial countries show a lot of daily and weekly volatility, whereas there is a fear of floating in the developing countries who try to keep their exchange rates fairly close to they all softly peg. We can see fluctuations in US dollar against euro are high and against Swiss franc are very high by comparison. Therefore, despite the IMF's warnings not to peg softly to the dollar, these countries by large have gone back to doing that.

What I would like to discuss briefly is what the rationale is for them doing this contrary to the IMF's advice. So we know the dollar is widely used for invoicing commodity trade. But the dollar has a second function in the world system. That is as a nominal anchor for countries who peg to the dollar (see Figure 3), so they can stabilize their own price level somewhat more easily. So back in the 1950s and 1960s, all the European industrial countries and most developing countries, outside of the Communist Socialist world, declared formal par values for their currencies under Bretton Woods. So the exchange rates were very stable. During the 1950s and 1960s, America had a very stable price level. So countries that did peg to the dollar could import that price stability. Then the system broke down at the end of the 1960s. Inflation became very high in the US. And President Nixon insisted that the dollar be devalued against all the other major currencies. So we had a period of high invariable inflation in the world economy, wildly fluctuating exchange rates and high and very volatile interest rates, up to the early 1990s. But now you can see that the American price level has stabilized again. Maybe we have to put aside the year 2004. But in the 1990s through 2003, it has become quite stable. So it is more attractive for other countries to peg to the dollar to anchor their own price levels. So this macroeconomic

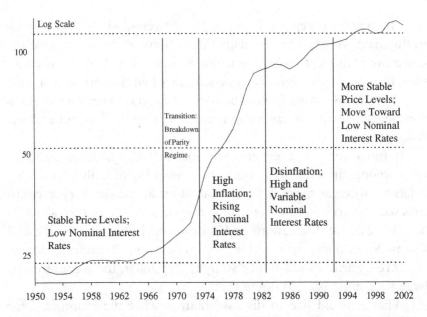

Figure 3.   The World's Nominal Anchor: US Wholesale Prices (1951–2002)

sense there is an incentive to peg to the dollar. But from the point of view of avoiding risk in the foreign exchange markets, there is another form of incentive to help exporters and importers hedge their risk.

So two American economists, Barry Eichengreen and Ricardo Hausmann, have identified the problem of "original sin" in debtor economies who are less developed. And "original sin" means essentially that if you were debtor economy, you can not borrow in your own currencies. If you run trade deficit, you build up debts to foreigners. All those debts will be denominated in foreign money but not in your own money. So as with the East Asian countries before 1997 and Latin America now, when they build up large debts, they are dollar-denominated. Then these countries become very vulnerable to an attack or they have a forced depreciation of their currencies against the dollar. They can not repay the dollar debts. This attack can cause widespread bankruptcies through their financial systems. It turns out when you build up dollar debts it becomes impossible to hedge through forward exchange transactions the exchange risk. And even though the domestic bond market might be relatively good, the forward market in foreign exchange is not well developed. So governments respond by just trying to keep this spot exchange rate fairly stable through time as a method of giving a bit forward cover to importers and exporters.

But we now know in the East Asia since 1997, all the East Asian countries collectively had been running big trade surpluses with the US. So the problem has changed from being dollar debtors to suddenly being large dollar creditors and piling up liquid claims against the US. So "conflicted virtue," which is difficult to translate into Chinese, refers to the fact the creditor economies like China, Japan and Korea do not lend their own currencies to foreigners but rather they build up dollar claims on foreigners, mainly the US. They become vulnerable to a different form of attack — a rush out of dollar into the domestic currency with a potential of a forced appreciation in these Asian economies.

So we have a problem of translation. And let me first start with the "original sin." A student suggested that the original sin is a Christian concept; there is a Buddhist concept which is very similar, called "sin from the past life." This concept whether Buddhist or Christian means that something you were born with. Not necessarily your fault in this life, anyway, but something you were born with. And it takes the form for debtor economies of not being able to borrow in terms of their own currencies, but having to use somebody else's currency. And in the present world where you have dollar dominance, maybe euro dominance as you mentioned, for borrowing or lending, it is very hard for other countries with their own currencies to actually use them in the borrowing or lending process. Once this system is set up with the two dominant monies, it is very difficult for other monies to break in like the Japanese yen which is relatively little used.

Now when Eichengreen and Hausmann coined this term of "original sin" for debtor economies, and then I can see the East Asian countries are all becoming creditors, I felt there need to be a parallel term, a mere image term for "original sin." So I came up with the idea of "conflicted virtue."

So "conflicted virtue" sounds in English like the opposite of "original sin," virtue being the opposite of sin anyway. But in this context, virtue means high saving. So, virtuous person is a high saving person. So, all these East Asian countries, very high savers like China, are virtuous. But right now the US is very un-virtuous or improper, because it saves so little. But unfortunately we just could not come up with the Chinese translation directly of "conflicted virtue"; maybe you could help us on this.

So we are using the translation of "high saving dilemma" to apply to East Asian countries. Now as we have said the high saving East Asian countries lend to foreigners, in the form of having trade and current account surpluses, they build up claims on foreigners. But then foreigners start complaining about the build-up, as if it was a misvalued exchange rate. And the domestic holders of dollar assets become very nervous and begin disholding and coming back to yen or into RMB. So as runs into the domestic currency begin, the government becomes conflicted, China's government, Japan's government. Because if they allow appreciation, a sharp appreciation, they lose mercantile competitiveness, and if as in the Japanese case, so these appreciations are repetitive, then they will get big deflation. Japan has had the problem of "conflicted virtue" for much longer than any other Asian countries running big trade surpluses with the US in the early 1980s right to the present. They have been forced into serious appreciations by American pressure, talked by Secretary of Treasury, and this is what pushed Japan into the big deflation in the 1990s and the zero interest rate liquidity trap. But if a country comes under American pressure to appreciate and it does not appreciate, then there is a threat of trade sanctions imposed by the American government. And this happened several times in the 1970s, 1980s until in the mid of 1990s. Fortunately China has been much more stand fast than Japan in resisting this pressure and keeping the RMB stable at 8.28 yuan to the dollar, whereas in Japan the yen has been all over the place and there is much less confidence in the government can actually hold the rate.

The next 3 slides provide very detailed data (see Tables 3, 4, and 5). They simply show this huge build-up of foreign exchange reserves in

Table 3. Comparison of East Asian (EA) to US Current Account Surpluses, 1990–2003

	1990	1991	1992	1993	1994	1995	1996	1997	1998	1999	2000	2001	2002	2003 (Preliminary)
							Percent of GDP							
Japan	1.4	2.0	3.0	3.0	2.7	2.1	1.4	2.2	3.0	2.6	2.5	2.1	2.8	3.1
Singapore	8.5	11.3	11.9	7.2	16.2	17.7	15.2	15.6	22.6	18.6	14.5	19.0	21.5	27.7
Taiwan	7.0	7.1	4.1	3.1	2.7	2.1	3.9	2.4	1.3	2.9	2.9	6.4	9.1	9.8
Indonesia	-2.6	-3.3	-2.0	-1.3	-1.6	-3.2	-3.4	-2.3	4.3	4.1	5.3	4.8	4.2	4.0
Korea	-0.8	-2.8	-1.3	0.3	-1.0	-1.7	-4.4	-1.7	12.7	6.0	2.7	1.9	1.3	1.9
Malaysia	-2.0	-8.5	-3.7	-4.5	-6.1	-9.7	-4.4	-5.9	13.2	15.9	9.4	8.3	7.6	12.1
Philippines	-6.1	-2.3	-1.9	-5.6	-4.6	-2.7	-4.8	-5.3	2.4	9.5	8.2	1.8	5.4	4.4
Thailand	-8.5	-7.7	-5.7	-5.1	-5.6	-8.1	-8.1	-2.0	12.7	10.1	7.6	5.4	6.1	5.8
China	3.1	3.3	1.4	-1.9	1.3	0.2	0.9	4.1	3.3	2.1	1.9	1.5	2.9	1.9
Hong Kong	n.a.	n.a.	n.a.	n.a.	n.a.	n.a.	n.a.	n.a.	2.7	7.5	5.5	7.5	10.8	9.9
							Billions of US Dollars							
Total EA Current Account Surplus	54.3	73.5	117.3	117.8	132.9	93.8	44.2	129.4	246.4	233.8	215.8	181.5	242.3	269.9
US Current Account Surplus	-79.0	3.7	-48.0	-82.0	-117.7	-105.2	-117.2	-127.7	-204.7	-290.9	-411.5	-393.7	-480.9	-541.7

Table 4. Official Foreign Exchange Reserves in East Asia, 1990–2003

billions of US dollars

	1990	1991	1992	1993	1994	1995	1996	1997	1998	1999	2000	2001	2002	2003
Japan	69.5	61.8	61.9	88.7	115.1	172.4	207.3	207.9	203.2	277.7	347.2	387.7	451.5	652.79
Singapore	27.5	33.9	39.7	48.1	57.9	68.3	76.5	70.9	74.4	76.3	79.7	74.9	81.4	94.97
Taiwan	72.4	82.4	82.3	83.6	92.5	90.3	88.0	83.5	90.3	106.2	106.7	122.2	161.7	206.63
Indonesia	7.4	9.2	10.2	11.0	11.8	13.3	17.8	16.1	22.4	26.2	28.3	27.0	30.8	34.74
Korea	14.5	13.3	16.6	19.7	25.0	31.9	33.2	19.7	52.0	73.7	95.9	102.5	120.8	154.51
Malaysia	9.3	10.4	16.8	26.8	24.9	22.9	26.2	20.0	24.7	29.7	28.6	29.6	33.3	43.47
Phillippines	0.9	3.2	4.3	4.5	5.9	6.2	9.9	7.1	9.1	13.1	12.9	13.3	13.0	13.33
Thailand	13.2	17.3	20.0	24.1	28.9	35.5	37.2	25.7	28.4	33.8	31.9	32.3	38.0	40.97
China	28.6	42.7	19.4	21.2	51.6	73.6	105.0	139.9	145.0	154.7	165.6	212.2	286.4	403.25
Hong Kong	24.6	28.8	35.2	43.0	49.3	55.4	63.8	92.8	89.6	96.2	107.5	111.2	111.9	118.36
Total	267.9	302.9	306.4	370.7	462.9	570.0	665.0	683.6	739.2	887.6	1004.4	1112.9	1328.7	1763.02

Table 5. East Asian (EA) Current Account Surpluses and Changes in Official Reserves, 1991–2003

										billions of US dollars per year			
	1991	1992	1993	1994	1995	1996	1997	1998	1999	2000	2001	2002	2003
Total Reserve Changes	35.0	3.5	64.3	92.2	107.1	95.1	18.6	55.6	148.5	116.7	108.5	215.8	451.1
Total Current Account	73.5	117.2	117.8	132.8	93.8	44.2	129.4	246.4	233.8	215.8	181.5	242.3	269.9
Japan Reserve Changes	-7.7	0.1	26.8	26.4	57.3	34.9	0.5	-4.7	74.5	69.5	40.5	63.7	222.1
Japan Current Account	68.2	112.6	131.6	130.3	111.0	65.8	96.8	118.7	114.6	119.7	87.8	112.4	132.0
China Reserve Changes	14.1	-23.2	1.8	30.4	22.0	31.5	34.9	5.1	9.7	10.9	46.6	74.2	116.8
China Current Account	13.3	6.4	-11.6	6.9	1.6	7.2	37.0	31.5	21.1	20.5	-7.4	35.4	25.5
Taiwan Reserve Changes	10.0	-0.1	1.3	8.9	-2.1	-2.3	-4.5	6.8	15.9	0.5	15.5	39.4	44.9
Taiwan Current Account	12.5	8.6	7.0	6.5	5.5	10.9	7.1	3.4	8.4	8.9	17.9	25.7	28.8
Korea Reserve Changes	-1.2	3.3	3.1	5.3	6.9	1.3	-13.5	32.3	21.7	22.2	6.6	18.3	29.5
Korea Current Account	-8.3	-3.9	-1.0	-3.9	-8.5	-23.0	-8.2	40.4	24.5	12.2	8.2	6.1	9.8
Singapore Reserve Changes	6.4	5.7	8.4	9.8	10.5	8.1	-5.6	3.5	1.9	3.4	-4.8	6.5	14.9
Singapore Current Account	4.9	5.9	4.2	11.4	14.8	14.0	14.9	18.5	15.2	13.3	16.1	18.7	25.6

East Asia. And in 2003 and 2004, the build-up of exchange reserve is really much bigger than the current account surpluses of these East Asian countries because of disholding in private sector in China and private sector in Japan switching out whatever dollar assets they own into the local currency. So the problem of "conflicted virtue" is one or another sort of balance sheet mismatch, or you build up dollar assets which are quite high, whether in the banking system or insurance companies, relative to the domestic currency assets. But it is not disequilibrium in the flow sense when your price level and productivity is misaligning with your trading partners. So if we look at China and Japan, from the point of view of international competitiveness and whether price levels are aligning and wage is rising right away, we see that there is no evidence of serious undervaluation of these currencies.

So when we want to look at the extremely rapidly growing economy, very high productivity growth, like China. Outsiders often say if you have high productivity growth, you should be appreciating your currency. That is the sort of simple minded way of looking at it. But the fact is that there is quite a better adjustment mechanism — relative wage adjustment that works best when the exchange rate is fixed.

We see this in the period of Japan's very high growth 1950–1971 which was just as high as in China now, with the exchange rate fixed at 360 yen to the dollar just as what we will see for the Chinese data (see Table 6). So we see in the 1950–1971 period for Japan the labor productivity in manufacturing grew very rapidly, 9% a year, but money wages in Japan also grew very rapidly, 10% a year. So the rapid growth in money wages just offset the effect of higher productivity growth in Japan. So Japanese prices remain quite well align with American as you can see the rate of wholesale price inflation, tradable goods inflation, was close to 1% in each country.

But Japan then was a much less open economy than China now. So for the service sectors in Japan and a lot of small skilled industries we see protection. And thus, when wages in the manufacturing sector rose so fast, these relatively backward industries had to raise their prices. And that is why the Consumer Price Index in Japan then rose faster than in the US. Economists have a name for this when the price

Table 6. Key Economic Indicators for Japan and the US 1950–1970

Wholesale prices		Money wages		Consumer prices		Industrial production	
US	Japan	US	Japan	US	Japan	US	Japan
1.63	0.69[a]	4.52	10.00	2.53	5.01	4.40	14.56
Real GDP		Nominal GDP		Narrow money		Labor productivity	
US	Japan	US	Japan	US	Japan	US	Japan
3.84	9.45[a]	6.79	14.52[a]	3.94	16.10[b]	2.55	8.92[c]

[a] 1952–1971; [b] 1953–1971; [c] 1951–1971

of services rises relative to the price of manufacture on a growth path. It is called the Balassa–Samuelson Effect. And this is what we see with the high increase in Japanese consumer prices, but there is no disequilibrium in the balance of payments, because the international competitiveness remains balance with the high wage growth in Japan.

And Japanese money growth remained extremely high in that period, because the Bank of Japan was targeting the exchange rate with its monetary policy, not the rate of growth of money supply. So money supply was just an endogenous variable reflecting the very high saving propensities in Japanese as they became richer they want to hold bank accounts in monetary assets.

We now do the same table for China, but for the modern time period 1994–2002 (see Table 7). We see very similar effect. So in the lower right-hand corner, we see China's labor productivity growth is about 10.77% per year, which is very high. But then if you look on the money wages, they are rising about 10.8% per year. So this is very high growth in average money wages in China. I am not saying marginal for poor, un-skilled workers but the average money wage growth in manufacturing has been very high, the same order of magnitudes as productivity growth.

China is a much more open economy where service sector is less protected now 1994–2004 than Japan was in the 1950s and 1960s. Part of the openness is foreign retailing firms coming in and putting a lot of pressure on the service activities in China keeping the prices

Table 7. Key Economic Indicators for China and the US 1994–2002

Wholesale prices		Money wages		Consumer prices		Industrial production	
US	China	US	China	US	China	US	China
1.10	1.24[a]	3.02	10.80	2.45	3.22	3.35	12.17
Real GDP		Nominal GDP		Narrow money		Labor productivity	
US	China	US	China	US	China	US	China
3.19	8.41	5.04	10.51	3.80	17.82	2.49	10.77

[a] Ex-factory price index

down. Major retailers like Wal-Mart, IKEA, Carrefour and so forth are all in China. This is one reason why China's CPI has not risen relative to its WPI in the same way that happened earlier in Japan.

Now because the People's Bank of China was targeting monetary policy towards the stable exchange rate, this meant that the money growth could be endogenously determined by how fast the economy was growing and the demand that wealthier and wealthier households had for bank deposits and other financial assets. So you can see the growth of narrow money in China, 17.82% per year, is like Japan's, even slightly higher, but nothing to worry about.

So you can see once China got over its inflation in 1997 that China's CPI has actually been falling a bit as American Consumer Price Index rose, but the WPI in China, an Ex-factory index, which is not generally available, has been falling quite a bit through this data which ended in 2002 (see Figure 4). So again we repeat in this diagram, although the RMB has been pretty well fixed at 8.28, Chinese money wage growth is really quite remarkable (see Figure 5). So there is a natural balance in the international payments in the flow sense, just as in Japan in the earlier case. And this wage growth is quite well dispersed across Chinese industries. So we see here that various industries, all the things are moving together (see Figure 6). And it is actually easier to get this kind of high wage growth adjustment if the nominal exchange rate is fixed.

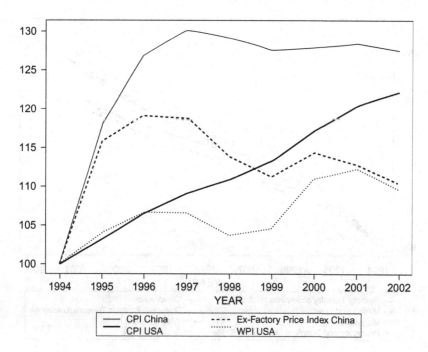

Figure 4. CPI and WPI for the US and China

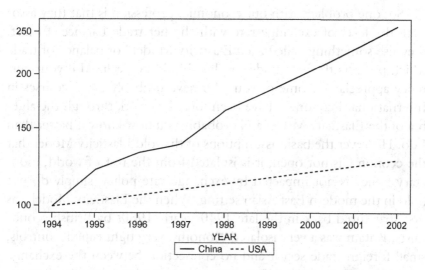

Figure 5. Nominal Manufacturing Wage Growth for the US and China

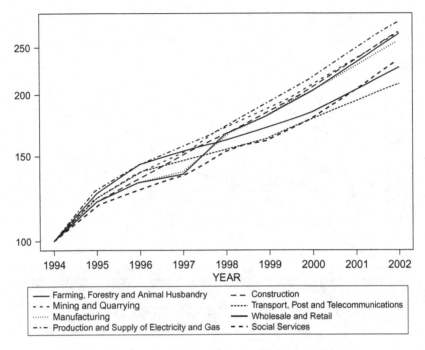

Figure 6. China: Nominal Wages Across Different Sectors

So, one problem with our economics profession is that they associate the level of exchange rate with the net trade balance. In fact,
they use something called the "Elasticity Model" of balance of trade
which projects the year trade surplus should be declined if your currency appreciates. Some of you who have probably taken courses in
International Economics have been forced to work through the alge-
bra of the Elasticity Model and probably you now know it better than
I do. However the basic assumptions of that old Elasticity Model that
the economy is not open, it is isolated from the rest of world, monetary policy is not impacted by exchange rate policy, simply do not
hold in the modern East Asian setting. When the Elasticity Model was
first structured back in the late 1940s, early 1950s by British economists, Britain was a very isolated economy, very tight capital controls,
small foreign trade sector and no connection between the exchange
rate and monetary policy. But economists are somewhat like the generals. You know, generals are always prepared to fight the last war but

not the coming one. So our economists with Elasticity Model, they are thinking of a very isolated economy of the late 1940s or early 1950s, not the very widely open economies we now see in East Asia.

So it is necessary to dispose the idea that you can change the exchange rate and think that the net trade balance will change in a predictable way. Although I can not provide equations and models here, the host will not permit, we can look at the experience of Japan in the 1970s, 1980s and mid-1990s, continual appreciations of the yen of 360 to the dollar all the way to 80, and by the end of that period, its trade surplus, current account surplus was much bigger than it was in the beginning.

But there are other things changing the exchange rate China can do at the present time and modifying its policies to take away some of the pressure coming through the foreign exchanges. And one is simply to speed up the trade liberalization associated with the WTO entry and remove many import restrictions and export subsidies. And it is fine now for China to run a trade deficit, although difficult with the US pre-empting the world trade deficits, but it is fine because of the huge inflow of foreign direct investment. So there really should be a trade deficit, which is the counterpart of the foreign direct investment inflow.

When foreign direct investment comes in, it has been valuable to China, brings foreign technology, managerial skills and patterns, and so forth. But what should be changed with the FDI is the amount of money that foreigners bring in. We do not need for companies borrowing in New York, London and bring the money in. We just want their technologies. So allow them more to borrow from Chinese banks instead. This would reduce the rate of liquid dollar assets owned by China increase if there is less foreign money associated with the FDI inflow.

China has been right to maintain high domestic demand for output, so there is very fast internal monetary growth and high economic growth through 2003. But now in 2004 the economy is clearly overheating. There are two basic problems. One is made in Washington where the US Federal Reserves Board of Governors has a very easy monetary policy with interest rates set up much too low, even for

America's own good. The second is probably excess bank lending within China itself.

So right now we hope the next meeting of the US Federal Reserve Board of Governors in early June, they agree to raise interest rates. That would solve much of China's problem. But in the meantime, there is excess growth in money and the People's Bank of China should continue its efforts to sterilize this excess money growth and they create new instruments, central bank bonds, which they sell to banks to take away monetary base from the banks. I think there is also room for greatly raising reserve requirements as the People's Bank of China imposes on commercial banks above the current 7.5% rate and at the same time pay a high interest rate on required reserves, so it does not damage the profitability of the banks.

But none of these suggestions involves changing the exchange rate. So keep the 8.28, there is a lot of reputation and creditability built up with the 8.28 rate. And we can slow the liberalization of capital controls because there is too much money coming in. We should also slow the entry of foreign banks into Chinese markets because they are also a vehicle by which foreign capital being brought into the economy.

We were at a meeting with IMF officials two days ago in Dalian and their consensus opinion was China should have a more flexible exchange rate. In English the word "flexible" has a very nice connotation because the opposite of "flexible" is "rigid," and nobody wants to be a rigid person.

So to satisfy the IMF that China is becoming a bit more flexible in the foreign exchanges but also to do the right thing, my suggestion is that there be a narrow band, maybe 1% or 1.5% on either side of the central 8.28 rate. So in the long-run we do not want to change the 8.28 rate. But we want this narrow band around it which broadens the characters of foreign exchange markets within China, move things away from the Bank of China and the People's Bank of China to variety of other financial institutions. Once the bad loan positions of the domestic banks are more or less corrected, then in the longer run it is good to have competition from foreign banks, but even more importantly from new Chinese banks that do not have any history of making bad loans. Because the bad loans in the big 4 banks were not necessarily what the big 4 did voluntarily but it was local government and central government forced them into it. Therefore they have to be protected during this period of liberalization.

As all of you know when China was faced with the great deflationary pressure from the Asian Crisis 1997–1998. Fortunately they did not devalue the RMB like many foreigners like Professor Joseph Stiglitz wanted them to do. But instead Zhu Rongji kept the exchange rate and announced a huge expansion of public expenditures amounts into 1 trillion dollars in March of 1998. This policy was enormously successful, because that not only it prevented China from suffering from downturn of the other East Asian economies, but because China did not turn down or did not devalue, it meant the other East Asian economies could recover more quickly. Indeed, we have a theorem by professor Robert Mundell called the "Mundell–Flemming Model," which shows that fiscal policy could only really be effective in an open economy if the exchange rate is stable and you have stationary expectations with regard to prices and interest rates.

But now it's time to realize the over-heating of the economy requires for a Keynesian fiscal contraction, that is Zhu Rongji policy mark two, but with a minus sign in front of it. So I think at this time it should be mainly a cut back in marginal government expenditures, infrastructures spending leaning on the banks to make even more loans that should all be cut back. So this would work better because of the fixed exchange rate when Mundell–Flemming Model still holds but we just put the machine into rivers.

So everyone here is used to Americans being quoted in the press coming to China telling them what should they do, right? I think we should consider the matter the other way around. What should the US do at this juncture? The most immediate thing is to get rid of the ultra easy American monetary policy with the short term interest rate at 1%, because inflation in the US economy is picking up and commodity price inflation has risen 30% year over year. So this change to monetary tightening in the US by raising interest rates would reduce the capital inflow into China, make it easier to sterilize excess money growth. And also in the world economy, it would tend to dampen inflation and commodity prices.

So I think going to a tighter money policy in the US is very much in American self-interest of letting things get under control, and it happens to be even more so in China's best interest if they embark on tightening money policy. But regaining fiscal control is not so easy to rationalize.

So it is easy to show that the very large American fiscal deficits made much larger under the George W Bush administration and very low personal saving in the Americans is responsible for the very large current account deficit that the America has, the large current account surpluses East Asian countries have, and the conflicted virtue that the East Asian countries have. But many Americans do not see a problem because they can borrow so easily from foreigners even though the government is running huge deficits. You have the People's Bank of China buying all the US dollar treasury bonds. The Bank of Japan, the Bank of Korea, and the Bank of Thailand... All these countries are now buying US government securities and so the American government does not see any problem with running deficits in financing in this way.

So trying to persuade Americans that this is doing damage to their economy is difficult. And many political opponents of the current government keep predicting that if these deficits continue, there will be a big rise in interest rates in the US, the credits squeeze, the down-turn, but never seems to happen — that has been going on since the early 1980s actually. So this is a peculiar era of world dollar standard. The US is the only country that has an almost unlimited line of credit with the rest of world.

One thought I have had, not worked out very well, is to appeal to the American politicians and government by saying the shrinkage in the American manufacturing base is greatly aggravated by the current account deficits of the US, which is largely transferred from the East Asia in the form of the big trade deficit in manufactures. There is a little example of the shrinkage in American manufacturing base. When I returned from Dalian yesterday, there was a ceremony that delayed the take-off of flight because China Southern Airlines has just bought a new Airbus A19 to replace the old Boeing that they had been flying. And Airbus more generally has been taking the line share of the market for new aircraft; the Boeing is now falling away behind.

So I would like the president of the Boeing Corporation to go to Washington and convince George W Bush to raise tax revenue and cut spending. But anyway one thing the Americans can do is simply stop talking about the exchange rates. It is not going to solve any problems that either country has at the moment.

Thank you very much.

Review

Huang Da

Huang Da, Professor of Renmin University of China. Current Honorary President of RUC School Administration Committee; Consultant of Social Science Committee, China Ministry of Education; Honorary President of China Society for Finance and Banking. Former President of RUC; Deputy to the 8th National People's Congress and Member of Financial and Economic Committee; Member of the 2nd and the 3rd Academic Degrees Committee of the State Council; Member of National Philosophy Social Science Economics Subject Planning Group; Chairman of Humanity Social Science Research Expert Consulting Committee, China Ministry of Education; Member of the 1st Monetary Policy Committee, People's Bank of China; Member of the 4th and the 5th Securities Issuance Examining and Verifying Committee, China's Securities Regulatory Commission, etc.

Professor Huang has devoted to teaching and researching in the field of finance and economics since 1950. He published textbooks and academic books, including *Money and Banking; Economics of Money and Finance; An Introduction to the Comprehensive Equilibrium of Public Finance and Credit; Topics of Socialist Fiscal and Financial Problems*; etc. Professor Huang won multiple state prizes, and ministry and commission prizes as well. He is also Winner of the Sun Yefang Prize in Economics.

"Will Renminbi become the third power currency of the world?" It is subtitle of Topic 4 at the international forum being held by Renmin University of China on May 30, 2004.[1] At that time, people had a craze for this subject. It is indeed not an issue unworthy of serious thinking. But a question like this sounds quite pressing — urging you to give a direct answer of "yes" or "no" right here right now. Professor McKinnon and I were the two speakers for this topic. I was not trying to make a quick positive or negative response, yet did "answer the question." I chose the title of "RMB Meeting with the Great Opportunity" and gave my opinions about RMB, i.e., as long as China's current economic development status sustains, it will for sure support RMB to enter in the international power currency club and then through all kinds of frictions to compromise, to coordinate, and to explore the way of cooperation and improvement. As to Professor McKinnon's lecture, it had nothing to do with the RMB's position among global currencies. At the conference hall, McKinnon just outlined his points as what I heard on the spot; while a comprehensive talk was made for students, teachers and the press at Elite Forum, Phoenix TV one day before, unfortunately I was not there. According to the memo, in reply to the reporter's detailed inquiry, McKinnon said: "I think China has many years off from RMB being an international currency... there are so many important things to get prepared in the future decades... I think trying to get collective exchange stability within East Asia as the first step, and then introducing 30 years

---

[1] On May 30, 2004, in Beijing, Renmin University of China was holding China Forum on the Humanities and Social Sciences — The Path to the Future: China in the World Economy and Financial System. This article was then for Topic 4, with the heading of "Currency Internationalization: Benefits, Risks, and Path — Will Renminbi Become the Third Power Currency of the World?"

from now an Asian 'euro' as the last step, for trying to get complete monetary harmony within East Asia. Then you will be independent of the dollar standard somewhat more like the Europeans are."

However, Professor McKinnon delivered his lecture in a broad perspective to overlook world economy and financial system. He pointed out how to correctly understand, analyze and explain the most important 20th century academic subject in international economy and international finance ever since World War II, especially for the recent two and three decades. What he presented was a very knowledgeable, very profound, and very instructive speech. As a matter of fact, he showed far more wisdom in this way than making an easy compliment of how RMB will turn out in the future. McKinnon did not entitle his lecture by himself; still, people in charge of paperwork herein put a name not that appropriate.

Anyway, something of McKinnon's speech once again impressed me deeply.

Firstly, regarding dollar's position in the world, McKinnon gave us a simple comment, "… given this dollar dominance for historical reasons; just happens to be a fact of life." For the first half of the sentence, we should fully understand — it was by good luck that various factors in history for at least one century accidentally cooperate to accomplish what dollar is like today. For the second half, there was an extremely frank saying there — just a fact of life we have to live with. The truth is, without serious analysis, talking about displacing dollar as world monetary standard is nothing more than a fantasy.

Secondly, "conflicted virtue" is a brief and to the point description of the international economic and financial situation between America and East Asian countries as well as the situation among East Asian countries with China included. Six months later, McKinnon published a book concentrated on this issue.[2]

From 1970s and 1980s, such a structure gradually came into being: East Asian countries' (including China) savings ratio

---

[2] *Exchange Rates Under the East Asian Dollar Standard: Living With Conflicted Virtue*; the Chinese version of it was published by China Financial Publishing House in April, 2005.

progressively rose and stayed high continuously, with China being the most outstanding one, while America kept an extremely low — some analysts believed sometimes actually "negative" — savings ratio the whole time. In international trade, East Asia has a huge surplus, whereas America was running long term deficit. According to McKinnon, because of the increase of East Asian foreign trade as a share of world total trade, the East Asian surplus corresponded directly to the American deficit; moreover, because most of the foreign trade comes from China importing from the rest of East Asian economies, processing and then exporting to America, the whole East Asia's surplus towards America appeared as China's trade surplus towards America. Therefore, he said, "China has become very visible in the American politics, particularly economy of the trade surplus."

Probably there are various theories from one analysis to another, but one thing without doubt is China's extremely and continuously high savings together with America's extremely and continuously low savings is the ROOT of Sino-American trade situation. In the early 20th century, America is very rich and China is very poor. No way for the two countries back then to have current contradiction like this. China has changed a lot after reforming and opening-up; although it is still way behind America in richness and powerfulness, yet China becomes creditor of America. Current Sino–American situation is described as "imbalance." Then what kind of balance we have lost — is it the sharp contrast between the rich and the poor, the powerful and the weak? Obviously, that balance is impossible to go back to. If not so, then what kind of situation could be called balance? Maybe we should take this: current structure is a new balance which is built up after the original balance was broken through. Of course, current balance will not last forever either; sooner or later it will be replaced by an updating one.

If we admit the forming of such a structure has sort of inevitability, then we should go for ways and rules to deal with all kinds of conflicts of interest — in tag lines, go for "win-win" or "win-all" situation. Some Americans (maybe some Europeans as well now) ignore the "root," reluctant to face the fact of their own too low savings, but wish by themselves to play the old Plaza Accord trick to press RMB to appreciate. McKinnon made a clear point here that "look at the experience of Japan in the 1970s, 1980s and mid-1990s, continual appreciations of the yen of 360 to the dollar all the way to 80, and by the end of that period, its current account surplus was much bigger than it was in the beginning." Among those Americans pressing RMB to appreciate, it's not likely that no one knows this. Knowing it yet still pressing, then no doubt they are for something else.

In the meantime, some people among us are aroused to criticize our "high savings ratio." It seems "high savings ratio" will do, or has already done, somewhat harm to China, including continuous huge trade surplus. Sure too high savings would lead to various conflicts. But the strange thing is that in their minds what high savings truly means to a struggling developing country seems to be and not to be so. Expanding domestic demand is the proper policy decision. But to carry out policy of expanding domestic demand effectively, it is not possible, neither right, to pull the high savings down awkwardly within a very short period to achieve the so called balance of import and export.

Thirdly, speaking of exchange rate and import-export issue, McKinnon warned students majoring in Economics about the basic assumptions of Elasticity Model and said: "It is necessary to dispose the idea that you can change the exchange rate and think that the net trade balance will change in a predictable way."

Elasticity Model is very often referenced. Using it to analyze the relation of exchange rate and import-export under the assumption of "ceteris paribus" is brief and clear. However, if someone believes directly based on this model that adjusting exchange rate can adjust import and export, and then can adjust the basic situation of international economy and finance, more or less he is attempting to do what is actually far beyond his power. In the economics profession, including China's, many people dote on this model. Don't buy what they said? It means you do not understand economics. Now one of the authorities of modern western economics said so. I wonder how they who dote on this model would think of it.

Fourthly, McKinnon proposed maintaining a steady exchange rate regime in response to the current situation of international economy and finance. To prove his point, he adopted a quite complex analysis framework, including many variables such as exchange rate, price, inflation, productivity, wage, and so forth — all of these are needful important variables to analyze modern international economic and financial relations. His analysis exhibits meticulous scholarship what an economist should have. Anyone who would like to keep up with McKinnon's analytic thinking, may follow this speech as a lead to further study.

Fifthly, he provided China with two suggestions.

One is to keep the 8.28 rate to dollar, which is also many world famous economists' advice at that time, and meanwhile consider a flexible band of 1% or 1.5% on either side of the central 8.28 rate. The lecture was made in May, 2004. But a year later, RMB is on the way of appreciation: from July 22, 2005 untill now in October, 2007, RMB has been appreciated by more than 10%. Did we take the other path? Indeed there are just two paths about various suggestions of RMB: one is the Plaza Accord way, which is sharp appreciation; the other is to withstand strong pressure yet harmful to the world as well as related countries' economic development, which is stable RMB. The essence of RMB steady appreciation is still a way to keep the world exchange rate regime stable.

The other is for Chinese to tell Americans what to do. Such as, getting rid of the ultra easy American money policy, making Americans and American officials realize that unlimited borrowings from abroad do have problems, letting America no more meddle with others' exchange rates, remaining neutral in the exchange rate issue, etc. We should thank Professor McKinnon for his supporting Chinese to argue with America. Chinese did make certain requests in various situations from time to time, unfortunately seldom or never "worked." McKinnon himself had no alternative but to admit: "Trying to persuade Americans that this is doing damage to their economy is difficult", and "One thought I have had, not worked out very well, is to appeal to the American politicians and government by saying..." I guess in America, very likely that the same thing as an old Chinese saying goes happens too — when a scholar meeting a warrior, he is just unable to vindicate himself against an unreasonable opponent.

Chapter 6

The Analysis of the Influential Factors on Economic Growth: Some New Evidence

Robert J. Barro

Biography

Robert J. Barro is a senior fellow at the Hoover Institution, the Paul M. Warburg Professor of Economics at Harvard University, and a research associate of the National Bureau of Economic Research.

Barro's expertise is in the areas of macroeconomics, economic growth, and monetary theory. Current research focuses on two very different topics: the interplay between religion and political economy and the impact of rare disasters on asset markets and macroeconomic activity.

He has written extensively on macroeconomics and economic growth. Noteworthy research includes empirical determinants of economic growth, economic effects of public debt and budget deficits, and the formation of monetary policy.

Recent books include Macroeconomics: A Modern Approach, Economic Growth (2nd edition McGraw Hill, 2008) written with Xavier Sala-i-Martin, Nothing Is Sacred: Economic Ideas for the New Millennium, Determinants of Economic Growth (2002), and Getting It Right: Markets and Choices in a Free Society (1996).

Barro is coeditor of Harvard's Quarterly Journal of Economics and was recently president of the Western Economic Association and vice president of the American Economic Association.

He was a viewpoint columnist for Business Week from 1998 to 2006 and a contributing editor of the Wall Street Journal from 1991 to 1998.

Before his appointments at Harvard University and the Hoover Institution at Stanford University, Barro was a professor of economics at the University of Chicago and at the University of Rochester.

Barro received a PhD in economics from Harvard University and a BS in physics from Caltech.

Speech

To great pleasure to be here. This is my first trip ever to China. It has been a great trip by being traveling now for three weeks and I have been to six cities in China, and I have been very impressed with the pace of economic growth and with the great potential of this country. I was also promised that if I give a lecture in Renmin University, that will greatly increase the probability of my getting the Nobel Prize in Economics.

Correct forecast, but do never know. I want to speak today about an empirical research I have been doing for some time about factors that help to determine the rate of economic growth in a country. I would rather be considering a variety of factors and I am going to be considering evidences now available up to the year 2000. So this is new updated settle results on empirical determinants of economic growth. Well, I wanted write down one thing, but let me just say what that is and otherwise I will use the projector to describe the results for today. Some are going to think about how to rate economic growth's determinant, within the frame work of the well-known neoclassical growth model, due to the work of Robert Solow and many other economists. For the framework that comes from this model determines the rate of economic growth from two kinds of factors, one can summarize the results of the model with a very simple analytical framework. You can write the rate of growth as a function up to types of things. One is about where the economy is today, for example, represented by its level of per capita real gross domestic product. The second element is something about where the economy is going in the long run, something about the target, long run position where the economy is heading. The neoclassical model predicts that given this long run or target position and that a lower value of where we are today, for example a lower per capita gross domestic product implies higher rate of economic growth.

This is a simple relationship that I have in mind. On the left hand side, you have the rate of economic growth represented by Dy. So empirically I measure this by the rate of growth, per capita gross domestic product, for various countries over various time periods. On the right hand side, the first variable Y represents where an economy is today, represented for instance by the level of per capita gross domestic product. The minus sign below it indicates that a poorer country with lower per capita product tends to have a higher rate of economic growth, tends to go faster, therefore it tends to converge or catch up to the richer economies. In the neoclassical model, the main reason for that fact is the diminishing returns to accumulating capital. A poorer country has relatively less capital in the form of machines, buildings, human capital that has higher return on investing in capital that tends to spur higher growth rate in the poorer places. This fact is reinforced by the potential for a less developed economy to imitate the technology that have been developed or discovered in the leading countries. In other words, the potential for diffusion of the technology, technology adaptation, is another advantage of being behind and is another reason why poorer economies can grow faster and converge to richer places. However, in the neoclassical growth framework, this potential for convergence also depends on having some basic policies, institutions, national characteristics being favorable for economic development. It is represented by the second variable Y^* in that simple equation. It represents things that are favorable, for example, from the framework government policy, whether or not the economy is open to free markets, whether the institutions allow people to accumulate property because property rights are respected, whether people are willing to save, whether people are willing to have relatively lower rate of population growth. A variety of elements like that determine whether or not the

underlying climate in an economy is favorable to economic development. Other factor that might matter under the name of this one
variable Υ^* would include whether the economy is open to international trade, what is the nature of state financial markets, perhaps
whether international financial transactions are relatively open. So the
general idea of this model represented by this one equation is that if
you hold fixed all these factors that determine the underlying growth
potential the Υ^*, then if you start behind with a lower Υ meaning
lower per capita GDP level, you tend to get higher economic growth
and convergence. But it is important to recognize that convergence
is only predicted in this conditional sense, it is called conditional
convergence in literature. It is not enough just to be poorer to grow
fast, if you are poorer but you also have bad policies, bad institutions,
low saving rate, you will not grow rapidly. Using that simple framework, I want to summarize the kinds of empirical finding I have been
getting about what matters through economic growth across the
world.

Just quickly to describe the data, I am looking at about 100 countries, it is a group of countries for which I am able to get the data I need
for the empirical estimation. And I am looking at these countries over
the period from 1960 to 2000, which is also the period over which
there are pretty good national account's data for a large number of
countries. In the detailed estimation, I am observing economic growth
which I measure by growth of per capita real gross domestic product
over 3 ten-year periods, the first, 1965–1975, then 1975–1985, and
finally 1985–1995. So I have, roughly speaking, 100 countries, 3 time
periods, about 300 data points, it is what really constitutes the data that
I will be using in the main study. You can do the estimation instead, for
example, over 5-year time periods, you can take the five years from
1965 to 2000, there will be 7 five-year time intervals. The results turn
out to be quite similar, as 3 ten-year time periods, it turns out we do
not get a lot of additional information, particularly about longer term
economic growth from looking at five-year periods or ten-year ones.

Just in the term of describing some of the data, I have this first
table which shows 20 countries which had the lowest growth rate of
per capita gross domestic product over the thirty years from 1965 to

1995 which is the main sample that I am using. Have you looked at the level of per capita gross domestic product, across the world in 1960 or 1965? Here are amusing purchasing power adjusted numbers for gross domestic product which are put forward by Summers and Heston in the well known cross-country dataset. Having the brought pattern at the beginning, 1960 or 1965, is that the poorest countries in the world are mainly in Sub-Saharan Africa and also in the Asia. So China for example was among the world's poorest countries in term of level of per capita GDP at the beginning of the sample. Several other Asian countries such as South Korea, India would be in that category, and the other main group would be African countries. From perspective of convergence, predicted by the neoclassical growth framework, you might expect that the countries that began as the poorest in 1960 or 1965 would grow fastest in the following thirty or forty years. Surprisingly from that perspective, most of the countries that were in the lowest growing group over the period 1965 to 1995 were actually in Sub-Saharan Africa which was also among the world's poorest countries at the beginning in 1960 or 1965. In the early 1960 for many Africa countries became independent from colonial rule, there was a lot of optimism that many of those countries would grow rapidly. For example, there was a famous comparison made by World Bank between Ghana and South Korea and the bank felt that Ghana was very promising and would grow rapidly and develop while South Korea was view as being more or less hopeless and probably would not do very well. In fact, remarkable instead outcome is that many very poor countries in Africa also had the lowest growth rate, so when you look at the group of 20 lowest growing countries over the thirty years, most of them are in Sub-Saharan Africa, and nearly all countries had negative growth rate on average for per capita gross domestic product over thirty years. For example, the lowest growth was from former Zaire, now the Democratic Republic of the Congo, which managed to grow at negative rate of 3.5% per year for thirty years, it is very difficult to grow negatively at that much rate for so long. I should say, however, if we look starting from 1970s until now, the country with the lowest average growth rate of per capita GDP is actually Iraq, which has managed something like minus 6% a year for twenty-year period, which is even a great achievement in negative direction if we want to look at that way. Here you have, by contrast, 20 most rapidly growing countries over the period 1965 to 1995, and it's quite well known this list is dominated by countries of East Asia. The fastest growth over thirty years which ended in 1995 was South Korea, whose average growth rate per capita was almost 7% per year. South Korea and some other economy in Asia did a little worse because of the Asian financial crisis in 1997 and 1998, but still you get a pretty similar picture even a few extend sample to the year 2000. If you want to think as a quick numerical interpretation, what I mean is to grow at 6.9% per year for thirty years, you use the famous rule of 69 which comes from the factor that the natural logarithm of 2 is 0.69, so you divide the growth rate 6.9% per year into 69 just by accident happens to be a very convenient number 10, it means that it takes 10 years to double the per capita GDP when growing at that rate. So Korea managed to grow at that rate over thirty years which is three ten-year period, which means it doubled three times, two for eight, for managing to increase the level of per capita GDP by a factor of eight over thirty years, which seems to be about the most one kind of accomplish over that kind of time interval. So you can apply that reasoning to China. For China, at least the data I am looking at another a lot of questions about national account data in China, the data I am looking at showed per capita real GDP at the end of sample in 2000 was 4000 US dollars in 1995 prices. The richest countries in the world such as the US, some other countries in Western Europe are little a bit over 30,000 US dollars per capita on the same measure in the year 2000 about the factor of eight higher than the current number listed for China. If you try the capacity for China to grow rapidly for a long time, if what makes up a factor of 8, it will grow 7% per year faster than the richest country for about 30 years, if you wanted to catch up in 30 years. The US, for example, we are not growing at all per capita, then China would have to do the same rate as what Korean has managed to do in 30 years. It would catch up at the end of that period. So the other high-growth country shown on the table, as I mentioned, many east-Asian economies, including Singapore, Taiwan (Taiwan is very difficult to get the data for, by the way, because it is not listed either by the World Bank or the IMF as a separate economy. But it is possible to get the data from Taiwan). There is also Hong Kong, which is thought of being a separate economy I guess now and also in the history. And you have places like Thailand, Indonesia, China and Malaysia. China's pattern here, according to the data at least, is that did not grow very rapidly in the first part of period. But then very well later on, and did remarkablely well period in 1995-2000 when many of East Asian countries are performing poorly. Japan is also on this list that actually only did well in the earliest of this sample, and was doing quite badly over the last 15 years or so. If you think of the contrast between the African countries which did very poorly and Asian countries, many of which did well in terms of growth. I am going to explain that in some sense in my empirical work. I will start from differences of the initial level of per capital GDP, which in many cases were similar. Difference about policies, institutions, saving, behavior, etc, which is much more favorable in Asia rather than Africa. If you look generally across the countries, one hundred above countries, and see whether or not the convergence in absolute sense, you get this kind of diagram. The horizontal axis has the level of the per capita growth to gross product, it's on the proportion scale from 1960; the vertical axis shows the rate of growth of per capita GDP, in this case from 1960–1995, there's basically no relationship between the two variables. In particular, there is no tendency for countries that started up poor on the left, on the horizontal axis to grow faster. And I mentioned a particular example of that is African countries, which start up as poor but also have low rate at economic growth. To find the kind of convergence presented in the neo-classic theory, you really have hold constant, a lot of other factors, which I represented formerly in one equation by that concept Y^*. And then my main empirical challenges of excise was trying to measure a number of variables across countries which would hold constant that long round of target position of Y^*.

The empirical results along this line are shown in this table, but I want really try to go through the details of the number shown here. The main idea, is I am trying to explain economic growth about 100 countries, 3 time periods as mentioned, and I have a number of

determinants of growth, aside from the starting level of per capita of
G (GDP), which enter into this system. The kinds of variables that are
in here, which I will go through in sequence using figures in a
moment, I will first make some measure initial level of human capital
in the form of schooling and health. There is a measure of the fertility
rate, which tells you about the growth rate of population in this
economy. There are measures of government policy. The government
policy measures that am using here, one has to do with the size of it
in terms of consumption outlays, another has to do with the extend
to which rule of law is maintained in this economy, which has to do
with the presence of property rights, and law order. Another one has
to do was the extend of democracy, in the sense of freedom and civil
liberties. Other factors that are considered here have to do with
the extend of international openness, with the development in terms
of changes and in the term of trade, which relate to the export and
import prices, with the economy saving rate, and finally would a
measure of macroeconomic stability, which are measured in this particular system by the rate of inflation. Other factors that have considered, which are not contained in the basic system shown in this table
have to do with the development of financial markets, with the size of
a country, whether that measures, and with some refinement measures of educational attainments, and a number of other influences.

This first figure shows you here what the relation between the
economic growth (again measured in per capita GDP growth) and the
level of per capita GDP is. But the difference from the previous figure
is that in this one, I am holding constant, although have other influences, which I went through a little bit, which are reported in that
table, and which I will go through in kind of sequence here. So I am
not looking here for absolute convergence, whether the poor grow
faster than the rich, but rather do the poor grow faster after holding
constant things, like education, health, government policies, macroeconomic stability, investment ratios and so on. So unlike the absolute
convergence which is not in the data, it does no prove that the poor
grow faster than the rich. There is a lot of evidence in favor of conditional convergence in the data-cross countries. That is what is shown
on the figure here. The negative slop tells you something about the

rate of conditional convergence. It is something about how fast a poor economy catches up to rich ones, if two of them have the same underlying political institutions, government policies, saving rates, population growth, and so on. From the perspective of this diagram, If you take a typical Sub-Sahara African countries, at the starting up the way on the left, they have very low per capita of GDP. But they did not grow fast, they were not way up in line that is indicated in this diagram. The reason is that, the typical African country also had low value of Υ^*, that is their variable policies, institutions, national behavior in term of saving rates. The whole array of variables turned out to be unfavorable to the development countries, that's what I meant by Υ^* being low in that circumstances. On the other hand, the interpretation is that many of the East Asian countries, which also start up poor, at least several of them in 1960s, have much more favorable Υ^*s like underlying policies, institutions, saving behavior, etc. So they were able to grow faster and converge as is indicated by the potential here in this conditional convergence relationship. China should mention as roughly in the middle now in terms of horizontal axis. So where they have large forces to converge earlier, and forces now weaker, although they are still in presence if you compare China with the most riches countries.

Independent variables I have used that I interpret as holding fixed the target position Υ^*, the first one relates to the initial human capital in the form of education, measured by years of school attainment at the beginning of time period that I am using. I do not actually find a lot of explanatory power, just from the years of education, which is the main data I have available to use to measure education. I think it is because years of school means very different, if one look across countries. I think it is not a good measure to the quality of education. I have some other results along this lines that I will mention later on, which come from using the result on internal examinations that are from students of different countries. I actually also find more explanatory power from different measures or supplementary measure of human capital which relates to the statistics of health rather than education. This particular setting uses the reciprocals of life expectancy as the indicator of health. You can interpret that as the measure of average of mortality rate. For example, point 02 along the horizontal axis means something like probability of dying is 2% per year. So this relation is saying that poor health which is a movement toward the right along the horizontal axis seem to predict lower economic growth. So lower human capital a net form seems to more precisely estimated as having the growth effect. Where there is more about a problem with respect to I think to the education results. The neo-classical growth theory does especially predict that people choose a higher population growth. That will be a negative in terms of growth rate GDP per person, that is, economic development in terms of the standard of living would be adversely affected. I have looked at here by using of the concept of the total fertility rate, which is the average number of perspective live births, for each woman and society over the perspective lifetime. That is the number comes from for example, like the UN. So I do find here a indication that higher fertility leading the higher population growth, is negatively related with the growth rate of GDP per capita, that is what is shown by the negative line here. I think it seems to be some support for the underlying theory. And I think this is something controversial in China, because part of reason the fertility rate has been reduced, I believe in China comes from the One-Child Policy, which perhaps force families to lower fertility than they might otherwise choose to have volunteerly. There is a quite regular relationship in the modern data across countries and over time, will by the countries develop, and particularly have more educations, the fertility rate tend to decline. However, the fertility number, most recently reported for China which is about 1.9, which is below replacement fertility, is in fact lower than we predicted for China, given the level of per capita of income and levels of education. I do not necessarily want to say that it is a good idea to have population control. But there might be some evidence that it support economic growth. However, economic growth is probably not the only objectives in mind to think about policy, such as whether or not to limit the number of children that families can have.

So I mentioned the other variables that have to do is the size government. The variables I have looked at is the ratio to the growth to gross product of government outlays on consumption activities. I take government consumption activities as an area that would likely not contribute directly to the productivity. Moreover, financing of government consumption would require taxation, which will tend to distort the economy. So I would anticipate the greater size of government in this context, would like be negatively associated with economic growth, by reducing Υ^* concept that I mentioned before. Some evidence in data that variable is negatively related to growth is not that stronger relationship. China is relatively high in terms of share of GDP that goes to government consumption. It is something like about 17% of this number. I should mention the measurement of government consumption, I have subtracted out the expenditure for public lays for education, national defense, which I do not think should be viewed as consumption as they are usually measured in national accounts.

A lot of economists now think that legal system is important for economic functioning. In particular, a lot people think that government should make rule of law, which is on property rights, and what have law and order more generally. The challenge has been really to try to measure these concepts. In some way, it is comparable across country and over time. And I attempted to do that here in this empirical work. The measure I used as this variable, comes from a international consulting firm, which is basically in the business of advising potential foreign investors, about which country provide the favorable climate for foreign investment. Indicators produced by the company related to the nature of legal system and to various other factors. And the index I used from them, has to do with the make of law, which is referred to the as general provision of general law and order. The particular measure as the subjective one, it originally comes from seven different categories. 0 here means the poorest made of the inside rule of the law, while 1 means the most favorable climate, and additional, there are also 5 in between. That's why you have a funny experience in this diagram, because the underlying variable only takes one of the seven possible values. But there are some general indications that are statistically significant. The improvement in the rule of law, measured by at least the consulting services, is positively related with the economic growth. It is also turns out to be positively related to investment, if you look at the share of investment in the GDP. It is also predicted positively by this measure the rule of law. And the rule of law has to do with property rights, it has to do with whether you can enter into the contracts that are actually enforced, and it has to do whether the long and order presence in the society.

Conceptually, that kind of idea is very different from democracy, which many people have looked at it in the concept of relations with economic growth and development. Here I am using the measure of democracy, which comes from freedom house, which is subjective indicators of electoral freedom, civil liberties, going back to the 1970s. In terms of theoretical reasoning, I think it is pretty straight-forward to anticipate a positive relation between the rule of law and economic performings. But the relationship between democracy and economic growth, I think, is much more complicated. It is not obvious that more democracy, for example, electoral freedom, will be accompanied by faster economic growth. There are a variety of theories in the political economic literature, some predicted democracy will be negative for growth. For example, in the majority voting system, it is tendency for majority to vote to transfer rich from minority, which would be quite poor from the standpoint for property rights and incentives for work and invest. Therefore, in those models, more democracy tend to reduce economic growth. But there are other theories that have the opposite implication. For example, it is often thought that in the full dictatorship, there are too much attemptation to steal the resources from people, and have a lot of official corruptions. That is not a good environment for investment and economic growth. In these kinds of models, the prediction seems to be democracy will increase the economic growth. The free-house data, I mentioned, have both electoral system and also civil liberties, two of them are so co-related with the data that I can not separate them in terms of their relation to economic growth. The one I have used here is the one related to electoral rights, the extent to voting in order to elect office-holders basically. But the results is much more similar, if instead I have used the measure of civil liberties, which has to do with freedom of speech, freedom of the press, freedom of assembly and freedom of relation among other thing. The reason I can separate out the fact of democracy, or electoral rights, from the rule of law, because those two concepts are not co-related in data. You can find examples of countries that are Strong on the rule of law, and weak on democracy, and vice versa. China is the example of that. The most recent on rule of law data, coming from the consulting firm I mentioned, China is in the second category out of 7. While in democracy, China of course is very low, in fact, is one of the lowest according to freedom house. There are many other examples. For example, Singapore, which is in the highest category in the rule of law, property right, is not very high on democracy. If you look back in earlier periods, counties like South Korea, Economy of Taiwan, were low in the democracy, but pretty high in rule of law. More recently, these countries become more democratic. If you look at Chile, in the 1970s through the 1980s, it was very low in democracy, 0, but was quite good in rule of law. You'll find quite a lot of examples like that. The President of Singapore often argues that it is a good idea, if you do not want too much democracy, but it is a good idea to have property rights, and protection especially for foreign investors. So what do I find for democracy? Basically the overall relation between economic growth and democracy is about 0. In particular if you look at the bottom, Where there are very few political rights, the democracy is very low, but you find some examples of high growth, some examples of low growth. It is also true that as you have more democracy, I also find some evidence on non-linear relationship shown from the solid curve in this diagram, which comes some fact that I enter into this system. Not just the democracy in the linear form, but also pediatrics that had square term. Initially, if you start with no democracy, you have no democratic sound, you get stimulus to economic growth, it's positive. It curve peak somewhere in the middle, then later on it starts to decline again. So some of the democracy looks like it is favorable to growth, but too much democracy look like it is adverse to economic growth. It is shown from the results. I would not push that so far, because statistically is not that reliable, but there's something there. Another thing to say that is that from the point of view to maximize the economic growth rate, it is seems like some level of middle democracy is corresponding to that. Middle democracy as measured is the countries like Malaysia, Mexico in some earlier times (Mexico is much more democratic recently), but in terms of growth maximization, it seems to give you the best outcomes. Of course there might be reasons for higher level of democracy, but I do not think it can be justified from the standpoint of growth permission.

Since I am running out of time, I will try to be more quick to some of other results. I do have a positive relationship between Growth and the extent of international openness related to trade and goods and services. It is really about export and import as a ratio to GDP. I get a positive relation of that openness to growth, but it is a weaker relationship than I would expect. So I was surprise that I did not find a more powerful, positive relationship of growth to international openness. As a related matter, I have looked at how the evolution in terms of trade relates to economic growth. So it is measured by the change over time in the ratio of export to import prices. Also actually interacted with the stand on the international openness, which shows you how important international prices should be for a economy. I do find a significantly positive relationship with growth and the improvement in terms of trade in a period. That is what is shown in this figure. However, the change of trade has not been so important for China in the recent period according to my estimate. It is also true with the in previous diagram that China is roughly in the middle with respect to the international openness variable. So China wasn't a particular high or low in terms of particular measure as I had for the openness.

Some of the East Asian countries that grow rapidly have high saving rate and investment ratios, it is particular true with Singapore, and later, in the period true with South Korea, Taiwan, it is actually true with all the East Asian countries that grow rapidly. For example, it is not true with the economy of Hong Kong. The number I have here is investment ratio, the ratio of investment to GDP, which is closely related with saving rate. The number I have for China is not that high, abut 23%, but other people told me that the saving rate is much higher than that, and I do not understand the point of discrepancies between this figure to that number, and I hope to learn where they are coming from. In other case, I found the relationship between growth and investment ratio is positive, but not that powerful, so you certainly could not say that rapid growth to have a extremely high investment or saving rate, even though some of the East-Asian country have that. It does not seem to be necessary to get high economic growth.

These figures show the relation between growth and inflation rate. The relation is negative, but it is really mainly important for very high inflation. For example, one on horizontal axis means the 100% per year inflation rate which is extremely high. For moderate range of inflation there is only a little bit of evidence that relates closely with economic growth in the negative direction. For China, recently, the inflation rate has been low, earlier was more like 10%, but I do not really find from these result, that you can see there is a big growth difference, associated with that kind of difference in the inflation performance.

A couple of results that are not in the basic table, one is that the size of a country does not seem to matter much for per capita growth. So if you add measure of countryside based on population on the horizontal axis, it explains nothing about per capita growth. Small countries and rich countries seem to grow at the same rate. So you do not need a bigger country, a bigger scale of domestic market in order to grow in a high rate. That is not in the evidence. I mentioned before my disappointment in the results related to the education. It turns out that if you use different measure of human capital in the form of schooling, based on the results of international comparables, exams on minister of students, you find that much more the positive relationships with economic growth. So I have the test scores on the horizontal axis 0.5 means 50%correct for example on this exam. This measure, which perhaps approximate for the quality of school, or at least for ability, seems to be very reliably positively related to economic growth, on the vertical axis. The exam I have in mine is in three fields, science, mathematics, and reading. They have been minister to a growing number of countries over time. I believe that China have never participated in any of these special examinations. The particular feature of these exams is that they try to cover the materials in the way that internally comparable, so you can make comparisons. It is done in different grade levels. For example, the eight level is one of the regular times at which the exam is ministered. The main problem of using the results is that they are only apply to relatively small number of countries. When you use, you will lose have of the observations in terms of the statistical estimation. I should say that the East Asian countries that have participated in these examinations have done particular well on it, notably on science and mathematics. It turns out science and mathematic results are one that have predicted content with economic growth, not the reading. I guess China will do relatively well on these examinations if you participate. But that just conjecture, because China never participated in it.

Another thing I have looked at is the development of financial sector. Whether the development of Financial market is related in the special way to the economic growth, which is sometimes been argued. I have measured the development of financial sector, using the information from the World Bank, partly on the private credit, that is presence in the economy, in relation to gross domestic product, and partly in looking at the amount of deposits that has been created through financial institutions of the country. I do not find the any relation of either private credit variable, or deposit variable, to economic growth. So I do not get the evidence that it is special rule from the development of financial sector, in terms of promoting overall economic growth.

Some other controversial topic I have looked at in relation to growth, which turns out to be not that related to growth. First, a measure of the extent of official corruption presence in the economy, I do not think that is related to growth once you hold fix things like the rule of law as I already mentioned. I also do not find the grade of income inequality is significantly related to the rate of economic growth. So if you hold things that I have been describing, enter into the addition measure of the income inequality, that is not one thing significantly related with economic growth. In terms of theory, as with democracy, there are some theories that say the inequality should be harmful to growth, and some actually say that it will be favorable. In empirical evidence, I do not find reliable relationship between the inequality to economic growth.

My current research is on another sensitive topic, which is particularly on the rule of culture factors related to religion and how that interact with economic performance. I have some results now on that question. But I do not really have the time to go into that today, which has to be a topic in future talk. Perhaps I will return to China and I will talk about that.

The conclusion I would like to leave with you is that there are many factors that matter for economic growth. There is not one single secret to growth success. There is not one single element that matters, but I think the empirical work has isolated a number of factors, including some under control of government through public policy, that can matter for economic growth. Using these results, I think one can get some guidance about what a good idea about underlying public institutions and policies. But the modest claim I would make is that the policies would be followed, if your advice from analysis of these results would be followed, it would make the expect or probable of economic growth higher, but certainly there will be no insurance that economic growth would be better. Because even though that the kinds of influences that I isolated explain quite a deal of difference of growth across countries and over time, there are still a lot that are unexplained. So can not also be the case that even the countries that end up doing things well, and doing things appropriately in terms advancing and growth, in some periods be disappointed. But I do not think there are better advices that one can get from the world experiences, at least I do not know it as opposed to the kind of results that I already been described today. So I finished with my formal remark. If anybody has a couple of questions, I will be happy and try to answer and respond to them.

Review

Guo Qingwang

Guo Qingwang is a Professor of Public Finance in the School of Finance, Renmin University of China. He obtained his Ph.D. in Economics from Dongbei University of Finance and Economics. He has been a senior visiting scholar at Australian National University and Tilburg University.

Professor Guo is currently the Dean of the School of Finance, Renmin University. He also served as Vice Chairman of the China Association of Public Finance, Vice Chairman of the Chinese Taxation Institute, etc.

Professor Guo's research interests include public finance and taxation, macro-economic theory and policy, economic growth theory, etc. His recent work has been published in *Social Sciences in China, Economic Research Journal, The Journal of World Economy, Management World* and *China and World Economy*.

Professor Guo was awarded as Yangtze River Distinguished Professor by the Ministry of Education in 2009 and the New-Century National Expert by the Ministry of Human Resources and Social Security in 2006. He began to receive the special government subsidy from the State Council in 2004.

On some level, modern economic growth theories and modern economics are developed together. Founders of modern economics, such as Adam Smith (1776) and David Ricardo (1817), all include modern economics growth theories in their studies. Ramsey (1928) is the first one who succeeded modeling modern economic growth theories in his classic paper "A mathematical theory of saving." Harrod (1939) and Domar (1928) tried to add economic growth factors into Keynesian analysis framework, which made it a "long-term" analysis, so that succeeded to form the most popular Harrod–Domar model. Solow (1956) and Swan (1956) contributed more to the economic growth theories with Solow–Swan model in 1950's. Assuming labor is combined with capital according to a fixed ratio (Cass, 1956), Harrod–Domar model takes capital as the only production factor to study the relationship between economic growth rate and capital accumulation growth rate. However, Solow–Swan model believes economic growth depends on not only capital growth rate and labor growth rate but technology development (Guo, 1995, p. 3) based on neoclassical production function, which assumes that different factors could be substituted, especially capital and labor. Further development by economists such as Cass (1965), Koopmans (1965) formed neoclassical growth theory later. From 1960s to 1980s, "growth theory, which used to be very hot topic, turned to be frozen" (Barro, Sala-I-Martin, 2000, p. 12), which might because growth theory used too much analysis technique and lack of empirical application. This situation lasted to the middle 1980s when Romer (1986) and Lucas, (1988) work broke the silence. Their study, leading to endogenous economic growth theory, focused on finding determinant factors on long-term economic growth. They believe that long-term growth rate is positive because of accumulation, human capital accumulation, R&D, technology spreading and so on. The reason why endogenous economic growth theory got widely accepted is not only this theory make clear determinants on long term economic growth but also, comparing with previous growth theories, "paid more attention to meaning of experience and the relationship between theory and data" (Barro, Sala-I-Martin, 2000, p. 13). The studies that Barro spent more than ten years on are, basically, analysis on relationship between different factors and economic growth from empirical angles of different countries.

Barro believes that there are a bunch of factors that could determine economic growth, some of them are directly, and some of them are indirectly; some of them are strong, and some of them are weak. He put these factors into two catalogs: the first one is "how is the economy going on today, mainly using the per capita GDP to describe"; the second one is technology factors. As far as the first catalog is concerned, the poor countries that used to have very low per capita GDP developed pretty quickly latter with the exception of Sub-Saharan Africa. It is very complicated about case of Sub-Saharan Africa, but the factors in the second catalog are the things that matter a lot.

The second catalog, technology, is the most important determinant on long term economic growth. But there is a condition on the effect of technology, the environmental factors in the first catalog. In barro's speech, he described these conditions (environmental factors) as economic factors, policy factors, system factors, social factors and culture factors. Economic factors include human capital (health or birth rate and death rate, education level), trade openness (import/export value by GDP, trade condition), macroeconomic stability (inflation), financial market development (mortgage by GDP, save by GDP), save rate, investment rate and government scale (public consumption by GDP); policy factors include fiscal policy, infrastructure, public administration; system factors include economic system, law system (foreign investment attracting capability, property right protection), democracy level (voting right); social factors include country size (population), income unfairness, corruption; culture factors are mainly religion. Barro believes the relation between the factors above and economic growth is mixed, some of them are positive, some are negative, some are strong and some are weak.

There are three conclusions of Barro's study on economic growth determinants that impress me very much. And these should be paid more attention to if China wants to keep a growth rate as 7% in the process of building xiaokang society.

First, in order to get long term economic growth, not only high save rate, investment rate, low inflation rate, but further economic system innovation, healthy law system, orderly and competitive market economy are needed. Especially, Barro believes, healthy law system is a powerful factor, whereas economic growth rate might not be higher with higher democracy level.

Second, public policies have effect on economic growth. Neoclassical growth theory believes long term economic growth is decided by exogenous factors. No matter what policy was taken, there will be no difference for a long term. However, endogenous economic growth theory believes the long term growth is determined by a series of endogenous variables, which are sensitive to public policies (especially fiscal policies) (Barro and Sala-iMartin, 1995; Romer, 1989). It is not only because both knowledge accumulation (including human capital accumulation, production and quality improvement of new product) and R&D have spillover effect or technological externality, but also because knowledge itself has some nature of public goods, which needs a positive fiscal policy to be taken by government (Guo and Zhao, 1999, p. 221).

Third, the ideal economic growth: the best, not the fastest. I want to cite Parro's last word to finish mine. "For economic growth, it does not mean good when it is fast. For a country, it is enough to get the best effect of economic growth, no need to make it as fast as possible."

Chapter 7

The Lessons of the Asian Financial Crisis

Frederic S. Mishkin

Biography

Frederic S. Mishkin is Professor at Business School of Columbia University and NBER Research Fellow. He obtained his Ph.D. in MIT and taught in many universities, such as University of Chicago, Northwestern University, Princeton University and Columbia University. He is also Honorary Professor of Renmin University of China. From 1994 to 1997, he was Executive Vice Chairman of Federal Reserve Bank of New York in charge of research and worked as economic advisor of FOMC.

The main research area of Professor Mishkin is monetary policy and its impact on financial market and macroeconomy. He is the writer of the best seller *The Economics of Money, Banking and Financial Markets*, which is a textbook on monetary economics. Other books by Professor Mishkin include: *Inflation Targeting: Lessons From the International Experience*; *Money, Interest Rates and Inflation; Financial Markets and Institutions; A Rational Expectations Approach to*

Macroeconometrics: Testing Policy Ineffectiveness and Efficient Markets Models. Moreover, he has more than 100 papers published in economic journals.

Professor Mishkin is the Editor of many leading academic journals including *American Economic Review, Journal of Business and Economic Statistics, Applied Economics and Economic Policy Review.* He is also the Associate Chief Editor of 8 economic journals. He has been the Advisor of FED, World Bank and IMF and also advises for many other countries' central banks. He used to be member of South Korea's International Advisory Board of Financial Regulatory Committee and now he is the member of economic advisory team of Federal Reserve Bank of New York.

Speech

From July 1997, financial crisis in Thailand, Indonesia, Malaysia and Korea caused huge damage to the economies of these Southeast Asian countries. The economic growth of these countries exceeded 5% before 1997, but in 1998 this figure turned negative. Even now we are still not sure when theses economies will stop the declining trend and start a new round of growth.

These countries used to do a good job in wiping out poverty and were part of "Asian Miracle," but now facing severe economic decline. Why? I think the fragility of the information of the financial market is the key factor underlying the crisis. After giving an asymmetric information framework of the crisis, I will use it to analyze what we can learn from the crisis.

(1) *Asymmetric information framework of the Asian financial crisis*

A financial system plays a key role in a economy because when it functions properly, money can be effectively channeled to people who need productive investment from those who have surplus funds. The major obstacle hindering the financial system to fulfill this task is the problem of asymmetric information, namely the two sides of the financial contract do not have the same information, which will cause the problem of moral hazard and adverse selection. From the perspective of asymmetric information, a financial crisis happens if a financial market cannot conduct funds to people who have the best productive investment opportunities when the problems of moral hazard and adverse selection caused by asymmetric information seriously deteriorates.

Here, we will use the asymmetric information framework to analyze the Southeast Asian financial crisis. This framework attributes crisis to some fundamental factors, especially those inside the financial system. Our analysis is in accordance with former studies by Corsetti, Pesenti and Roubini (1998), Goldstein (1998), and Krugman (1998) and does not deny the view by Radelet and Sachs (1998) that illiquidity and multi-equilibrium may also play some role in it. However, the main point in our framework, which may surpass other studies, is the mechanism through which the financial crisis causes severe decline of real economic activities.

For most crises, especially the Southeast Asian financial crisis, the key factor that aggravates asymmetric information and finally causes the financial crisis is the deterioration of balance sheets, especially the balance sheets of financial institutions. Just like the former crisis, such as similar analysis of 1982 Chile crisis and 1994–1995 Mexico crisis, the sharp rising loans supported by capital inflow of financial liberalization are the right beginning of the crisis. Once the constraint of interest rate ceiling and lending type are relaxed, lending rises sharply. As mentioned by Corsetti, Pesenti and Roubini (1998), Goldstein (1998), World Bank (1998), and Kamin (1999), the expansion rate of domestic credit in Asian crisis countries is by far exceeding their GDP growth rates. The problem of rising loans is not the expansion of credit but the too rapid credit expansion and the risk involved that may cause future loan losses.

There are two reasons for Southeast Asian countries to undertake excessive risk after financial liberalization. First, when faced with additional loan opportunities brought by financial liberalization, the managers of financial institutions lack the corresponding experience of effective risk management. In addition, when loans increase quickly, financial institutions cannot increase the necessary managerial resources (such as well-trained loan makers, risk estimation systems, etc.) in a very short time to monitor these new loans effectively.

The second reason of undertaking excessive risk is the unsoundness of a supervisory system. Even if there is not explicit government financial safety system toward a banking system, there is obvious implicit safety system in Asian crisis countries. This will cause moral hazard problem. Depositors and foreign lenders know that governments of these countries will come out to protect them, so they do not have incentive to monitor banks, which in turn encourages domestic financial institutions to undertake excessive risk and look for new loan opportunities progressively.

Emerging economies, especially Southeast Asian countries, usually have inadequate financial rules and supervision. When financial liberalization brings along new risk-taking opportunities, these weak systems cannot control moral hazard caused by government protection system and the result is the excessive risk taking behavior. The rapid expansion of credit and the limited resource faced by financial regulators will make this problem even worse. Because banks keep on starting new businesses and these new businesses develop very fast, financial regulators face the same problem that the limited regulatory power (well-trained inspectors and information system) cannot keep in pace with growing regulatory responsibilities.

Capital inflow makes this problem even worse. Once emerging economies liberalize their financial systems, foreign capital will rush into the banking sector because of high expected returns and the protection of government safety systems. These government safety systems are provided by the governments of emerging economies or by international financial institutions such as IMF. In this way, capital inflow will cause credit expansion in astonishing rate and some banks will be encouraged to undertake excessive risk. This is exactly what we see in the Asian financial crisis: from 1993 to 1996, capital inflow amounted to 50 billion to 100 billion dollars. Folkens-Landau found that in those Asian emerging economies, which had enormous private capital inflow, there, was also considerable expansion of the banking system.

The rapid credit expansion after financial liberalization results in large sum of loan loss and the subsequent deterioration of banks' balance sheets. For Southeast Asian countries, the unpaid loans were up to 15–30% of the total loans (Goldstein, 1998). The deterioration of banks' balance sheets is the key factor that pushes these countries to the financial crisis.

In emerging economies like Southeast Asian countries, there are two channels through which banking sector problem causes the financial crisis. First, the deterioration of banks' balance sheets will lead banks to restrict their loans to enhance capital asset ratio or directly cause systematic banking crisis that will make banks unable to pay their debt and this in turn undermines the banks' capacity to make loans.

Second, the deterioration of banks' balance sheets will trigger a currency crisis, because the central banks can hardly defense their exchange rates in face of speculative attacks. Raising interest rate will cause further damage to banks' balance sheets, so any instrument used to defense exchange rate by increasing interest rate will put the banking system in a worse condition. Due to mismatch of funds maturity, the credit risk increases as the economy declines, which will have a negative effect on banks' balance sheets. In this way, when the currencies of emerging economies are under a speculative attack, if the central bank increases interest rate to the level enough to defense exchange rate, the banking system will crash. When investors realize that one country's fragile banking system makes it impossible for the central bank to successfully defense its exchange rate, they will attack the country's currency even more actively with the expected return of short selling. Therefore, speculative attacks are probably successful when the target country has a fragile banking system. Many factors will encourage such kind of speculative attack, of which is the huge deficit of current account. Therefore, the deterioration of the banking system is the key factor causing the currency crisis.

Because of two key features of the debt contract, the currency crisis and devaluation will lead to systematic financial crisis in emerging economies. In emerging economies, debt contracts usually have very short maturities and denominated in foreign currencies. The features of debt contract formed three mechanisms, through which the currency crisis of merging economies aggravates asymmetric information in credit market and finally lead to financial crisis.

The first mechanism is a direct impact of currency devaluation on firm's balance sheets. When domestic currency depreciates, the debt contract denominated in foreign currencies will aggravate firm's debt burden. On the other side, because assets are mainly denominated in local currency, they will not increase at the same time. The result is the deterioration of firm's balance sheets and the declining of net assets. This will aggravate adverse selection, because the diminution of effective guaranty will lower the protection on lenders. Moreover, the decrease of net worth will lead to moral hazard, encouraging firms to undertake more risk because they will lose less when loan increases. Because the lenders face higher default risk, the credit supply will decrease. Then the investment and economic activities decline too.

Just like the 1995 Mexico crisis, the damage of devaluation caused by foreign currency crisis to the balance sheets is also a major factor leading to the decline of Southeast Asian economies. Because the currency of Indonesia depreciated by 75%, the rupee debt denominated in foreign currencies became 4 times as before. In this situation, this mechanism is very obvious. Under such attack, if a firm has a lot of foreign debt, it will become insolvent although the original balance sheet was very good.

The second mechanism that the currency crisis leads to financial crisis is the higher inflation caused by devaluation. Because many emerging economies have the experience of high and unstable inflation, their central banks are not anti-inflation worriers worth believing. So the rising pressure of price brought by large decrease of exchange rate after the speculative attack will lead to rapid increase of real or expected inflation. After the foreign currency crisis in 1994, Mexico's inflation raised up to 50%. In Indonesia, the most heavily beaten country, we saw almost the same situation. The increase of anticipated inflation after the currency crisis will deteriorate financial crisis, because it will lead to higher interest rate. The mutual interaction between short-time debt and rising interest rate will increase firms' interest expense, worsening their cash flow position and further exacerbating the balance sheets. So, just as what we see, when the asymmetric information problem deteriorates, credit and economic activities will decrease sharply.

The third mechanism that the currency crisis leads to the financial crisis is that the local currency devaluation will further exacerbate balance sheets of the banking system, triggering large scale banking crisis. When the currency crisis happens in emerging economies, banks usually have a lot of debt denominated by foreign currencies. On the other hand, the problems of firms and households mean that they cannot pay their debt, which will lead to loan loss on the asset side of bank's balance sheets. The result is, under the pressure from both the asset and liability side of bank's balance sheets, the net worth of banks will decrease consequently. Another problem faced by banks is that a lot of debt denominated by foreign currencies have short maturities, so the sudden increase of debt will cause banks' liquidity problems because these debts must be paid shortly. The further deterioration of banks' balance sheets and undermining capital base will force banks to cut credit. In extreme situations, the financial crisis caused by asset deterioration forces many banks failed, which directly restricts banks' credit creation capacity. Because banks play an important role in overcoming moral hazard and adverse selection and are probably the only credit source for many firms, in this sense, banks are very special. Therefore, once the bank credit crashes, economic crash will follow.

The basic conclusion from the asymmetric information analysis is that the Asian financial crisis is a systematic crash. This crash is due to deterioration of balance sheets of both financial and non-financial institutions, which aggravates the asymmetric information problem. The result is that financial market cannot channel funds to those who have productive opportunities and this in turn causes huge damages to the economies of those crisis countries.

Lessons

The above asymmetric information analysis about the causes of the Asian financial crisis and economic decline can be used to generate several lessons to prevent such crisis from happening again and to come out with the right solution when crisis happens. The first lesson is to stabilize the financial system through government intervention: for emerging countries, they need an international lender of last resort. The second lesson is that the loan condition of the international lender of last resort must be properly specified to avoid excessive moral hazard that leads to financial instability. The third lesson is that capital flow may relate to crisis, but this is only phenomenon instead of root, so foreign capital control may has little effect in preventing future crisis. The forth lesson is that pegged exchange-rate regime is dangerous to emerging economies, which makes financial crisis more easily happen. Now let us explain these lessons respectively.

(1) *About the international lender of last resort*

We already see that the information failure with the financial crisis will lead to economic disaster. In order to restore the economy, the financial system needs to restart to channel funds to productive investment. In industrial countries, central banks can do it by using expansionary monetary policy or the lending of last resort.

The asymmetric information perspective argues that the central banks of emerging countries do not have this capacity. Therefore, in order to solve the financial crisis in these countries, it will be necessary to have an international lender of last resort. However, even if there is an international lender of last resort, its action will cause serious moral hazard problems and increase the probability of the financial crisis. It will be even worse if the international lender of last resort cannot solve the moral hazard problems effectively. We will return to this point in the next section.

The financial systems of emerging economies have their own institutional character, which makes the central banks hard to help the economies recover from the financial crisis. In the early part of this lecture, we have already mentioned that many emerging economies have foreign currency denominated debt. In addition, they used to have high and unstable inflation and their debt contracts usually have short maturities. In this situation, expansionary monetary policy will lead to rapid increase of expected inflation.

As a result of their institutional character, the central banks of emerging economies cannot adopt expansionary monetary policy to recover the economies in face of the financial crisis. Imagine what will happen if such a country chooses to use expansionary monetary policy. Obviously, expansionary monetary policy is easy to induce high inflation anticipation and sharp devaluation of the local currency. We have seen that the devaluation of the local currency deteriorates the financial statements of companies and banks because their foreign currency denominated debts will aggravate debt burden and decrease net worth. We have also seen that rising interest rates lead to increasing interest expense and the cash flow of both companies and households declines. And this in turn makes the financial statements of companies and household even worse and banks' potential loan loss will increase too.

If an emerging economy of such institutional characters adopts expansionary monetary policy, the result is that the financial condition of households, companies and bank are all harmed. Therefore, expansionary monetary policy leads to deterioration of financial condition and makes the problems of moral hazard and adverse selection more complicated. For similar reasons, the measures of the central banks of emerging economies may not be so successful as developed countries. When Fed operated as the lender of last resort, such as in the 1987 stock crash, the market sentiment did not anticipate higher inflation. But emerging economies face another situation. Given the former inflation record, when the central banks make loans to the financial system after crisis, the expansion of credit will arouse worries that the inflation may lose control. We already see that the anticipated rising inflation will lead to higher interest rates, devaluation of local currency and deterioration of cash flow and financial condition. All of these will make it harder to recover from crisis.

In an emerging economy of such institutional characters, the role of the lender of last resort is limited because the central bank's loan is a double-edged sword. The mentioned viewpoints argue that the central banks of emerging economies have very limited capacity to save their economy from financial crisis. In fact, rapid economic recovery needs foreign aid, because liquidity from overseas will not cause negative effects as provided by local agency. Foreign assistance will not lead to inflation or damage financial condition through cash flow. This is helpful to stabilize local currency and improve financial condition.

Since emerging economies need lending of last resort and the latter can only be provided from overseas instead of domestic agencies, there will be a solid theoretic foundation for the establishment of an international lender of last resort. If there is cross-border contagion in the financial crisis, then the theoretic foundation for the establishment of an international lender of last resort will be even more convincing. But danger will not be limited to any single country and a successful attack toward one currency will lead to another speculative attack toward another currency. It is possible that more and more currencies will crash under such attacks. In this way, it is probably that the currency crisis may expand like a snowball. In addition, once these currency crises become systematic financial crises in emerging economies, dangers of contagious effect among countries do exist. The international lender of last resort has the capacity to provide international reserve for those countries under attack, thus stabilize currency value and prevent crisis from spreading. The help from the international lender of last resort is useful to prevent crisis and even the spreading of financial crisis.

(2) *Operation of the international lender of last resort*

From the viewpoint of asymmetric information, we can generalize several guidelines to solve the Asian financial crisis: (1) reintegrate the financial system to restore its function, namely conducting funds to people who have best productive investments; (2) provide liquidity in time for this; (3) reconstruct the financial structure of both financial institutions and non-financial companies to alleviate asymmetric information; (4) take actions to solve the problems of moral hazard caused by the crisis resolution.

In order to resolve a crisis such as what we experienced in Asia recently, those guidelines will be very useful to specify the operations of international lender of last resort. Just as the first guideline suggested, in order to reintegrate the financial system, the international lender of last resort must inject adequate liquidity into the financial system to restore the capacity of making new loans. However, there is another important factor involved: restore people's confidence toward the financial system. In order to realize this aim, the liquidity assistance from the lender of last resort is not enough. Assurance that financial institutions will not undertake excessive risk is equally important. This means that the lender of last resort must persist in the loan condition that the crisis countries improve their supervisory systems, which will play an important part in the process of restoring confidence and resolving crisis. To discourage the excessive risk taking behavior, insolvent banks must be closed because they will have strong incentives to pursue more risks if they are allowed to continue operation but actually have nothing to lose. On the other hand, to restore people's confidence toward the financial system means to convince them believe that their money in other banks is safe when some banks are liquidated. Indonesia did not follow this rule when closing 16 banks in the early stages of the crisis, which was sharply criticized by IMF.

One of the historical features of the successful operation of last lending is that the more quickly loans provided, the less amount of rescue money needed. This fact supports the second rule that liquidity should be provided as soon as possible. It is an excellent example what happened after the American stock crash in October 19, 1987. Close to the ending of the trading day, security companies needed to borrow several thousand million dollars to keep regular trading. This situation had never happened before and banks worried about making loans to these companies again. When realized this, the Fed acted as the lender of last resort immediately. Greenspan announced before the next trading day that the Fed "has prepared for providing liquidity support to economic and financial system." Besides, the Fed agreed to provide liquidity to banks lending to security companies. As a matter of fact, the most attractive part of the senario is that the quick intervention of the Fed not only stopped the stock crash but also suggested that the liquidity needed is not enormous (see Mishkin, 1991).

The Fed initiated the operation of lender of last resort within one day after the American financial system was shocked. It sharply contrasts with the recent slow action of IMF during the crisis. Because the design of IMF is to provide support only when the crisis country encounters imbalance of payments, it usually involves a bargaining process and may cost several months before funds are actually in place. This will make the situation even worse. The result is that in order to overcome the crisis, much more funds are needed, which usually places IMF under a financial pressure. One of the reasons why central banks can act more quickly than IMF is that central banks usually have ready loan conditions and agreements on loan clauses and conditions. In order to utilize funds efficiently, the loan conditions of the international lender of last resort must be specified that funds will be provided as soon as the borrower satisfies the loan conditions. In fact, there are advices that IMF changes its emergency loan requirements so that liquidity could be provided more efficiently.

The third rule suggests that the financial structure of financial institutions and non-financial companies should be reconstructed to solve the financial crisis. The reconstruction of non-financial companies' financial structure requires an effective bankruptcy law to help these companies obtain financing capacity in credit market. Reconstruction of the financial structure of financial institutions may need injection of public funds so that healthy banks can buy the assets of failed banks. Entities such as DTCC must be created to sell the assets of failed banks to erase them from financial industry. The international lender of last resort and other potential international organizations may help during the process, such as providing technical support, encouraging the governments of crisis countries to establish better judicial framework and liquidation procedure for failed financial institutions.

The forth rule suggests that it is necessary to control moral hazard caused by the existence of the international lender of last resort. The existence of the international lender of last resort will bring along serious moral hazard because depositors and other creditors may think that they will be protected when the crisis happens. In the recent events of the Asian financial crisis, the governments of crisis countries use money from IMF to protect depositors and other creditors from loss. Such safety network will cause the well-known moral hazard, because depositors and other creditors lack enough incentive to monitor banks and will draw back money when banks undertake too mush risk. The result is to encourage these banks to undertake high-risk activities.

There is a tradeoff between preventing crisis and bringing moral hazard for the international lender of last resort, so lending should be given only when necessary. The international lender of last resort has an adequate reason to reject money requirements when the borrower is still in normal state. In other words, the role of the international lender of last resort will be more successful only when it is seldom used.

The problem of moral hazard can be controlled by a well-running common regulatory system: punishments for the management and stockholders of failed financial institutions, suitable accounting system and information disclosure, adequate capital asset ratio, prompt correction mechanism, prudential regulation of the risk management of financial institutions, and rule-based regulation.

However, in emerging economies, there usually exists political power to reject these measures, which may also be a problem in industrial countries. For example, the S&L crisis formed political pressure on weakening regulation (Kane, 1989), but in emerging economies, things will be much worse. We see that in Asian crisis countries, the political pressure on the proper regulation of financial institutions is very weak because politicians and their relatives are usually the real owners of these financial institutions. The international lender of last resort is very suitable for adopting the above measures to control moral hazard, because it can provide enormous leverage effect for those emerging economies that have borrowed from it or may ask for loans in the future.

If the international lender of last resort encourages emerging economies to adopt the above regulatory measures, the effects will be even better. There are two reasons for this. First, the actions taken by the international lender of last resort provide finance for governments of the crisis countries to sustain their financial industry. The international lender of last resort strengthens the financial safety network, which encourages financial institutions to assume more risk. This problem can be solved through strengthening financial regulations of these countries. Second, the reason why the existence of the international lender of last resort brings along moral hazard is that if the governments of the crisis countries know their financial institutions will be saved, they will not have enough incentive to prevent financial institutions from undertaking excessive risk. The international lender of last resort can declare that it will not provide liquidity support unless the governments of the crisis countries take effective measures to prevent excessive risk-taking of their banks. This will stimulate crisis countries to improve their financial regulations. Moreover, this is also helpful to restrict the capacity of these governments to protect the stakeholders of domestic financial institutions and large uninsured creditors, which will discourage the incentive of assuming high risk. Only when such pressures are imposed will the moral hazard brought by the international lender of last resort be controlled.

One of the problems that international organizations and foreign governments will take part in the operation of the lending of last resort is that they know emerging economies will experience an extreme hard time or even political turbulence if they do not give an helping hand. Based on this anticipation, politicians of crisis countries may play Chicken Game with the international lender of last resort. They reject the necessary reforms, wishing the international lender of last resort would finally give in. It is the case in the 1995 Mexico crisis. And in the Asian financial crisis, it is also one of the important features in the bargaining process between Indonesia and IMF.

The effects might be much better if the international lender of last resort declares that it will not play this game. Just like giving in to your children, it may be a good choice in the short run; but in the long run, it will do harm to children's growth. The international lender of last resort will not give in for humanistic considerations. Better policies will be adopted only when the emerging economies cannot escape the necessary reforms. In a financial crisis, if the international lender of last resort give in to a country, it will be more difficult to control moral hazard when other countries see that they may also escape the necessary reforms.

The asymmetric information analysis of the Asian financial crisis points out that in the operation of the lending of last resort, those macroeconomic and microeconomic economic policies unrelated to financial industry should not be over emphasized. IMF has already been criticized for imposing harsh constrictive policies on East Asian countries. As currency and financial crises develop, what kind of macroeconomic and non-financial microeconomic policies should be adopted is not very clear and this becomes a hot topic in recent debate. No matter what the right policies are, there are two reasons not to emphasize them if the international lender of last resort wants to be successful the in stabilizing the financial system.

First, the fundamental driving force of the crisis lies in the micro aspect of financial industry. So macroeconomic policy and financial-industry-unrelated microeconomic policy are useless in solving crisis. Second, staring at severe policies and other microeconomic policies might lead to political disaster. Politicians tend to refrain from tough-ing the difficult part of the financial reform, especially in Southeast Asian countries, because many politicians' crony and even their fami-lies will suffer from loss during reform. If severe constrictive policies imposed, these politicians will depict the international lender of last resort (IMF in the Asian financial crisis) as anti-economic growth or even anti-Asia. This will help politicians mobilize public to oppose the international lender of last resort thus to escape from the real neces-sary reforms of their financial industry. If conditions focus on micro-economic policies related to the financial industry, the international lender of last resort will be recognized as the helping hand to aid emerging countries to establish more efficient financial systems.

(3) *Capital flow and capital control*

In the Asian financial crisis, crisis countries have experienced enor-mous capital inflow before the crisis and enormous capital outflow after the crisis. After the crisis, much attention was given to the ques-tion whether capital flow is one of the radical origins of financial instability. The asymmetric information analysis of the crisis suggests that international capital flow plays an important role in the propaga-tion of financial instability. But just as we have already realized, the major reason is that the existence of government safety network and inadequate banking supervision encourage capital inflow, which causes sharp loan increase and excessive risk taking behavior of banks. In line with this view, Gavin and Hausman (1996) and Kaminsky and Reinhart (1996) found that the sharp increase of loan is an indicator of banking crisis. But this does not means that capital inflow will actually cause sharp increase of bank loans, of which the latter deteriorate the balance sheets of banks. In fact, Kaminsky and Reinhart (1996) found that financial liberalization, not the international capital, is more likely to be the important indicator for banking crisis.

(4) *The danger of pegged exchange-rate regime*

A regular way to obtain price stability is to peg its currency to the currency of another low inflation country. Under some circumstances, this strategy involves pegging one country's exchange rate to another currency with a fixed price so that its inflation goes down to the level of the pegged country. Under other circumstances, this strategy involves crawling peg or target ratio of currency devaluation. If a country devalues its currency according to this target ratio, its inflation rate can be maintained above the pegged country.

Though it is a very successful strategy to use fixed exchange-rate regime or pegged exchange-rate regime to control inflation, the asymmetric information analysis of Asian crisis suggests that this strategy is dangerous for an emerging economy that has enormous foreign debt. Under pegged exchange-rate regime, after a successful speculative attack, compared with floating exchange-rate regime, the devaluation of local currency is sharper, faster and more unpredictable. For example, in the recent Asian financial crisis, the most seriously attacked currency of Indonesia decreased to 1/4 of its pre-crisis value within a short period and the loss of balance sheet is also huge after devaluation. In Indonesia, the value of foreign debt increased by 4 times after currency crash, which made those Indonesian companies that have increased foreign debt cannot maintain solvency. The deterioration of the balance sheets of non-financial companies causes further deterioration of banks' balance sheets, because the probability of payments of loans becomes smaller. The result of the crash of balance sheets is rightly the severe economic recession we have already seen.

Another potential danger caused by pegged exchange rate is that it encourages capital inflow because it provides a more stable currency value, which gives foreign investors a sense of low risk. These capital inflows may be conducted to productive investments and thus promote growth, but they will also lead to excessive loan making, which shows up as sharp rising of loan. This happens because domestic financial institutions, such as banks, play a key role in intermediating these capital inflows. Further, if bank regulation procedure is very weak, as we see in emerging economies, the safety network of banking institutions set up by governments will encourage excessive risk taking and the probability of sharp loan increase caused by capital inflow will be even bigger. Because of inadequate bank regulation, the possible outcome of loan increase is huge loan loss, the deterioration of bank balance sheets and the probable financial crisis.

The volatility of exchange rate under floating regime is more evident than that under fixed regime and this is an advantage of floating exchange rate regime. In fact, the daily volatility of exchange rate under floating regime has the following advantage: it gives a signal to private companies, banks and governments that foreign currency denominated debts have obvious risk. In addition, the devaluation of exchange rate sends an early warning message to policy makers that their policies must be adjusted to prevent financial crisis.

The conclusion is that pegged exchange-rate regime may add to financial instability of emerging economies and transition economies. However, this conclusion does not exclude that fact that under some circumstances, the fixed or pegged exchange rate regime can be an effective way to control inflation. In fact, for countries that have bad inflation history, inflation can only be controlled when the rigorous pegged exchange-rate regime adopted. Moreover, in order to control inflation successfully, it is necessary to adopt policies improving the bank system. In addition, if a country has an institutional structure of its fragile banking system and enormous foreign currency denominated debt, it is probably dangerous to adopt pegged exchange-rate regime to control inflation.

Conclusion

Southeast Asian financial crisis is not only catastrophic to the economies of this region but also push the global financial system under enormous pressure. Here our asymmetric information of the crisis comes up with several lessons: first, there are sufficient reasons to have an international lender of last resort; second, restrictive conditions of loans must be properly specified, or the operation of the international lender of last resort will cause moral hazard and thus financial instability; third, though capital flow is conducive to the development of financial crisis, it is only the symptom not the cause of crisis, so the regulation of exchange rate is less likely become an effective way to prevent crisis; forth, pegged exchange-rate regime is a dangerous strategy for emerging economies because it makes financial crisis more likely to happen. I sincerely hope what we learn from the crisis will help us avoid making the same mistake again. These mistakes have caused enormous costs in the recent events.

Review

Chen Yu-lu

From the year 2000 to 2001, as a senior visiting scholar of the Fubright Program, I was studying in Colombia University in Manhattan, New York. This old university, brought me not only with rich academic wisdom and inspiration but also unforgettable life experience. When the horrible disaster of 911 suddenly attacked this city, I was there sharing the same feelings with people. Now nearly two years has passed since I left Colombia University, but memories about there and time spent there never evade as time goes by. Today, I am glad and feel great honor to have the opportunity to comment on Professor Mishkin's lecture *The Lessons of the Asian Financial Crisis.*

Professor Mishkin used to be my co-worker in Colombia University and he was also the former Vice Chairman of the New York Fed. He has worldwide academic reputation for his study and excels in macroeconomic theory, money and banking, and international financial theory. As the Chief Editor, his textbook *The Economics of Money, Banking, and Finacial Markets* is not only widely used in the United States, but also earns good reputation in China. When the Asian financial crisis broke out, Professor Mishkin showed a great interest and made much progress in exploring the causes and countermeasures of the crisis. In today's lecture, he uses the information theory to analyze the causes of the Asian financial crisis and comes up with several policy suggestions for developing countries that may be threatened by such a crisis.

Professor Mishkin gives a complete new view to look at the Asian financial crisis. He argues that the problem of asymmetric information is inherent in the financial system itself and the financial fragility of developing countries further worsens moral hazard and adverse selection, which arise from the asymmetric information between debtors and creditors. Because of the dysfunction of the financial institutions, money in the surplus sector cannot be efficiently conducted to the deficit sector to support the productive investment and the crash of financial system causes the turbulence of the economic system and even the political system.

Based on the analysis of the causes of financial crisis mentioned above, Professor Mishkin's suggestions are mainly provided for international financial institutions, crisis countries and potentially threatened economies.

From an international perspective, we need an international financial institution to act as the lender of last resort and further measures must be taken to ensure that it functions efficiently and scientifically.

The reasons why we need the international lender of last resort are based on the following considerations. First, the central bank of developing countries can hardly save their countries from crisis when the crisis already broken out or prevent the crisis when their economies slide to the edge of the crisis. This is because most developing countries have their unique institutional structures: in order to stimulate economic development, these countries attract a lot of foreign capital, which usually has short maturity and denominated by foreign currencies. Therefore, once a country is threatened by a financial crisis, central bank's expansionary monetary policy will cause people's anticipation of high inflation. The devaluation of the local currency and the rising interest rate will worsen the financial condition of enterprises and financial institutions. Second, along with the process of financial globalization, a financial crisis will spread to other countries from various contagion channels and thus threaten the stability of global financial system. The foreign reserve of any single developing country is just like a drop in the bucket in face of international speculative attack. Therefore, it's necessary that we have an international institution which functions as the lender of last resort.

But establishing international lender of last resort is not enough to save crisis from disaster, more important is to ensure that it functions efficiently and scientifically. This has already been evidenced in the Asian financial crisis. Professor Mishkin proposed four operative principles for the international lender of last resort: (1) reconstruct financial system to restore the financing function, including not only providing liquidity to the crisis countries but also improving the policy coordination and supervisory system to restore the confidence of domestic and foreign investors; (2) design the loan procedure scientifically to ensure the efficiency of resolving process. Slow action in the resolving process will cause even more loss; (3) provide technological support for the crisis countries to make their financial and economic system function efficiently. Such technological support includes the reconstruction of the financial structure of both financial and non-financial corporations and the design of exit mechanism of market participant; (4) take effective measures to alleviate the moral hazard problem caused by the international lender of last resort. Such measures include the punishment of managers and stockholders of failed financial institutions, the requirement of accounting standards and information disclosures, the requirement of capital adequacy, etc.

In his lecture, Mishkin criticized the deflationary policies that were imposed on Southeast Asian countries by IMF. The asymmetric information in the Asian financial crisis indicates that the fundamental problem involved was due to the micro-financial side. Therefore, macroeconomic policy and those unrelated microeconomic policies would do no good to solve the crisis. Moreover, when deflationary policies were imposed on crisis countries, the economic conditions of the crisis will even deteriorate more.

For the governments of developing countries, Professor Mishkin proposed the following policy recommedations:

(1) Managing capital flow. After the Asian financial crisis broke out, the third generation theory of currency crisis by Krugman argues that the unstable financial system of developing countries will cause the problem of external diseconomies. In this background, if capital is allowed to flow freely, any change of real exchange rate will aggregate the negative shocks to real economy. Therefore, the radical solution to avoid crisis is to employ capital control. Professor Mishkin's analytic framework based on informational economics shows that capital flow is just the symptom but not the cause of the financial crisis. Therefore, capital control will not prevent financial crisis. On the contrary, capital control will disturb the inflow of productive investment and thus enervate the power of economic development. Moreover, as time goes by, capital control imposed on households and enterprises will cause policy distortion and the inefficient allocation of economic resources. Therefore, the right choice for developing countries is to strengthen the management and monitoring of capital flow and improve the efficiency of capital utilization.

(2) Improving the management and efficiency of the financial system. Now most developing countries have their financial safety networks for the banking systems, which will cause the moral

hazard problems, undermining the incentives of depositors and foreign investors to monitor banks. Once the banks assume too much risk, a financial crisis will follow. Therefore, it is important for developing countries to improve their financial legislation, strengthen their financial supervision, impose better information disclosure and enhance transparency.

(3) Improving the risk management of the financial system. In fact, the asymmetric information of the financial system is the same in every country, but mature economies gradually formed their own solution during the long process of economic development. Therefore, the cost of the financial crisis in developed countries is much lower than developing countries. It will be an effective way for developing countries to prevent financial crisis by exploring and enhancing their risk management techniques.

China and Southeast Asian countries are all developing countries and have a lot in common in economic structure and economic development, so, many issues that Professor Mishkin mentioned in his lecture do exist in china, such as the governmental implicit protection of the financial system, the opacity of financial management and the low level of risk management. These factors caused large sum of non-performing loans in Chinese banking system, which will lead to financial crisis if not properly resolved. Moreover, along with the opening process of domestic capital market, we must prepare for the pressure of the international capital flow on Chinese banking sector. How to minimize the impact of capital flow and alleviate the fragility of the financial system (especially the banking system) to avoid financial crisis is an important issue that deserves attention of both policy makers and academic scholars. Today, Professor Mishkin gave us the right way to further study it.

Of course, some of the points in his lecture deserve further discussion. For example, Professor Mishkin argues that the assistance of the international lender of last resort will weaken constraint on market participants, encouraging their risk-taking behaviors and thus causing moral hazard. This happens because, if policymakers believe that the international lender of last resort will finally bail out their failure, they will pursue even more risk. But I think this presumption is short of evidence. In fact, in the Asian financial crisis, those crisis countries paid great economic and political costs and most loans from overseas were used for regrouping and some loans were even suffered a loss. It is hardly to believe that the governments of the crisis countries and the international investors will undertake so much risk just because there is potentially finance from the international lender of last resort. However, concerning the policy suggestions Professor Mishkin proposed for reforming the international financial system, I fully agree.

Capital outflow is also considered as one of the causes of currency crisis. As we see, the latter probably leads to financial instability of emerging economies. According to this view, when foreign investors move away their capital, the resulted capital outflow is rightly the driving force of the local currency devaluation. However, as pointed out earlier, one of the major factors triggering the Asian financial crisis is the problem of financial sector, which attracted speculative attacks and capital outflow. Based on this view, the capital outflow that accompanies the exchange rate crisis is only a symptom of the radical contradictions lying behind, not the cause of the currency crisis. A lot of studies (see Kaminsky, Lizondo and Reinhart, 1997) support this view, for empirical foundations suggest that capital flow and current account data have no use in predicting currency crisis while those more fundamental problems such as the banking sector problem are more useful for prediction.

Therefore, the analysis here does not provide foundation for capital control, such as that adopted by Malaysia recently. Capital control is just like dumping bath water and baby together. Capital control has an undesirable feature that it will stop productive investments from flowing into a country. Though capital control may restrict rapid loan increase brought by capital flow, it will lead to obvious distortion and inefficient resource allocation when households and firms try to escape these regulations as time goes by. In fact, in today's environment, because of trade liberalization and financial instruments that make escaping these regulations easier, it is rather doubted whether capital control can be effective.

On the other hand, there are adequate reasons that bank regulation should be improved to decrease the probability of rapid loan increase and excessive risk taken by banks. For instance, the increasing rate of bank loans can be controlled to offset the effects of capital inflow. These prudential controlling measures can be considered as forms of capital control, but they are very different from typical foreign currency control in that they focus on financial instability instead of its symptoms. This kind of the regulatory control can improve the efficiency of the financial system instead of worsening it.

Chapter 8

Imagination, Futures and Financial Futures

Leo Melamed

Biography

Leo Melamed, Chairman Emeritus of CME Group, Inc. is recognized as the founder of financial futures markets. At the close of 1999, Melamed was named by the former editor of the Chicago Tribune, among the ten most important Chicagoans in business of the 20th Century. Chicago Magazine included him among the century's top 100 Chicagoans. In 2003, Pensions & Investments included Mr. Melamed in the list of 30 individuals whose contribution "made the most dramatic difference" in the management of money during the last 100 years.

Leo Melamed was an immigrant child who found safety in the US during World War II. The story of his escape from Bialystok, Poland where he was born, as he and his parents miraculously outwitted the Gestapo and KGB, was an odyssey that took two years. The escape spanned three continents, seven languages, the Trans-Siberian railroad, and Japan — courtesy a life-saving transit visa from Japanese Counsel General to Lithuania, Chiune Sugihara. Happily, the journey concluded in the US in 1941.

As chairman of the Chicago Mercantile Exchange (CME) in 1971, Leo Melamed revolutionized futures markets by launching the International Monetary Market (IMM) — the world's first futures market for the express purpose of trading in financial instruments. Currency futures at the IMM began trading on May 16, 1972. In the years that followed, Melamed led the CME in the introduction of a diverse number of financial instruments, including Treasury Bills in 1976, Eurodollars in 1981, and stock index futures in 1982. Twenty years after their inception, Nobel Laureate in Economics, Merton Miller, named financial futures as "the most significant innovation in the past two decades." In 1987, Melamed spearheaded the introduction of Globex®, the world's first futures electronic trading system, and became its founding chairman. The Chicago Mercantile Exchange, today known as the CME Group, is the world's premier futures market, where Mr. Melamed serves as a member of the Board and is chairman of its Strategic Steering Committee.

Mr. Melamed has written extensively on financial markets. Many of his essays and lectures can be found on the website www.leomelamed.com. Mr. Melamed's memoirs, *Escape to the Futures* have been translated and published in Chinese, Japanese as well as Korean. Mr. Melamed is the recipient of many awards including the 2005 Fred Arditti Innovation Award of the Chicago Mercantile Exchange. In 2008, Leo Melamed became the recipient of the Ellis Island Medal of Honor, as well as the William F Sharpe Lifetime Achievement Award. He holds an Honorary Professorship at Renmin University, Beijing, and in 2007 was appointed Honorary Dean of Peking University.

Leo Melamed is an attorney by profession and an active futures trader. He is Chairman and CEO of Melamed & Associates, Inc., a global market consulting service.

Speech

My theme of today's speech is imagination. Although I have not made any preparation for this topic, before meeting you, I had a communication with your President Linghui Feng (the Vice President of Renmin University of China), who led me to deliver a speech in this field. You are in the very ages so that you will take charge of the future of the new century. One cannot keep ahead of the new era unless he is full of imagination. Therefore do you know what I would do if I could restart my life? There is no doubt that I would be a student in Renmin University of China, for I could acquire a lot of knowledge here.

It is well-known that computer technology develops fast. In less than 50 years, revolutionary development occurred to this technology, which really filled another gap in the history. With the invention of chip made by three young Americans in the middle of the 20th century, the first transistor was born. And 50 years later, we have the internet. Looking more closely at the cases, we can find that all of these happened without much imagination. That means when you are young, you must use your imagination properly. Once you get older, you are not willing to take risks, and then you will be dull. Do you know why you can bear the risk when you are young? That is because you have a long way to go in your life and you can do many other things until you succeed even if you failed today.

My father took some risks when the Second World War broke out. I was born in Poland. And my father managed to rescue us after we had been Nazi's prisoners. So maybe he is the most admirable people I have met. Succeeding in rescuing his children and wife, he took them across Soviet Russia in one a year and a half, walked across the Siberia to Vladivostok. After that we arrived in Japan for a brief stopover, and then we finally moved to America. In this process, my father exerted a lot of imagination. Few people could escape from Nazi, but we were lucky. I came to America and was grown up in the most wonderful country in the world. When I entered school, I was speaking my seventh language. Try to figure that when I was born, I spoke two languages. One was Jewish language for I was a Jew, the other was Polish. Then we started our escape. We reached Lithuania first. My parents were teachers. For them the worst thing was letting their children out of school. Therefore, I studied in Lithuanian school. Later, we studied in Russia and Japan. And finally I furthered my studies in America. That was why I could speak several languages when I was in America.

After I graduated, I became a lawyer and engaged in this field for a period of time. However when I was studying in law school, I had already tried to do some other things. I was working in Chicago Mercantile Exchange to do the most basic work, and that was to deliver the bill of exchange between the front desk and counter. For I had to pay back the tuition fees, and that was my first job. It was at that time the market fascinated me all of a sudden and I began to feel interested in the market. Being a student studying in law, although I had never studied in economics school before, I experienced the charm of the market and understood the basic law of demand of supply, how it worked and the fluctuation of market and its causes. Then I began to read all the financial-related books I could get. In 1969, I managed to be the Chairman of Chicago Mercantile Exchange. I am quite sure at that time many of you have not yet born, so let me tell you something related to imagination.

In 1969, there were only some agricultural products in the future market, since what they operated in the beginning were agricultural products. So people could only trade these products in the future market at that time. What we operated were eggs, butter, pork, beef, grain, wheat and soy. The future market had been existent for nearly 5,000 years. The reason why I said that it had a history of 5,000 years was that I was quite sure about it. Do you have heard the story of Joseph and Pharaoh in the Bible before? Do you know how Joseph reached Egypt and told Pharaoh that there would be poor harvest that would last for 7 years? Do you know what he told Pharaoh to do after his prediction? He told Pharaoh to store some grains in order to survive that 7-year adversity. And this was the first futures transaction.

5,000 years ago, people traded grains through future trading. So it was very natural that grains dominated this market later. Until 1969 when I was the Chairman of Chicago Mercantile Exchange, I asked myself the question why there were only agricultural products in future market. No one could give me a satisfying answer. After considering it seriously, I figured out the reason and that because I was not an economist. I could not understand the question that was understood by Professor Chen, and that was why people could only deal with agricultural products in future market. There must be a real reason. But you know I cannot find it out by myself. But according to my imagination, I thought future market should achieve better results in other financial fields if it could smooth its function for agricultural products. One can understand it easily if one person has the belief that the fluctuation of mark, yen and US dollar is not likely to depend on the weather. However the growth of grains depends on weather. But no one can forecast the weather accurately. Even if one is weather forecaster, he will also make mistakes. By contrast, there is no point for anyone worrying about the weather in financial sector. On the contrary, people can get the only exact answer by applying to mathematics. I was quite confident to say one gentleman could give me the answer for in my opinion, there was rarely anything he did not know in financial sector. And he was Professor Milton Friedman. Maybe some of you have heard of the name before, he just lived on the same street where University of Chicago located, the one I often paid visits to. Although I was the Chairman of Chicago Mercantile Exchange, just like you, I attended the class taught by Professor Milton Friedman. I paid nothing for they did not check on the attendance. That was why I could often listen to his lecture at the back of the classroom. A few years later, Professor Milton Friedman was famous for his well-known statement that there is no free lunch. The very reason why this statement was famous was that one must cover some costs if the person wanted to get something. Several years later, I told him that maybe free lunch really existed in the world for my free opportunity to attend his class. But he replied no and told me that I needed to study more. At last, I asked him the question why there was not any financial future market and I told him I was the Chairman of Chicago Mercantile Exchange, I wanted to establish financial future market and I wanted to put forward the new products-financial futures.

It is widely accepted that currency plays a very important role in future market. For example, if you are a manufacturer of some certain products in China and you want to sell your products to German and expect them to pay in mark, you will receive the mark payment in six months or a year or two years from now on. Maybe you can get the payments two or three years after you deliver your products. But the value of mark fluctuates everyday. So you may bear a loss if the clearing price is declining to some extent that the settlement price is lower than the agreed price. However, we cannot expect that will happen when delivering products. You are lucky if mark appreciates while you are unfortunate if mark depreciates. However, the production costs remain the same in this period. Maybe you hope that your actual profits are equal to the one you figured out at the very beginning.

Then how to avoid risks if you want to get that given profit? That is achievable through the financial instruments in future market. So I told Professor Milton Friedman if we established a foreign currency market, then enterprises could avoid exchange rate risk with the instruments in this market for the exchange rate may vary at any time. Professor Milton Friedman replied that this was the most perfect idea and asked me why not did it? You know as to me, this was just like the god was talking with me. It was Milton Friedman gave me the encouragement. So I established the first currency future market.

Furthermore, we made a special market sector for financial products, and that was International Monetary Market. Many people thought I was mad and considered this was a crazy idea. They stuck to the point that future market was fit for agricultural products rather than financial one. What was more, I was 30 years old, and elder people did not trust young people in this age. Therefore they did not trust me either, was not it? You can take risks and use your imagination for you are different from me at that time. You are less than 30.

Now you know I established this market and got it work. But at that time, I told myself no worry. Why should not we apply it to interest rate as we did to exchange rate if the market functioned well with the latter? Also, the interest rate varies from time to time. Through learning, we know the value of anything change owing to the changes of interest rate, such as the value of investment, the purchasing value and selling value. Nearly the value of anything depends on interest rate. And of course, they also depend on the country's social and political conditions and the economic situation. It was the same with the idea that I wanted to get currency involved in future market. In light of my imagination, I believed maybe we could get interest rate in the market. But there was a small problem, caused by a law in America, which says one must trade for practicalities if he intends to trade in future market. Therefore, you can trade francs or Italian lira in currency market. But what could we deal with interest rate? How could we trade interest rate in future market? There seemed to be no solutions. But I was interested in trading interest rate all the time, maybe you felt interested in the value differences between two different interest rates as well, did not you? Different value accounted for this difference. If your expected profit margin of an investment is 5%, while the real profit margin is 7%, then you can gain 2% more. Do you want to get it? If you want this 2%, this is what you are actually seeking for. Thinking twice, I believe maybe you can handle such transactions with cash rather than practicalities. That is to say, we can finish these transactions with cash instead of trading interest rate.

Therefore I found the corresponding Government officials.

> "Authorizing us the cash disposal right, we will establish non-in-kind transactions. When we do beef business, we must use the beef to trade; when we do grain business, we must use the grain to trade; when we do currency business, we must use the currency to trade. Please provide us the right of trading nothing but difference in exchanging value."
>
> "Get out! You are crazy! " They answered at first.
>
> "Why?" I asked.
>
> "Nobody wants to trade the interest rate, what do you want to let the value represent for?"

After a while, I cannot but to convince them. But my imagination had still not been realized. It was until 1981 that the federal government passed a law saying that "can be." Having the power to dispose of cash, we created today's interest rate market.

But after having the cash disposal right, I was thinking: "Is the cash disposal right only restricted in the interest rate market?" No, the cash disposal right can be used in any field. Because, once you can use the cash disposal right, you can use the index. Therefore I was thinking whether I do need one stock market index. Having this index means we have one kind of ability, because the index could not be traded. What is the index? It is a complex created with the value of various elements. Although you cannot trade the index, but can actually trade the price discrepancy. Obviously, the index will sometimes rise, and sometimes drop, which causes losses. But in each project, you only need to pay attention to the difference in the amount of currency, types of currency and the cash disposal right. Therefore the stock index futures market was established in Chicago Mercantile Exchange.

Today, the stock index futures market has existed all over the world, and I am sure that it will emerge in People's Republic of China soon. This is exactly why I am here, and if allowed, I will also go to Shanghai and other places. The Chinese government will welcome these financial instruments including stock market index. As China wants to develop, it is necessary to use these financial instruments rather than speculation. Of course, there are indeed many speculative behaviors, so it is also important to avoid speculation. But the real reason to avoid speculating is promoting economic development through risk transformation. You can gain related knowledge from books and our website. I am sure your professor will find and explain them to you, and the key point is that China must develop.

I believe that China has the greatest potential in the world. Why? Because this country has you, the greatest resources to the country, and if all China's younger generation can learn, live and use imagination like you, they can create what I have never thought before. You may ponder boldly, grasp the opportunity and undertake the risk. If you are wrong, you still have time to correct, as I had done. Of course, I have won fame now, but it is insufficient to speak high of myself. What I am most excited is talking with you, and bringing you the information of imagination.

A few years ago, I decided to write a science fiction. I have always been a faithful reader of science fiction. During my growth, I like science fiction movies, and have read lots of science fictions, which is my hobby. How many of you have read science fictions? I think I am able to write better science fiction, and I have finally completed this novel. But do not try to buy it, because it is no longer printed, and has few copies. After the publication of the novel, I told my living father, "I have really completed a great thing — I have published a science fiction." But he who has been paying close attention to my financial innovation looked at me, saying: "No, you do not... you have been creating science fiction including those markets, but with the exception of this novel. Therefore, you should not be too proud, thinking that you have exerted imagination fully." Therefore, I also hope that you can exert really scientific fantasy, and utilize your imagination fully in the real world.

Review

Chuanlun Wang

Leo Melamed is a success in financial circle of the US. The financial future market was established under his guidance, making the great expansion of Chicago Board of Trade and its international good reputation. He toured around the world. He visited Beijing and delivered this speech in School of Finance, Renmin University of China, adding the unique distinction to this academic activity.

His speech aroused our great attentions.

He gave us details of the evolutions from the spot trading to future trading of commodities like grains, from the future trading of common commodities to currencies, from the trading of normal currency futures to the trading among different currencies and from the trading of normal currency futures to the trading of compound financial futures. The process mentioned above permeated to the western market economies within 50 years, becoming a non-neglectable issue in economic realities.

What are the driving forces to this development? An important factor Leo Melamed mentioned in his speech was the motivation of risk aversion. Risks existed in all trading. Only could a trade securitize the benefits of a transaction if he managed to control relative risks. The gradual development of financial futures trading was driven by this fact. The nature of financial futures trading was transacting the combination of financial commodity itself and its risks in the market.

Although trading of financial futures cannot eliminate risks, it can definitely disperse risks. There are traders expecting more returns while taking fewer risks and willingly having more risk exposures in the market. Both parties share the market risks through the trading of financial futures, which makes the contribution to the stability of financial market.

However, it is apparently that it do more harm to the stability of financial market if one takes advantage of the private information or adopts other unfair and immoral tactics to manipulate market, getting more returns for oneself while imposing risks on other investors. Leo Melamed raised this problem in his speech and expressed the significance of avoiding speculations.

Like most successful people, Leo Melamed recalled the whole life and regarded himself as the success of financial innovation. And financial innovation is the irreversible trend, which cannot be made by any single person. But Leo Melamed proposed an important point, and that was imagination, which was also the theme of the speech. And it is beyond question that imagination plays a significant role in Chinese economic society, and especially important to the young scholars.

Chapter 9

The Interconnection and Pricing of the Internet

Jean-Jacques Laffont

Biography

Jean-Jacques Marcel Laffont (1947–2004) was a French economist specializing in public economics and information theory. Educated at the University of Toulouse and the Ecole Nationale de la Statistique et de l'Administration Economique (ENSAE) in Paris, he was awarded the Ph.D. in Economics by Harvard University in 1975.

Laffont taught at the Ecole Polytechnique (1975–87), and was Professor of Economics at the University of Toulouse I (1991–2001). In 1991, he founded Toulouse's Industrial Economics Institute (Institut D'Economie Industrielle, IDEI) which has become one of the more prominent European research centres in economics. From 2001 until his death, he was the inaugural holder of the University of Southern California's John Elliott Chair in Economics. Over the course of his career, he wrote 17 books and more than 200 articles.

Laffont made pioneering contributions in microeconomics, in particular, public economics, development economics, and the theory of imperfect information, incentives, and regulation. His 1993 book, *A Theory of Incentives in Procurement and Regulation*, written with Jean Tirole, is a fundamental reference in the economics of the public sector and the theory of regulation. In 2002, he published (with David Martimort). *The Theory of Incentives: The Principal-Agent Model*, a treatise on the economics of information and incentives. His last book, *Regulation and Development*, discussed policies for improving the economies of less developed countries.

Speech

Good afternoon, ladies and gentlemen. I am honored to give this lecture.

For those who have this little book on telecommunication, they must have noticed on page 256, we mentioned a problem of internet. The research I would like to report today has been done in last year on the question of pricing intercommunication in internet. It contains some new results that show you how fast the topic is changing.

In the internet, most of the communication is made for backbones, b-pipe that connects cities. Currently, pricing of the communication to these backbones is done according to so-called Pareto, which means simply that it is internal transmission between backbones in which there is no charge for interconnection. So the situation is very different from telecommunication where the pricing of interconnection is a big issue. But things are changing. Some backbones are beginning to charge some little ones, some little backbones and also when they wonder if the need for better quality for internet, videoconferencing or other services will not require better interconnection. So it is very important to question if pricing in internet should be different. But when we start this research, there was absolutely nothing written on this topic. The purpose of this paper is to start thinking about this question. And advantage of this talk is to open a new field and probably a lot of opportunities for research for college students.

The major difference between telecommunication and internet is that in internet, you have two types of users: you have consumers who call and websites which provide contact. And backbones or networks compete over the two types of costumers: laptop consumers, websites and tie to connect them. So we want to analyze the pricing strategies of backbones as well as the impact of the access charge eventually different from zero, and welfare and profits.

To think about this problem, I am going to take a very simple example. Here you have LA and here you have NY. So you have two backbones, one here connecting LA and NY. This backbone has 2 kinds of consumers: laptop consumers like you and me as well as websites. You have websites in LA and NY and consumers in both cities. And you have another backbone here with the same characteristics, two points of interconnection, one in NY and one in LA. So we are going to simplify also the so-called balance-calling pattern, which means that our consumers are equally interested in both websites. They are not particularly interested in either of the websites or backbones. They are interested in all of them. So we are going to assume, since the problem is comparatively simple, that the charge is the same in each direction, which calls reciprocal access charge. Let's look a little bit at the cost structure, where a consumer in LA, want to call a website in NY. There is a characteristic of internet, the hot-potato behavior. In the interconnection between the two backbones, the assumption is that if a backbone receives a topic from backbone2, which is supposed to reach consumers of backbone1, backbone1 carries all the topics as soon as he gets the topic. So you are in backbone1 and you want to call websites in backbone2, the backbone1 carries the topic to the closed interconnection with backbone2. For example, if you are in LA, backbone1 simply has a local cost C'. Backbone2 carries across the US and also down to the website in NY So that the consumer is downloading the pages. Backbone2 has the same characteristic, which means in NY, it will simply bear the local cost to give it to backbone1 and backbone1 carries back the topic down to the consumer.

To simply letters, neglect the call, because the call is very short. What is really taking a lot of time and resources is downloading, so let's forget about the call. If a consumer call a website and download some pages, what is the cost incurred? The backbone which owns the website that you call will only bear this cost, which we call the origination cost Co. The topic originates from the website and these backbones pay $C' = Co$. The backbone to which the consumer belongs will have to pay $C'' + C'$, that we call the intermediation cost. And the intermediation cost a total cost C. So the key point here is when the consumer of backbone1 calls the website of backbone2 imposes a cost, a negative externality on backbone2. Let's now look at demand side of the problem. And to start, let's assume that two networks, the two backbones are perfectly substituent for the consumers of the website. They do not care about which one they are subscribed to. It is the first assumption. The second assumption is that there is an inelastic demand. That is for each website the consumer reaches, he gets some utility, some value V from each unit of topics he gets. The website gets some utility Vt for each visit he gets from consumers. For example, for the moment, let's think about advertising utility. So assume that each time there is a match between a consumer and a website. The total value which generates V for the consumer and Vt for the website is larger than the cost of transmission C. To study the pricing strategies of the backbones, let's call Pi the price charge by backbonei to consumers, Ps the price charged by backbonei to the website, αi the share owned by backbonei of the consumer markets, as the share of website markets owned by backbonei, and finally we will introduce reciprocal access charge that backbone has to pay the other backbone when demand meets supply.

Let's do a little bit of accounting to see what the proper function of the backbone is. This is a profit of backbonei. Backbonei has a share of consumers and a share of websites. With the assumption balance-calling pattern, the topic between these backbones is proportional to the market share. For this proportion, what is the profit of the backbone? This is internal profit. It is from consumer of the backbone to website of the backbone. It consists of payment from consumers, payment from websites and the cost C. Then you have topics between backbonei of which the consumer of website on backbonej is proportional to the number of consumer on backbonei and the number of websites on backbonej. For this topic, backbonei receives a payment from the website but because of the hot-potato behavior, it gets a Pi cost from consumer when a consumer calls the website. Backbones have to pay intermediation cost Ct. But it is partially compensated by the access charge. And then we have final set. The topic from consumers of backbonej to websites of backbonei, for which backbonei get to price charge to the website minus the origination cost C_o, because the backbone has to send back the topic which come to its own website. In addition, it has to pay the access charge to get the topic to the consumer websites. All this simplifies when you have full access to the website. You can decompose the profit in two parts, which we can call the consumer business and website business. It is exactly as if when you have a consumer, you receive the price P_i and you cost intermediation charge of C_t minus access charge. For website business, you cost origination cost plus access charge.

Now we are going to study competition with the following time. First the access charge is determined, then the backbone set price in a competitive way and end users, websites and consumers, select the backbones. Now when we study competition, we get a result that is quite striking and we have called the off-netting cost pricing principle. In fact, it is logic of adding on competition which works here. Despite the fact that these two markets are interconnected, what we obtain is that there is a unique similarity in which two backbones charge for consumers $C_t - \alpha$, for websites $C_t + \alpha$. Of course, with competition we add on, you have zero profit. And the intuition that we will explain in a minute is simply that competition leads to pricing which are such that price equals to opportunity cost of serving a consumer. But usually in economies of a firm, the opportunity cost is simply production cost. But here, because of externality I mentioned, the opportunity is more complex. Let me know explain the intuition. Suppose backbone1 steals a consumer, not a website, on backbone2, this consumer on backbone2has two kinds of topics: topic inside backbone2 and topic toward backbone2. Topic is inside backbone2. Backbone1 does not have any cost or gain. But now when the consumer is in backbone1, it has to bear the cost. Each time the consumer visits the website of backbone2, it has to pay for the internal topic, the intermediation cost C_t. On the other hand it receives the access charge. So the opportunity cost for stealing a consumer is $C_t - \alpha$. When there was other type of topic, remember he consumer was in the other backbone, so it was topic to backbone1. Now that the consumer is in backbone1, the cost in backbone1 is the total cost because the consumer is calling a website of the same backbone. So it is $C + Ct$. Now if you compute opportunity cost, you find again $Ct - \alpha$, just like here. So the key is to compute opportunity cost. Once you compute the opportunity cost, it is simply the logic of adding on competition, which leads to price equaling opportunity cost. The price for consumers will be $Ct - \alpha$, the price for the website will $Ct + \alpha$, and you see some of the prices equals to the cost. So the result is that we add on competition and no elasticity. The only thing that access charge does is to share the cost between the consumer and the website. The high access charge is good for the consumer $(Ct - \alpha)$ but it is bad for the website $(Ct + \alpha)$. For this framework, it has no effect on the welfare.

This principle, the off-netting cost pricing principle, is found to be robust to manage generalization of this model. You can have any number of backbones. That does not change anything. You can have mixed topic but remember we neglect the outgoing topic which you call. We just look at internal topics. You can have a value of demand as the function of the price. You can have multi-homing, which means website can locate itself on different backbones with a price which will be a combination of individual prices. You can have quality of services if you can differentiate quality. You can also deal with intermediation cost if the cost to which is price discrimination. I will say a few more word about price discrimination.

A very natural idea is to price discriminate. You do not price a consumer the same price if he calls a website that is inside or outside the network. Then you have two prices. But we find in this case the same result the off-netting cost pricing as long as you impose stability of. You get to gain the off-netting cost pricing principle. If in the asymmetry world, the access charge are different, then there is no, which we have not really thought very much about if you do not use reciprocal access charge. So one may wonder why the results look so different from telecommunications. In 1996, we worked on the problem of reciprocal access pricing for competing networks into a theory of access pricing for competitive networks, which is basically Chapter 5 of this book. And in this lecture, we assume that the receiver of cost do not pay anything so you have a price which is equal to perceived marginal cost, because when you have a consumer which calls another consumer, you have to pay a cost and for the share of the market you do not have for the consumer of the other network that you call. You pay the eventual price if the access charge exceeds intermediation charge. So in this work, the perceived marginal cost, which is going to be equal to the price, is different from the cost, which is always C. And this difference creates a lot of problems, in particular, instability of competition. The result we obtained is that if the access charge is too high, the final price is too high and it opens a room for price discrimination.

So in fact, it is as if three was a missing price, the price of receiver and the theory for internet turns out similar, though not the same, to what we obtained for telecommunication if you start pricing receivers for telecommunication of calls. And as you know, the receiver calling principle is something much more debatable in HK, US, and in China mobile tele-company. And we have written a paper very recently on extending this work to where the receiver of calls get utility and also pay the theory obtains also something similar to what I explain today.

So far, we have simplified this analysis by looking at the situation where there is no price stability. Now we are going to look at the place where there is price stability. Now let's first consider a simple case where consumer demand elasticity depends on price but as before website demand is not elastic. I do not have to do the Ramsey analysis. In this case, you will want to tax the inelastic segment because each time you increase the price, you do not decrease the demand for this segment. You decrease the price for the inelastic segment, so you increase demand and then you increase welfare. So in this case, the access charge equals the valuation of the website minus the origination cost. This looks very traditional. You tax the inelastic side, like any principle but in fact, there is something much more interesting and quite different behind it. Now, we double the elasticity, elasticity on both sides. We consider the case where each consumer wants to consumer one unit of each website which is available and it has a valuation V for each of the consumption. And similarly, each of the website has a valuation V'. But the difference now is that there is a distribution of valuation: not every consumer has the same valuation. So $F(v)$ is a cumulative distribution function describing valuation of different consumers, and $F'(v)$ is the cumulative distribution function describing valuation of different websites.

Now we come to this pricing theory. The target is a net consumer surplus, that is, the consumers' consumer surplus plus the website's consumer surplus, and minus the charging fees. It is also a marginal cost minus a positive externality. Obviously, for the consumers' price, we can not price it according to marginal cost pricing but a little lower than that. For the same reason, the pricing of website is a little lower than marginal cost, as the positive externality should be minus. The price I pay cannot be higher than the price I think I should pay. Now we take the assumption that websites cannot lose money into consideration, using the Lagrange method to calculate. The net marginal cost is the marginal cost minus the positive externality. Assuming that we increase the pricing for customers, then the consumers' needs are damaged. At the same time websites' consumer surplus will decrease. According to the Equimarginal principle, the websites' damage to customers, which is the decrease of need, should be the same as the websites' damage to main operator. We previously talked about the uniqueness of equilibrium price, the pricing for consumers should be the agent price minus switch-in price. But the pricing for websites should be the initial price plus switch-in price. We already relax the previous assumption that the main operator and the consumers have the full elasticity. Under this circumstance, it is ought to charge high prices for those who have high demand elasticity, which is the result of principle of optimality.

Next we talked about the market's monopoly power. Consumers can choose between different websites. The relational between websites is horizontal competition, which is a standard space competition model. Consumers and websites are continuously and uniformly distributed between main operators, as is the basis for our discussion.

Now let's look at websites' utility function, that is, the net utility of the websites' customers minus the transportation cost. We reach at the conclusion that, first, if the choice of outside websites is not bigger than the current two main operators' utilities, then the consumers' price will equal the current price minus switch-in price. Consider the point that competition between websites is incomplete, the result is that the price will deviate from the previous marginal cost. The total profit of main operators on the web has no relationship with switch-in choice. Second, when outside main operators' choice can attack inside main operators, government should control the level of switch-in price. Let's look at a very specific situation first, that is, the websites can provide customers service, but cannot charge directly from customers. This problem is very like the pricing problem of public goods. As the basic facilities the government provided will be consumed by a lot of people, how can the government charge fees from individual customers? Image such a technical, if we can charge fees according to the time the consumers knock keyboard, then the previous problem will be greatly adjusted. If one day it is like to control the traffic: who enjoys the service, who pay for according service, then the websites' pricing problem will be solved, which is the same as the charging side and the paying side are matching. There is another situation, which is when selling goods on the internet, the time on the internet will be associated with the buying quantity. In this way the charging problem will be solved. This is like a micro pay plan.

My conclusion is that if there is no micro paying plan, the called party is not paying. Then switch-in price will influence the distribution of interest. At this time the switch-in price is very important. If only let the main competitor price, it is not possible to reach Pareto Optimality. If there is micro pay plan, the government has no need to interrupt. This is the main contribution of my speech.

Review

Liu Manhong

Liu Manhong, Professor, School of Finance, Renmin University of China, Ph.D. of Consumer Economics, Cornell University, M.A. of OU Business School, University of Oklahoma, M.A. of Finance, Renmin University of China, B.A. Finance of Renmin University of China.

Pricing Theory of Internet Access

On "Huang Da–Mundell" lecture series, held by the fiscal and financial policy research center of Renmin University of China, Professor Laffont introduced his research on pricing theory for internet access. Based on non-technical but in-depth economics theory, Professor Laffont developed a framework for Internet backbone competition. He believes that given the lack of payment mechanism between websites and consumers, access pricing actually helps to allocate communication costs, and that business operators set prices for their customers as if their customers' traffic were entirely off-net. By comparing the socially optimal access charge with the privately desirable one, he found that the operators lack of social incentive to choose the optimal access prices when they are in a monopoly.

Professor Laffont analyzed the off-net-cost pricing principle beginning with a simple model with constraints. Based on certain assumptions on consumer demand and the inelasticity of network supply, Professor Laffont examined the correlation among consumers, backbone operators and the network, he noticed that it's obviously that backbone operators can form "between balance" in this framework. As a result, the change of access price will only affect the benefit distribution between Web site and the consumer, and has nothing to do with the social welfare. Professor Laffont has proved that when access pricing is based on differential pricing, the basic model of equilibrium price is no longer relevant.

Professor Laffont further analyzed the stability of tax structure in conjection with the principles of Ramsey pricing. Ramsey pricing principles are: to price under the social welfare optimization model, we need to consider not only the demand elasticity from both sides of the competition but also externality as well. Laffont's analysis shows that when one side lacks of price flexibility, it should be taxed; but if both sides have price elasticity, the side with higher elasticity should be taxed, according to the principle of Ramsey pricing.

The book *A Theory of Incentives in Procurement and Regulation* (written by Jean-Jacques Laffont and Jean Tirole) makes the new regulatory economics accessible to average readers, and offers insights into the theoretical idea of regulation economics. The book is the most authoritative reference to regulation economics by far, known as the "the Bible of regulation theory." And the view of "competition in telecommunications" by Laffont and Tirole, has an extensive and far-reaching effect on telecommunication reforms in many countries in the world.

Chapter 10

The Rising of Behavior Finance

Robert J. Shiller

Biography

Robert J. Shiller, receiving his Ph.D. in Economics from the Massachusetts Institute of Technology in 1972, is now the Arthur M. Okun Professor of Economics, Department of Economics and Cowles Foundation for Research of Economics in Yale University, and Professor of Finance and Fellow at the International Center for Finance in Yale's School of Management. He is also a senior member of the Econometric Society. His research works in economics cover a wide range of fields, including financial markets, financial innovation, behavioral economics, macroeconomics, real estate, statistical methods, public attitudes, opinions, and moral judgments regarding markets. In particular, Professor Shiller is one of the founders in the behavioral finance area. Differing from the "rational man" assumption in conventional finance, behavioral finance puts emphasis on psychology and behavior to study and explain phenomena in the real financial market. At present, behavioral finance has become one of the most active areas in modern financial research and its method and some conclusions have already been accepted by more and more experts.

Apart from a large number of papers in various kinds of economic and financial authoritative magazines, Professor Shiller has also written many famous books in related areas. His 1989 book, *Market Volatility* (MIT Press) is a mathematical and behavioral analysis of price fluctuations in speculative markets. Offering detailed analyses of the stock, the bond, and the real estate markets, Shiller discusses the relations of these speculative prices and extends the analysis of speculative markets to macroeconomic activity in this book. His 1993 book, *Macro Markets: Creating Institutions for Managing Society's Largest Economic Risks* (Oxford University Press) proposes a variety of new risk-management contracts, such as futures contracts in national incomes or securities based on real estate that would permit the management of risks to standards of living. This book has acquired Samuelson Prize conferred by TIAA-CREF. Although both the two books contain a large number of financial terms and advanced mathematic tools which are very difficult for the mass population, their academic value has received recognition from academic circles.

The stock market of US has presented an unprecedented prosperity when stimulated by the new economic mythology in the late 1990s. Dow Jones Index, S&P500 Index and NASDAQ index have continually broken the record under the investment enthusiasm of American investors. As a economist, Professor Shiller discovered the crisis under the surface prosperity. His book, *Irrational Exuberance* (2005) is an analysis and explication of speculative bubbles, with special reference to the stock market and real estate. This book was a broad study, drawing on a wide range of published research and historical evidence, of the enormous stock market boom that started around 1982 and picked up incredible speed after 1995. In this book, Professor Shiller compares the P/E ration in the recent 140 years US stock market and indicates that the skyrocket of US stock market index is abnormal. He also analyzes the causes of this abnormal phenomenon in details. US stock market crashed just when the book got published. Dow Jones Index jumped from 11,700 by approximately 20% in a few weeks. And NASDAQ index has also been trapped in a same situation, jumping from 5078 on March 24, 2000 to 3227 on April 17, 2000. The public became very interested in *Irrational Exuberance* at that time and meanwhile, *Business Week, New Yorker, New York Times* and *Financial Times* all made positive comments on the book. This book had also been recognized as a best selling non-fiction book by *New York Times*. And media had paid much attention to

Professor Shiller. He was invited by *CNN*, *ABC* and *PBC* to talk about his views in two weeks. There was a hidden story about the book's name: In December of 1996, Professor Shiller and his colleague expressed their pessimistic expectation on the US stock market to the FED president, Alan Greenspan. Two days later, Greenspan used the phrase "irrational exuberance" to express his worrys about US stock market.

Irrational Exuberance also received a good comment from the economics theoretical circles. The Nobel Laureate of 2001, Joseph Stiglitz confirmed that this book [is] "undoubtedly the most important work in this important field." The famous American columnist, Peter Bernstein also highly praised the delicate economic technique presented in the book.

After the success of *Irrational Exuberance*, Shiller paid attention to another more complicated question — what is the direction of the financial development during the 21st century? In his latest book, *The New Financial Order: Risk in the 21st Century*, he gives his answer. Professor Shiller delivers his warning to the mass population: people harbor overdue faith in stock market; everyone wants to earn a fortune through stock market. However, this overdue faith in stock market will only lead to instability of financial system. The warning contains a point which has been omitted occasionally, stock market is instable, and the ever changing of the share prices results in the instability of people's return. Meanwhile, people pay too much attention to the stock market that they often do not care much about the real economy, the outcome brought by human labor or real estate for instance. These all belong to the area of real economy and have much deeper impact on our life. With the development of globalization, the risks faced by these real economy factors have increased. Robert J Shiller provides us a prescription for these risks.

Professor Shiller indicates in *The New Finacial Order: Risk in the 21st Century* that the insights of finance have been applied in only a limited way. Risk sharing has been used primarily for certain narrow kinds of insurable risks, such as stock market crashes or hurricanes, or for managing the risks of conventional investments, such as diversifying investment portfolios or hedging commodity risks, benefits that often accrue mainly to the already-well-off members of our society. Finance has substantially neglected the protection of our ordinary riches, our careers, our homes, and our very abilities to be creative as professionals. Therefore, he raises six solutions to construct a 21st century financial order through modern information technology and senior financial theories. In the past, complex financial arrangements, such as insurance contracts and corporate structures, have been expensive to devise and have required information that is costly to collect. With rapidly expanding new information technology, these barriers are falling away. Computer programs, using information supplied electronically in database, can make complex financial contracts and instruments. The presentation of these contracts and instruments, and their context and framing, can be fashioned by this technology to be user friendly. Financial creativity can now be supplied cheaply and effectively. The new digital technology has made vast amounts of data about people's homes available electronically. Then the trading of these new financial tools can be used to disperse and solve the real economy risks.

This assumption is just like insurance. Both of them have made more people commonly avoid the risks through financial trading. However, the risks which Professor Shiller wants to disperse are all in the area where insurance dares not to enter. These bold thoughts may look unbelievable, but don't forget that people didn't show much interest in property insurance and life insurance a century ago either.

The most inspiring comment comes from another Nobel Laureate, George Akerlof in *The New Financial Order*, Professor Shiller tells us how new financial order improves everyone's condition through decreasing the economy indefinites. No matter the upper class, the middle class or the lower class, they can all share the benefits from new financial order. He indicates the direction of the finance's development in 21st century.

Besides writing books, Professor Shiller is glad to apply his theory to practice. He is co-creater of the Standard & Poor's Case-Shiller Home Price Indices, widel quoted as measures of the US housing market. He is also one of the founders of MacroMarkets LLC. This company, situated in New Jersey, US helped launch the futures market for single family homes at the Chicago Mercantile Exchange, and the MacroShares for oil and for home prices traded on stock exchanges.

In 2008 Professor Shiller published an analysis of the current US and world economic crisis, *Subprime Solution: How the Global Financial Crisis Happened and What to Do About It.* In 2009, with co-author George Akerlof, he published *Animal Spirits: How Human Psychology Drives the Economy and Why It Matters for Global Capitalism.*

His current research interests include: devising new forms markets to conduct large scale risk management and decrease income inequality; price index adjustment approach to protecting from inflation; social safety net; assets assessment (including financial assets assessment and real estate assessment); time-series analysis of asset prices and market psychology. We are all looking forward to the publication of Professor Shiller's next masterpiece.

Speech

I am very honored to be here as a part of the "Huang Da–Mundell" lecture series. And what I want to be talking about is something which is very dear to my heart, and that's this expanding field of behavioral finance. So I guess in your introduction you've heard something about this, but what I want to talk about is a new trend that's developed since around 1990s in academic finance.

I think behavioral finance is about the most exiting thing that's going on in finance these days, a really new perspective. It involves the introduction of a message from other social sciences, outside economics, into finance, notably psychology and sociology. And this is a reaction against trends that had developed in the finance profession. Over preceding decades, trends that had particularly been epitomized by the efficient market theory and finance.

The central construct of traditional finance is the efficient market hypothesis. I've looked for some time to find the earliest statement of the efficient market hypothesis. And I think the earliest I have been able to find is in 1889, when Mr. Gibson in the book about the stock markets of London, Paris and New York, said that "when shares become publicly known in an open market, the value which they require may be regarded as the judgment of the best intelligence concerning them."

So what Gibson was saying in 1889 was that the price you see in the stock market is like the combined intelligence of all the people in the world. So you should never try to outguess the market. The market is smarter than any one of us. That was expressed in 1889. I have evidence that by the 30s or 40s it was a popular view in academia. But at that point it was still not widely accepted.

I think the efficient market theory or hypothesis became first dominant in academia or scholar thinking about finance around 1970, when Eugene Fama published his article, "Efficient Capital Markets: A Review of Empirical Work." It was in that decade that Robert Merton published his article, "An Intertemporal Capital Asset Pricing Model." And Robert Lucas published "Asset Prices in an Exchange Economy." These were elegant mathematical models of financial markets that describe every person as very accurate and intelligent. So if you believe these models then market prices themselves would have to be highly intelligent and accurate. And that I think is the attitude prevailed in 1970s.

In order to test the efficient markets model, we have to have a formal representation of what it means. Unfortunately, it is a little difficult to know exactly what this theory means. The basic idea of efficient markets is that forecasting the stock market or any other expected market is a failure. Because the prices are already right. They can never be wrong. And so we have to represent what that means in terms of the model. And I think the various forms of efficient markets can be written as the fact that prices are the optimal forecast of the present value of future dividends (or sometimes earnings). So it is the present value model, and it says that the price is the best possible forecast of the present value. Others are alternative formulations of the efficient markets model that are different in terms of what interest rates are used to discount. One version is a constant discount rate, another one is a discount rate equal to interest rate plus constant risk premium, and a more complicated one relates discount rates to consumption growth rates. These are the main variations on the efficient markets model.

The problem with these efficient markets models is that they do not correspond very well to the data. Well I have a plot here. This is for the US for the years 1871 to 2003. The black line is the stock market that is the Standard and Poor's composite index in the real terms. You can see the stock market go up and down a lot. The blue line is the present value of dividends with constant discount rate. The green line is the present value of the future dividends with the market interest rate plus risk premium. And the red line is the present discounted value using a consumption growth discount model. The thing I want to point out is that none of those colored lines matches the black line. In other words, the market has never made any sense in the movements up and down and the stock market has never corresponded to movements. Generally they do not correspond to movements in the present value or future dividends. So I think we have to learn that the present value model or efficient markets model do not work with these data.

In particular, what I learn from the study of the data is that the stock market appears to be too volatile to accord with the efficient market theory. It moves too much. If people were forecasting one of those present values, they will forecast unsuccessfully. One should not be moving a forecast around if it is not a successful forecasting. But the prominent fact of the stock market is that it has gone up and down repeatedly through history, and it has not been matched by up and down movements in the present value. This means that the stock market is too volatile. There were two important papers in 1981. One was written by Stephen Leroy and Richard Porter, and another one was written by me.

I want to look at the access volatility in the stock market, something very visible and easy to see. I have a plot here now showing the US stock market back to 1871 and the earnings of US companies also back to 1871. The blue line is the stock market, and red line is the earnings. The stock market is supposed to valuing the present value of these earnings. The earnings have grown pretty steadily ever since 1871, but the stock market has done tremendous movements up and down. Notably, look at the1920s' up to 1929 and the crash of 1929. Look at the 1990s peaking in 2000 and then crashing after 2000. I will come back to discuss it in a minute.

Look also at the ratio of the stock price to earnings, with the earnings computed as an average over ten years, from 1881 to 2003. You can see that the ratio has been extremely variable. The ratio gets as low as around 5, and as high as 45. These variations in the ratio are evidence of access of volatility. This ratio predicts the stock in the way that it is inconsistent with efficient market.

I want to look again at the recent episode of the stock markets of many countries around the world. Let us look at the NASDAQ Index which comprises mostly the technology sector in the US. It shown here since 1984 until recently. What you can see that the technology stocks were increasing pretty steadily through the 90s and peaked at a dramatic peak in March of 2000, and since then they have fallen about three quarters that lost about 75% of their value. This is quite an impressive phenomenon which we call a bubble and its burst. This is the most dramatic example of the stock market crash. But I want to point out that the same event was pretty much a worldwide event. Not every country we will see but I want to see some other countries.

This is Germany. Again this is from 1990 to 2003. You know that the German stock market was rising rapidly until right around 2000. And then it broke at the same time that the US stock market broke, and lost most of its value.

This is the UK. Same thing peaked all around 2000 lost a great of its value.

This is the same thing for France. The market was climbing rapidly until around 2000 and it lost more than half of its value.

Japan is a different story because, as you may remember, there was a spectacular bubble that peaked at the end of 1989. And the market dropped more than a half within a couple of years. But that was an isolated event. It was not a worldwide event. Now it is easy to forget, but I want to point out that since 1999 Japan has looked just like all these other countries. Because if you look start in 1999 you can see that Japanese stock market was rising rapidly, peaked around 2000, and lost most of its value.

Brazil was a little different, but it was much the same story. It peaked around 2000 and lost half of its value.

This is Mexico. It only lost something like 15% of its value. It is similar to other countries, but less dramatic in Mexico.

There are exceptions. This is the Shanghai SSE Index in China. It did not move down after 2000. But if we moved to Hong Kong, we would see it again. Asia was disrupted by the Asian financial crisis. If there was not the Asian financial crisis, Hong Kong would perhaps look just like everybody else. The market was going rapidly up, and then this Asian financial crisis interrupted it. It recovered from that and was going up, and peaked again right around 2000, and lost close to half of its value.

So we must to understand why there are so many different countries that have experienced the same bubble, the same rapid increase until the day of 2000 and a sudden change after that. I am not going to present the efficient market model. I think that would be an incredible stretch to say that it reflects information and fundamentalvalue,

that is, information about the present value of future dividends or earnings. Instead I am going to give a story which is behavioral. And the
story is based on, firstly, precipitating factors, those are the things that
really changed to cause this and secondly amplification mechanisms,
things that make the factors have very strong impact on prices.

I gave these ideas in my book *Irrational Exuberance* in 2000
and listed the precipitating factors that I thought were important.
This was for the US, but I think that most of these apply to other
countries around the world. These precipitating factors which I listed
in my book Irrational Exuberance include: the Internet, triumphalism
after the Cold War, exaggeration of individual myth of becoming rich,
Republican Congressional Committee's plan of tax deduction, the
baby boom, optimistic analysts, defined contribution pension plans,
increase in mutual funds, decrease of inflation, decrease of transaction
cists, increase of a gambling culture etc.

Because there are so many precipitating factors, I will only talk
about the first one. The one I think the most important was the
psychological impact of the worldwide web — the Internet. And
what happened was a technological innovation, making it very
strong impression on us, and excessively strong in impression. The
internet was a technology that we all experienced. We got it in our
homes and offices. We were working with it everyday. We were using
it. So the impression that we got was that the importance was highlighted. Most important technological innovations are never seen by
the public. Most things that advance our economy are things that
like new kinds of structure of steel, new boilers, and new transistors.
And most people never find out about these. But the worldwide web
made vivid impression because we were using it ourselves. It gave us
strength to the idea that technology was rapidly changing, a new era
has come.

Now I am going to talk about the amplification mechanisms. The
first one is speculative price to price. In a bubbles the price (say a stock
price) goes rapidly up, it attracts attention, creates excitement and so
more people join into the market, which makes the prices go up further. This is a famous old story which has been noticed for hundreds
of years. It may not be mentioned in many finance text books, but it

is a very simple mechanism. When prices are going up, and when there is a story why they ought to be going up, people get excited. They come in to buy stocks and they make the prices up. So the price interests generate more interest. More people want to come into the market. We have an explosion of prices. It also works in another way, price to GDP to price. When he prices are going up, so people feel everything is successful. So they spend more. And therefore the growth of domestic product increases. The whole economy appears to be successful. Because the use of new technology, the prices go up further. Another is price to earnings to price feedback. It works like this: as prices are going up, people like spending a lot of money. So companies are making a lot of profit. But most people do not understand this feedback, and believe instead that this price increase says something about the fundamental economy or new technology. And so they spend more, and make the prices up.

The amplification mechanism is enhanced by the news media. The news media generate more communication and coherence of different people's reactions to the price increases. One thing that news media like to do during a speculated bubble is to tell a new era story. It is something that the readers are very interested to hear. The stock market is going up, and they love these stories. The news media are competing for readers' attention. So they give readers what they want which are the stories about this. A certain kind of story may be triedby one publication, and then if they get responses from readers, the other publications write the same stories. So the reason why these events covered so many countries of the world is partly that the Internet was everywhere and partly that the news media were writing the same stories. So that's why you can get very consistent response in many different countries. So I have told the story about feedback. I think this kind of story also helps you to understand how it is that the market turned so sharply in 2000 when there was no bad news about the internet at that time. The bad news seems to come from the market itself, and that's what happens when the bubble comes to an end. You have people buying because prices are going up. And then they lose interests when the price stops going up.

Another important aspect of human behavior has been highlighted by behavioral finance. It is the weaknesses of human judgment. It is our inner ability to apply attention. William James, a psychologist wrote in 1890 highlighting the importance of the attention. How the people know what to pay attention to is probably an aspect of our intelligence which is very hard to understand, but there is a social basis for attention. We can pay attention to the same thing that other people pay attention to. That is human nature. So stock markets in the talk that goes around are a little bit like a conversation among people. People in a friendly conversation at dinner tend to move from one topic to another, and after 20 minutes, someone may say how about we get down to this topic. In the unified world with so many news medium, the whole world is in a sense going through a conversation like that. So we start paying attention to one thing, and then later our attention focuses sharply on something else.

So I want to just conclude by mentioning a few new topics that are going on in behavioral finance today that help to understand these financial markets. There have been a number of papers recently about the importance of short sale restrictions, for example Jones and Lamont. The point is that in many countries of the world it is difficult to sell stocks short, which means to sell stocks that you do not have. And the fact is that when you can not sell stocks short, it is impossible for people who think it is overpriced to correct it, so stock markets can get too high. Many people know it is too high, and they can not take advantage of it. I think this must be especially important in China which does not allow short sales at all. There are other limits to arbitrage that prevent markets from being made efficient. Just like Andrei Shleifer and Robert Vishny in a famous paper recently emphasized that people who are aware that markets are mispriced may not have enough money initially to really exploit that. They only acquire a personal reputation over time by winning, by beating the market. By the time that they acquire a reputation the opportunity may be over. There are other papers about feedback trading. We need to work to understand the feedback mechanism. And a lot of other papers that are coming up now look at data of individual traders, and try to see what expand their feedback trading. And they have data that link their behavior in financial markets to other behaviors. And with all this research we eventually get a better picture that goes on in speculative markets.

Over the years I've been watching Behavioral Finance grow. When I started in the field, exactly 20 years ago, it's like that we were pretty hopeless minority that we didn't have much chance of impressing the profession. But it grows a great deal. And now there are many conferences and many papers are written on this field. I think there is a lot of work to be done in research in Behavioral Finance. But I don't think it should be isolated as a separate field. Some people ask if should we start a journal of Behavioral Finance. But I don't think it is a good idea. Behavioral finance needs to be integrated with conventional finance. It's hard to integrate the two, but that's what we have to do.

I think that one of the most important ways that Behavioral Finance can be used is in the design of new financial instruments and institutions. Because there is a lot to be done, this will be my next work. There is another emerging field which is sometime called Financial Engineering and that is really designing major new financial instruments and institutions that take account of financial theory. These people who do financial engineering usually don't pay much attention to Behavioral Finance. I think that is a big mistake. I think the two fields have to be blended together. Another thing is that I think the field of psychology, sociology, political science, and other social sciences really belong to economics. An economics profession has been somehow isolated. It seems up to me that the branch of economics has the most impact recently from psychology; another social science has been in finance. I think that all branches of economics ought to take more account of other social sciences. This has begun to happen, and I am optimistic that through this behavioral finance will grow and provide many tangible benefits.

Review

Chen Yulu

This speech was delivered by Robert Shiller at Mundell–Huang Da Forum on October 23, 2003, at the invitation of Renmin University of China. Our purpose was to invite this authority who specialized in Behavioral Economics to give us a lecture by himself on the subject of the logics of the formation of behavioral finance.

It seemed that there was some innate relationship between economics and rationality or rigidity. For a long time, a series of strong assumptions based on human rationality had been the basis of the mainstream economics. And it worked in any branches in economics. A lot of theoretical framework of finance had been established in light of the assumption that rational people were always seeking for maximized utility, such as capital asset pricing model, (CAPM) arbitrage pricing model, portfolio theory and option pricing model. However, more and more problems were discovered in these models in the process of empirical test. In 1977, Roll found that CAPM Model, which was the foundation of standardized finance, could not be tested as shown by the conflict between statistic data and the model. Later some statistical anomalies were pointed out to the well accepted theory of [EMH] that took considerable position in people's heart in 1980s and 1990s. Meanwhile another key concept in standardized theory of Finance — β coefficient was found that it only had some vague connection with the yield of stock. In 1992, being the father of CAPM, Fama withdrew his supports to CAPM. All of these events put the modern finance into a dilemma. People found that the so called rigid system was not perfect, if not incorrect. Finance was facing an embarrassing situation. Neither were there such models with the support of some rigid statistical data, nor empirical data that could be perfectly explained by existing theory. During the process of examining and reflecting the branches of economics, Behavioral Finance in which people researched financial activities from the perspective of psychology, sociology and behavioristics became the focus of the academic circle.

In fact, behavioral finance does not emerge only recently. In the rise and development of mainstream finance, behavioristics, being an important branch of social science, has already infiltrated finance. But at that time, it just dangled on the edge of financial research. As early as 1951, OK. Burell, Professor of Orlando Business School in the US, published a paper titled "An Experimental Method That Can Be Used for Investment Research," in which he first proposed the necessity of discussing theory by way of experiment. In the following 1967, Bauman from Oregon University published a paper named "Scientific Investment Analysis: A Science or Fantasy?" in which he criticized the one-sided reliance on models in financial research, and pointed out that the integration of financial study and behavioral study should be the future's direction of financial development. Other financial experts following their theory have also released some studies, but they were so scattered that they had not caused enough attention. Behavioral finance did not welcome its real development until the 1980's. As mainstream financial model has continuously deviated from the empirical study, Behavioral Finance accompanied by expectation theory which is created by Dainiel Kahneman from Princeton University and Amos Tversky from Stanford University has eventually became a breakthrough to the development of financial study. Kahneman was honored with the Nobel Economics Prize in 2002, which fully demonstrated the importance of behavioral economics and behavioral finance to the future development of finance.

Robert J. Shiller is a renowned economist in the US, professor of Yale University and one of the leading exponent in behavior finance. Since the early 1980s, he has devoted himself to integrating psychology with economics and finance, with particular emphasis on the influence of psychological factors in financial markets over investment behaviors and financial asset prices, and delivered a large number of influential theses. In 2000, Professor Shiller published his work titled *Irrational Exuberance* which based on behavioral finance theory. In this book, he found the crisis hiding behind the stock market prosperity in the late 90's in the US, and successfully predicted the serious bubble in NASDAQ market, which was highly praised by American economists. Professor Samuelson said that Alan Greenspan has been trying to make stock market functioning according to his wishes. Anyone who thinks it easy should read Shiller's *Irrational Exuberance*. Krugman said that Shiller, with his powerful theoretical analysis and an outstanding insight, has pointed out that the recent soaring of stock market is merely a sporadic Ponzi scheme in process, and it would finally end in tragedy.

In Mr. Shiller's speech, we should pay attention to three points:

(1) the role of the news media. When describing the amplification mechanism formed by asset price bubbles, Shiller repeatedly stressed the role of non-rational behavior, as well as the replication and amplification of news media rather than incomplete information, which inspired us a lot;

(2) short-selling mechanism in financial markets. If this mechanism exists, rational traders can sell short when the bubble increases, so as to curb extortionate prices. As far as our country is concerned, although the necessity of short-selling mechanism has been one of the focuses of debates, it is seldom discussed from the perspective of behavioral finance. It seems that this problem must be solved sooner or later;

(3) The status of behavioral finance. It is interesting that Shiller as a major figure in behavioral finance does not agree to develop

behavioral finance as an independent subject. Instead, he advocates integrating it in the mainstream finance and developing the latter. This is a valuable and scientific attitude, a kind of academic logos and breadth of mind.

Perhaps it is the academic quality that determine Mr. Shiller's broadly academic horizon. American economists are eagerly concerned about his new work, *New Financial Order: Risk in the 21st Century.*

Chapter 11

The Framework of the Retirement Risk Analysis

Zvi Bodie

Biography

Zvi Bodie was born on April 27, 1943. He is now Professor of Management College at Boston University. Professor Bordie is famous for his excellent study on pensions, especially on the finance and investment strategy of private pension, and on policies of public pension, such as how to make regulations of government pension. During 1979–1985, Professor Bodie was the leader of project on the national pension system, sponsored by US National Institute of Economic Research. He has been consultant for a number of institutions, including US Department of Labor, the government of Israel, and the World Bank. Professor Bodie is also an expert on the investment principle, investment strategy during Inflation, and some other areas, and he has published many articles on them. His book, *Investment*, which is co-authored by Bodie, is one of the most popular materials for MBAs, and is favored by white-collars in Wall Street. It has been published to the 4th Edition. Professor Bodie's research area has also extend to the theory and practice of financial accounting, and he is also a member of the US Financial Accounting Standards Board.

Professor Bodie has quite a lot of papers and books published, many of which were cooperated with his thesis mentor, Professor Merton, who was the Nobel Prize Winner in 1997. They proposed the famous functional view of financial system. Recently, they wrote a book for undergraduate students. Their teacher, Samuelson, will preface the book. The book is praised by him for its innovation and difference, and it is also highly recommended by the *Financial Times*.

Speech

This lecture will focus on some new tools and products satisfying people's old-age insurance goal. We analyze retirement planning models first, with the viewpoint that, fundamentally, many important uncertainty models mentioned by economists and financial specialists were not taken into consideration. Also, the most widespread risk management tools — hedging, insuring and diversifying — were seldom used by financial engineers when building up retirement plan. From the perspective of innovation, we examine a few financial products, which appear to offer new approaches against old-age risk, including inflation-linked annuities, survivor bonds, long-term care insurance and reverse annuity mortgages. Some of them come from combination of existing insurance products. We also believe that market could prevent pension fund from low increase due to market failure, institution rigescence and information obstacle, which restrict diversification of international investing. For us who study economics and finance, it has been an issue of great importance to study the costs and benefits of the retirement securing products created by the fund managers.

Advances in medicine and rising living standards promise longer life expectancies nowadays. Some people lead a life much longer than what we think to be "normal." Moreover, perhaps we can look forward to someday celebrating our birthdays when we are 100 years old or more. But a long retirement phase without income has been a big challenge.

Thus, in order to make the retirement period our "golden times," we have to prepare to face and manage the potential risk that may lower our life levels. The risks rise up from various aspects. Most people are aware of risk of low income and poor health. In contrast, however, also exist are the possibilities of increasing life expense and rising price and potentiality of unanticipated changes in old-age benefits promised by government, employer and other institutions. Factors mentioned above brought significant modification to worldwide retirement income plan, deepened the financial institutions' reform and caused the obvious problem of an aging population. These changes force policy makers, employees and retirees to develop new tools to assess retirement risk. Simultaneously, they give birth to new financial instruments, helping people and institutions to manage and avoid old-age economic loss. Some promising financial innovations used to raise the level of risk management will be taken into discussion.

As lifestyle and life level are changing, so too are the varieties of institutions available to provide support to elderly. Today, many diverse retirement income systems coexist around the world, each relying in proportions on one or more of the following institutional forms:

1) Support from family or community
2) Pension plans sponsored by employer and/or labor unions
3) Social insurance programs carried out by governments

Personal savings in the form of real and financial assets — equity in one's home or business saving accounts, insurance contracts, mutual funds, etc.

Many experts agree, however, that the mix of these institutional forms will exchange significantly during the next few years. This is particularly true for industrialized countries, such as those in Western Europe, as well as the US, the UK, Australia and Japan, where people are both living longer and having many fewer children. In these nations, people will find they can rely less on family and government support than in the past, and they instead will return to financial markets and related institutions by saving and investing for their own retirement. Even in emerging markets, new demographic and economic realities have promoted the beginning of widespread retirement system reforms, as seen in pension reform movements of Latin America and Eastern Europe and, more recently, in Asia.

In response to global population aging and financial deregulation trends, governments and financial firms are seeking to create new institutions and services that might afford better protection against the financial consequences of old-age illness, disability and longevity, and to insulate people against both inflation and asset price fluctuations. New opportunities will become available for older persons to continue employment, perhaps on a part-time basis, and to convert their asset, particularly housing wealth, into spendable income. For better or worse, these financial marketplace developments are paired with widespread financial disintermediation, meaning that people are being given more individual choice over their own asset accumulation and decumulation processes. For instance, participating directly in the pension funding plan offer employer the right to determine how much (if there is) to save for retirement, how much fraction of their assets going to stocks (if there are), when (or never) to change their assets allocation, and how much money (if there is) to be paid as annuities during the retirement period.

One strength of this type of retirement plan is that it make pension saving more widespread, but supporting financial policies should be improved. As these new financial instruments transfer more responsibility and choice to workers and retirees, it will be a challenge to frame risk-reward trade-off and cast financial decision making in a format that ordinary people can understand an implement.

Old-Age Risk Management

Some of the personal finance literature has cast the risks and rewards of retirement financial decision making in a risk management context. Traditionally, this term has referred mainly to the purchase of insurance and is distinguished from investment management.

However, from the analytical viewpoint, risk and investment management should be thought of in a more integrated manner, because the purchase of insurance is an integral part of the decision-making process in which risk and reward are trade-off if we analyze individual or family integrally. For example, one could decrease one's exposure to the risk of income loss by buying disability insurance; alternatively, one could insure against a decline in stock prices by buying put options.

In taking this broader perspective on risk management in the retirement context, it is useful to distinguish three methods of management risk: hedging, insuring and diversifying. Hedging against risk means eliminating the risk of a loss by sacrificing the potential for gain. For example, as a worker grows older, it is often argued that he should reduce the faction of his wealth held in stocks by boosting the fraction in risk-free bonds or annuities. In doing so, he is perceived to hedge against stock market risk. Hedging can take other forms, of course, including the use of derivatives such as futures and swap contracts. Thus, if someone held a portfolio of stocks and sought to hedge it without selling the stocks, he could do so by selling short a futures contract on stock index.

Insuring against risk means paying a known sum of money (the insurance premium) to eliminate the risk of losing a much larger sum. In this case the insured party protects against loss but remains potential for gain. To continue our example, if the investor bought put options on stocks instead of selling them, he would be insuring against stock market risk. If stock price went up by more than enough to offset the cost of the puts, he would come out ahead.

Diversifying, the third risk management tool, means investing in many different risky assets instead of putting all of one's money into a single asset. Diversification is useful when it reduce one's total exposure to risk without lowering one's expected rate of return. In practice, however, the power of diversification to reduce risk is limited by positive correlations across one's portfolio of risky assets. Thus, a stockbroker whose human capital returns depend solely on equity markets will be undiversified if his financial assets consist only of stocks.

In contrast to the integrated view of retirement risk management, some in the investment industry take a narrow view of retirement preparedness; the strategy instead has been to advocate diversification in the financial personal portfolio, to the virtual exclusion of hedging and insuring. To some extent, this attitude motivated by the relatively strong average performance of publicly traded US equities over the 1980s and 1990s. Nevertheless, there appears to be little public awareness of how risky stocks are, even in the long run. This leads to the observation that, in some cases, hedging and insuring may be at least as effective as diversification. This could be true in the case of longevity risk, the risk of wage and real interest rate shocks, inflation, and the shocks to the stock market as a whole. To illustrate this view furthermore, we turn next to a discussion of recent developments in risks faced by retirees.

Sources of Old-Age Economic Insecurity

People confront diverse risks as they seek to save for retirement when they are young, and also when old, when they seek to draw down their assets during the retirement period. It is well known that the life-cycle economic model suggests that workers build up assets during their work lives and gradually draw them down during the retirement period. In practice, however, this pattern is often difficult to implement. Some people find it unpleasant, if not impossible, to defer consumption, perhaps because they implicitly must face the fact of their aging when doing so. Only half of all working Americans say they have thought about saving for retirement, with the avoiders motivated by the fear of finding out how insecure they might be and by concern that they might have to make sacrifices (according to *Confidence on Life After Retirement*, 1999). Another explanation for undersaving when young and overconsuming when old is that people may expect that, in the future, the government will do what is necessary to cover old-age income and medical care needs. Unfortunately, social security system in many nations face insolvency and will not easily be able to pay tomorrow's elderly benefits equal to those paid to today's retirements. Furthermore, private undersaving is a major problem: US data indicate that older workers' wealth accumulations are substantially below retirement saving targets, and many retirees will be unable to maintain consumption levels in old age (Moore and Mitchell, 2000). These problems are global, with baby boomers in Europe and increasingly in Asia reporting that they have serious concerns about a comfortable retirement.

Another reason that people are sometimes poorly prepared for retirement has to do with the sheer difficulty of obtaining and processing information about the underlying risks that they face. Thus, human life expectancy has increased well above projections just a hundred years ago, and dramatic improvements are potentially plausible in the developed world in the future. Nevertheless, reasonable people have erred regarding mortality improvements in the past, and there remains much uncertainty regarding what to assume about future life expectance trends. To take another example, many workers and retirees are unaware of their likely future need for long-term care (e.g., nursing home), so they fail to make adequate provision for their own coverage. In the US, for instance, one-quarter of the elderly eventually require long-term care, yet many believe (wrongly) that nursing home coverage is provided by the government free of charge. In fact, in the US, only the indigent can rely on long-term nursing home coverage, requiring the elderly to exhaust most of their own assets before becoming eligible. Lacking correct information on such provisions, people may make serious mistakes by not saving for their own needs and not making provision for long-term care coverage.

One important risks facing workers and retirees — about which little is known — include the variability of, and correlations in returns to, human capital, financial capital, annuities, and benefits promised by other old-age programs. Of course, in practice, close linkages exist between worker's income, government taxation and benefits offered by public or private pension institution. These linkages merit much more exploration to determine their potential impacts on future old-age economic security. Study on correlation between human capital and old-age income shows that retirement incomes are directly tied to variations in lifetime pay levels, more strongly than differences in the length of lifetime employed (Levine *et al.*, 2000). In addition, recent research done by Davis and Willen highlights correlations between earnings and assets returns and also evaluates how aging changes how these correlations should influence investors' portfolio mixes. Relatively, ordinary people and their advisors are poorly informed regarding volatility in asset returns and inflation rates. For example, the US has experienced for some time a relatively low rate of inflation and rising stock prices, both of which have contributed to a widespread belief that equities sever as a good hedge for inflation. But during the 1970s, inflation rates reached double digits but stock prices fell by more than half in just two years (1974–1975). This is shown in Figure 1, illustrating that the inflation-adjusted NYSE stock index fluctuated substantially over the period from 1972 to 1984, and this may appear again. Similarly, Brown *et al.* (2000) reported that stock is not a good inflation hedge, at least in the short to medium term. As a result, retirees seeking to protect against the corrosive effect of inflation over a 25-year retirement period would likely benefit from investing a portion of their finance assets in inflation-protected bonds. We will talk about it later.

Developments in Retirement Planning Models

Institutional change and the process of financial disintermediation may herald a new era of "individual responsibility for retirement security" (Leibowitz *et al.*, 2001). In this environment, it appears to many that workers and retirees will require additional help confronting retirement risks and managing them effectively. Good retirement planning models can be useful in this regard, although designing them to make sense to average people is a challenge. It is worth planning models differ from behavioral economic models in that the former are prescriptive, while the latter are descriptive. That is, planning models embed objectives that the planner then tries to attain. For instance, one might want to smooth consumption before and after retirement, protect a widow's consumption after the death of a spouse, avoid running out of money in old age, and have a fund to bequeath to one's children (among other possible targets). By contrast, an economic model of behavior tries to explain observed behavior and predict how outcomes might change if initial conditions were changed. In the prescriptive context, a retirement planning model will typically offer the worker or retiree advice on how much to save, where to place one's investments and how much to consume, depending on the targets specified and the instruments available. Of course, such models can yield very different prescriptions about saving and investment, depending on how they are structured and the assumptions they use as inputs. The approach newly proposed by Leibowitz *et al.* (2000) formulates a user-friendly tool called the personal financing ratio (PFR). In this framework, a model user first specifies his target replacement ratio, or the ratio of postretirement to preretirement income. Such an income flow target can then be converted to a present discounted value and compared to actual assets in hand. From this calculation, asset shortfalls can be converted into increased saving objectives. This approach serves as a useful check on one's overall position, and it can offer the opportunity for sensitivity analysis as investment portfolios are changed.

Many other approaches also exist. An alternative one by Leibowitz *et al.* (2001) builds in a great deal of detail about the state and federal tax rules crucial for determining net-of-tax income streams. Although that model is very complete in important ways, it does not yet incorporate uncertainty regarding asset portfolio returns. By contrast, the financial engines model describe in Scott (2001) has as its primary goal the modeling of investment uncertainty. By selecting any one model, the worker risks concluding that he is "well protected" by following a particular saving and investment path, while that same retirement plan might be judged a failure by a different model (Bernheim *et al.*, 2001; Warshawsky and Ameriks, 2000; Moore and Mitchell, 2000). It is no wonder that many workers face retirement planning with trepidation.

Looking ahead, several key challenges remain in the retirement planning field. One is that it is essential to help workers and retires understand how to incorporate uncertainty into thinking about retirement needs and retirement assets. Another is that modelers need to better understand users' risk tolerance toward uncertainty and their willingness to change behaviors, given model prescriptions. But doing a better job in this arena will require new research to ascertain correlations across risky assets including human wealth, housing equity, and pension wealth from both public and private sources and measuring risk tolerances. Other research is also needed on how people process information and how they act on it. A confounding influence is that, as retirement planning models grow more elaborate, they also tend to become far too complex for ordinary people to use, particularly if they are not financially sophisticated.

Developments in Products to Increase Retirement Well-Being

Several financial products have recently been designed to provide innovative opportunities for people to diversify, hedge and ensure old-age economic risks. To illustrate these, we review key attributes of such products, including a form of hybrid pension plan as a means to structure pension wealth; the reverse annuity mortgage as a means to access illiquid housing wealth; and the role of international asset diversification as a means to protect investors against certain kinds of risk in old-age income streams.

Turning first to the pension case, pundits and policy makers have both praised and excoriated the variety of employer-provided pension known as the "cash balance" plan. The cash balance plan is sometimes called a hybrid pension, because it has elements of both a defined benefit and a defined contribution plan. It is not a particularly novel approach. In fact, it was first developed in 1985 for employers seeking to move away from conventional defined benefit pensions. More recently, the cash balance model has attracted public scrutiny when the IBM Corporation announced it was transitioning away from its traditional defined benefit toward a cash balance format. The old IBM plan rewarded early retirement with a relatively back-loaded benefit formula, whereas the new plan incorporates smoother benefit accruals across years of service with the firm, with no special reward for working up to the age of eligibility for early retirement. The trend toward eliminating early retirement subsidies is found to be widespread in survey results for 77 pension conversions examined by Clark and Schieber (2001). The companies adopting these cash balance plans offered larger and more portable benefits to younger and more mobile employees, and they virtually eliminated the spikes in accruals that had previously been offered to high levels of seniority. In this sense, the new plans are more age-neutral than those they replaced and, as such, they will tend to encourage workers to extend their employment careers. Of course, working longer is one way to help finance a longer anticipated retirement period, so these pensions may well be consistent with greater retirement security.

Moving from pensions to housing, we note that many older Americans have equity in their homes, which, for many, represents the most important source of personal wealth. For instance, Moore and Mitchell (2000) report that housing wealth amounted to about $150,000 for the median US older household is on the verge of retirement, while that population had few financial assets. This result gives rise to two questions: First, can older Americans use their housing wealth to finance retirement consumption? Second, if they cannot, could new financial products facilitate the conversion of this wealth stock into an income flow and, if so, how costly would they be?

The first question is explored by Venti and Wise (2001), who examine how housing wealth changes with age. One way that older persons might draw on their housing wealth to support consumption would be to "trade down" to less expensive dwellings. But there appears to be little support for the conclusion that older Americans who remain homeowners over time draw down their housing wealth smoothly as they age. By contrast there are sharp changes in housing wealth when life changes intervene, such as at the death of a spouse or when entering a nursing home. In other words, housing wealth appears to be used by the elderly as a type of self-insurance rather than as a liquid asset. This wealth discontinuity result may be due to high transaction costs imposed on home sellers and moving costs that may be quite substantial, particularly for the elderly.

In view of the difficulty people seem to have converting their housing wealth to income, economists have suggested the need for a product known as a reverse annuity mortgage (RAM). This instrument permits the homeowner to sell a portion of his net home equity to a financial institution, which in turn pays that individual a fixed monthly income flow in the form of a life annuity. The annuity is supposed to be structured so that the homeowner receives a cash flow equal in present value to the fraction of his equity secured, but he never must sell the house to access the equity value of the asset. At the homeowner's death, the financial institution sells the home and recovers remaining equity. RAMs are currently available in the US market but, as described by Caplin (2001), only some 50,000 of these products have been sold to date. It appears that the product's theoretical appeal is offset in practice by several problems, including limits on the total amount of homeowner equity that is accessible, up-front costs totaling 14% of capital, the risk of foreclosure and continuing uncertainty about the tax status of the product. These realities mean that, if this sort of financial innovation is to meet retirees' needs during the next several decades, it will have to be reconfigured to be simpler and more transparent, less costly and better regulated.

Next, we turn to the role of international diversification in retirement portfolios, a topic of growing interest to investors in Europe, Asia and Latin America. In their analysis, Srinivas and Yermo (2001) show how many countries explicitly limit retirement portfolio investments in nondomestic assets, with the restrictions motivated by diverse policy considerations. What is critical, of course, is that these investment caps and restrictions impose an implicit tax on investors by restricting them to a less favorable risk-return trade-off than they might have had from a globally diversified portfolio. In many cases, whether they might have preferred to invest globally is not observed, because currency controls prohibit this demand from being registered. In the specific cases examined by Srinivas and Yermo (2001), restrictions imposed by government regulatory constraints on key Latin American pension fund portfolios is shown to have exposed plan participants to lower returns with inferior risk exposure, as compared to the next best alternative. Their analysis therefore highlights the fact that political factors often influence retirement well-being by undermining what markets can do to help protect against retirement risk. Once again, institutional rigidities and barriers at times erected by government preclude implementing the most sensible risk management strategies from an economics and finance perspective.

Developments in Annuities and Bundled Insurance Products

A key reason that Americans invest in bonds and fixed annuities is that they seek to transfer resources safely through time. Three features of bonds and annuities are essential in achieving this objective: They must be free of default risk; they must match the spending target's maturity and time pattern; and they must match the spending target's unit of account. Hence, if someone plans an expenditure 20 years from now, the only way to hedge it precisely is with a default-free, 20-year, pure discount bond or its functional equivalent. Investing in a bond of any other maturity would expose the person to interest rate risk. Shorter maturity bonds would expose the investor to "reinvestment" risk when the bonds have to be "rolled over," and longer maturity bonds would expose him to "price" risk, because the bonds would have to be liquidated before maturity.

The reality, of course, is that nominal bonds and annuities have not always carried out their fundamental promise of transferring resources safely over time. Sometimes the issuers have defaulted on their promise to pay, or the payments have been confiscated through taxation. In other cases, bondholders have lost value because the currency used as the unit of account suffers from inflation. The problem of inflation risk may be dealt with by denominating bonds in units of constant purchasing power: that is, by tying payments to an index of the cost of living. Historically in many countries, however, private sector borrowers have been reluctant to issue bonds indexed to the cost of living. In consequence, financial economists have urged governments to issue inflation-indexed bonds to provide households with the much needed long run hedge for retirement saving.

For many years, the governments of no major industrialized countries proved willing to do so, but things began to change during the 1980s. In 1981, the British government began issuing inflation-indexed gilts (i.e., bonds) with the stated goal of providing a means for pension funds to hedge retirement benefits that were indexed to the cost of living. The government of Canada followed the UK's lead in 1994, and the US Treasury followed suit in 1997. Today, US Treasury-issued inflation-indexed bonds can be stripped by qualified financial institutions to provide a complete array of pure discount bonds with maturities of up to 30 years. By using these bonds, it is now possible for investors to completely hedge real spending targets as far as 30 years into the future.

A further development occurred in 1998 when the US Treasury also began issuing inflation-indexed savings bonds, known as Series I (or I-bonds). Although the interest rate on I-bonds is lower than on the Treasury's marketable inflation-protected bonds (known as TIPS). I-bonds have features that make them especially attractive to individual investors. 6 Among these are the fact that I-bonds are accrual-type bonds, so the holder receives all the interest and principal at redemption. Income tax is paid on I-bonds only at redemption; by contrast, on TIPS, income tax must be paid each year, and the tax is levied on both coupons received and the increase in the nominal value of principal due to inflation (both types of bonds are exempt from state and local income tax). Furthermore, the US Treasury guarantees a fixed schedule of inflation-adjusted redemption values on I-bonds, so the holder always receives principal plus accrued interest no matter when they are cashed in. By contrast, the Treasury guarantees the inflation-adjusted value of TIPS only at the maturity date; selling them before maturity requires engaging a broker-dealer in the secondary market. Consequently, if real interest rates have risen since the TIPS were issued, the holder will sell at a loss. Finally, the purchaser pays no fees when buying or redeeming I-bonds at the local bank at any time, whereas if TIPS are purchased after issue (or sold before maturity), the broker-dealer must play a role, and bid-ask spreads can be large.

If these products are as beneficial as they seem to be, one might well ask why the market seems so thin for them. One explanation is that they are not particularly well-known in much of the developed world. In the US, for instance, the Treasury has not marketed I-bonds or TIPS aggressively, and inflation-linked annuities have been slow to get started. By contrast, inflation-linked annuities are better known in the UK, in Israel and in Australia, among other countries. Another explanation may be that financial advisors have yet to recommend them to their clients, probably in large part due to low commissions and some illiquidity (at least for TIPS). A different argument has been that anticipated inflation, as well as inflation rate volatility, has been low for some time, so the real returns on these products seem relatively unattractive (Brown *et al.*, 2001). Also, investors may be attracted by the higher expected returns on stocks, believing that stocks are not risky in the long run; if so, stocks might appear to offer a higher risk-adjusted expected return than do I-bonds.

These questions become of key importance with the rapid growth of individually managed retirement accounts, which have resulted from changes in the corporate pension world and from the growth in individual retirement accounts. Currently, the individual annuity market is small in the US, but as Brown *et al.* (2001) point out, the fraction of the retiree population having self-directed accounts will burgeon during the next two decades. In many analysts' view, this asset growth will spur demand for annuities of many types. Supportive of this conclusion is the finding that administrative expense loadings on life annuities have fallen substantially. For instance, many years ago in both the US and the UK, as much as 25–30% of the asset value was devoted to administrative costs in a single premium immediate nominal annuity, but this figure is down to 5% today. The costs associated with adverse selection also appear to be lower than previously. Finally, the advent of TIPS and I-bonds means that insurers have the potential to now offer inflation-indexed annuities, which would do a great deal to protect old-age retirement consumption. The US market for such products is still nascent, but it is better developed in the UK, Australia and other nations.

A different approach to annuities is taken by Blake *et al.* (2001). Here, the risk of special concern is cross-cohort mortality risk, which differs from the within-cohort mortality risk that is normally the purview of life insurers. However, it is natural to ask if there is any way to protect an entire cohort against sudden mortality changes for the group as a whole and, if so, how this risk might be spread and financed. Private insurers may be able to pool cross-cohort mortality if they can invest in assets that permit hedging, but Blake and his co-authors surmise that enforcing cross-generational contracts of this sort might require government support. Of course, this in turn requires measuring and pricing appropriately for this insurance.

One reason that older people might not annuitize much of their wealth is that they feel they need to hold onto assets in case they have to finance nursing home care. The problem is that annuities, once bought, tend to be illiquid, so buyers cannot readily access the needed cash to pay for nursing home bills. In point of fact, longer life expectancies have coincided with increased health care costs near the end of peoples' lives, and the specter of needing two to three years of long-term care (LTC) figures prominently in many discussions of retirement planning. Warshawsky *et al.* (2001) discuss how an integrated instrument could help resolve this problem by combining a life annuity with long-term care insurance. They argue that combining the coverage mitigates the adverse selection that would occur in the demand for each of the two products on a standalone basis.

Conclusion

Common themes have emerged in our overview of retirement needs and innovative financial products to help people meet their old-age security goals. First, there is a profound need for better data on and understanding of retirement risks. Additional research must explore the entire range of retirement assets, both private and public, and include both financial and human wealth. Second, retirement planning models must devise and use the emerging data regarding retirement risks (including cross-asset correlations). Retirement planning modelers must also develop better tools to help users make more informed retirement planning decisions. Third, retirement planning analysts should use all the tools of risk management — hedging, insurance and diversification — to guide those making retirement plans. Fourth, users, modelers and policy makers all require broader perspectives of the retirement accumulation and decumulation process, and more financial education.

Despite these reasons for caution, several innovative financial products are beginning to offer interesting new opportunities for people to diversify, hedge and ensure their old-age security. Some of these products are currently marketed around the world. Others have yet to be brought to market; they include inflation-linked annuities, survivor bonds and reverse annuity mortgages. Some of the innovations arise from bundling existing insurance products — for example, long-term care insurance with life annuities, or possibly reverse mortgage annuities linked to market risk insurance. New products are also needed to protect retirement income, but sometimes market failures, institutional rigidities and information barriers have slowed their development. There remains a profoundly important role for additional economic and financial research to better inform all stakeholders on the costs and benefits of developing innovative products for retirement security.

Review

Zhu Qing

Zhu Qing, Professor of Finance, School of Renmin University of China, and Dean of the Department of Public Finance. He is also the member of China Social Insurance Association, Beijing Public Finance Association, and Senior visiting scholar at New York University.

Professor Zhu's major research fields include theories of public finance and taxation, social security, international taxation, China tax law and tax planning. His representative works are: *Taxation Economics* (1995); *Euros and European Economic Union* (1999); *Theory and Practice on China's Pension Reform* (2000); *Practical Operation of the Tax Inspector* (2000); *International Taxation* (2001); *Economic and Operational Analysis of Public Pension Fund* (2002). He is also the leading researcher of the following projects: "Study on the Operation of Public Pension: The Combination of Social Coordination and Private Accounting," "Development Strategy of Enterprise Annuity in China," and "Research on the Taxation Policy of Chinese Enterprise Annuity."

The lecture given by Professor Bodie mainly involves in two problems, old-age financial insecurity and investment management of retirement savings.

In economic view, an adult's lifetime includes working period and retirement period. If one has to arrange income and consumption during lifetime all by himself, rational individuals will save some of their earnings in working phase to maintain consumption after retirement. Otherwise, it is inevitable that they will face financial crises when retired. Although compulsory public pension plans have been carried out by governments in modern society, they can only meet the basic living demand after retirement, without considering expenses for nursing care. Therefore, in order to lead a comfortable life, the elderly have to join private pension plans and deposit some of their earnings. However, in fact, not all the people make full preparation for their retirement period. Some of them "enjoy the life today and leave all the worries till tomorrow" and others count on the old-age benefits provided by governments. Even in the US, where the economy and society are highly developed, these kinds of people exist. Just like what have been pointed out by Professor Bodie, "Only half of all working Americans say they have thought about saving for retirement, with the avoiders motivated by the fear of finding out how insecure they might be and by concern that they might have to make sacrifices"; "US data indicate that older workers' wealth accumulations are substantially below retirement saving targets, and many retirees will be unable to maintain consumption levels in old age." Of course, there are some objective reasons why senior citizens do not have enough saving, for example, lack of information on the underlying risks in old age. Professor Bodie gave two examples: the first is, many Americans hold the opinion that the government will provide them with nursing home coverage free of charge, but actually, this long-term nursing coverage is only available to the indigent; the second is, citizens are not aware of the risks in financial market. Some believe that stocks are a good inflation hedge, but what has been proved by American stock market is, "stocks are not a good firewall to keep from inflation."

Even if the elderly have prepared enough savings for their retirement time, they are also exposed to risks in investment management. Through different kinds of investment, retirement savings finally turn into a variety of financial assets, like stocks, bonds, insurance policies (annuities), and certificates of deposit. Safety, profitability, and liquidity brought by the investment are of vital importance to the old age, because once any of the three aspects meet with problems, retirement life of the elderly will encounter financial risks. Therefore, investment management of retirement savings is crucial to retirement risk management. That is why Professor Bodie said: "risk and investment management should be thought of in a more integrated manner." Generally speaking, there are three ways to manage risk: hedging, insuring and diversifying. Hedging means, as for the old age, they had better reduce the faction of their wealth held in stocks by boosting the fraction in risk-free bonds or annuities. In doing so, they are able to hedge against stock market risk. Insuring against risk means we can pay a known sum of money (the insurance premium) to eliminate the risk of losing a much larger sum. Purchasing policies in insurance companies belong to the insuring activity, as well as selling stock options while buying the stock. By doing this, people gain a certain return at the cost of option fees, so that they avoid risk from the stock market. Diversify means, "Do not put all your eggs in one basket," to prevent the loss caused by lack of diversification of asset. However, most of American investment managers take a narrow view of retirement preparedness, that is, they advocate diversification in the financial personal portfolio, with little attention on hedging or insuring.

Professor Bodie attributed this phenomenon to "strong average performance of publicly traded US equities over the 1980s and 1990s." But he criticized it, pointing out that managers fix their eyes on the return of stock without being aware of the risk. According to the data from *Stock, Bonds, Bills and Inflation Yearbook* (1996), during the year 1929–1995, average annual return of large companies' stocks is 12.5%, while the risk ratio is 20.4%; as for the small-sized companies, average annual return for stocks is 17.7%, while the risk ratio is 34.4%. In comparison, average annual return for corporate bonds is 6%, however, the risk ratio is only 8.7%. What the figure above tells us is, both the return and risk of stock market are high. That's why Professor Bodie proposed that we should use hedging and insuring more when managing the retirement asset.

In the developed countries, like the US, retirement savings are accumulated by both corporate pension plan and individual retirement saving plan, and both of them enjoy tax preference authorized by the government. Corporate pension plans can be divided into defined contribution plan and defined benefit plan. Pensions under defined contribution plans mean benefits given to the retirees are determined mutually by the contributions made by employers and employees, and by the investment return of the pension assets. Retirees will get more benefits if investment return is high, and vice versa. Therefore, employees bear all the management risk. When pension is under the defined benefit plan, the level of benefits received by the retirees is set beforehand. As a result, the contributions (a fraction of salary) made by employees should be prearranged by the sponsor of the plan according to the target replacement ratio and other factors. As long as payment rate is determined, benefits should be given to the retirees at the level set beforehand. If investment return is lower than expected, sponsors of the pension plans (employers) should use their own money to guarantee the level of benefits, so in this case employers bear all the risks. Before 1974, defined benefit plans were adopted by most of the sponsors of corporate pension plans. However, Employee Retirement Income Security Act (ERISA), enacted in 1974, required to establish Pension Benefit Guaranty Corporation (PBGC), to which should all the companies with defined benefit plan pay the insurance premium, and PBGC help them out if they can not afford the benefits. Many companies then abandoned defined benefit plans due to the sharp increase of expenses, and turned to defined contribution plans or even gave up their pension plans. In this circumstance, some types of new pension plans began to appear, for example, cash balance pension plan, which is mentioned by Professor Bodie. This plan can be generally categorized into defined benefit plan, while it has some characteristics of defined contribution plan. Part of the pension is paid as annuity, though most of it is lump-sum payment. This lump-sum payment is determined by the amount in the individual retirement account, which is closely related with age or employment record. Individuals who work longer for corporations will receive more benefits. Obviously, this plan creates incentive for employees to work longer, and help to increase economic securities for them after retirement.

Pensions plan contributions in the individual retirement accounts, no matter collected by corporate pension plans or by individual retirement saving plans, are managed by professional institutions (like insurance companies, pension fund associations, or fund management companies) as pension funds. These institutions invest in the capital market and choose investment portfolio that fit for the characteristics of pension funds. According to the investment principle, the strategy of investment should match investors' liability structures, in order that contributions and the return of assets match the benefits. Investors of pension funds have special liability structures. Employees deposit for rather a long period without withdrawing, so investors should find financial instruments that suit for long-term investment purpose. With the expansion of pension funds, more and more financial instruments suitable for pension fund investment appear in capital markets in the developed countries. From this perspective, pension plans play important roles in promoting the innovation of financial instruments. Professor Bodie mentioned this positive effect in this lecture. Take Reverse Annuity Mortgages as an example. This financial instrument allows the old age people to gradually sell out their house property to financial institutions, which pay them back a certain amount of money every month. After they have passed away, the institutions own the whole property and are able to sell the houses.

Indexed bond is anther example. In general, government bonds were not linked with inflation in the past. That's why pension funds are exposed to the risk of depreciation if invested in bond markets. In 1981, however, the government in England began to issue inflation-linked bonds to help avoid the risks for the pension funds. In 1997, American government also issued treasury inflation-protected securities (TIPS). The interest of these securities was paid annually, and interest rate was adjusted according to the inflation rate. In 1998, United States Department of the Treasury issued inflation-indexed savings bonds. Interest of these bonds was not paid every year, but paid altogether with the principal on the date due. These bonds or securities provide pension funds with chances to hedge value. Moreover, financial products in American markets, like zero-coupon bonds and interest rate futures contracts, are all connected with investment demand of pension plans.

Professor Bodie held a negative attitude towards the regulations made by some governments, which restrict investing of pension funds in foreign markets. Nowadays, for the purpose of reducing investment risks, many governments stipulate the ceiling of public funds invested in the non-domestic assets. For example, the ceiling is 4% in Germany, 30% in Japan, and 20% in Denmark and Switch. However, Prof. Bodie held the opinion that this regulation will "restrict them to a less favorable risk-return trade-off than they might have had from a globally diversified portfolio." He thought that "political factors often influence retirement well-being by undermining what markets can do to help protect against retirement risk... "Institutional rigidities and barriers at times erected by government preclude implementing the most sensible risk management strategies from an economics and finance perspective."

We can easily draw the conclusion, through Professor Bodie's lecture, that old-age retirement is not only a social problem but also involves in financial areas. Economic security of old people relies on highly-developed capital markets. Meanwhile, economic security plans play an important part in the innovation of a country's capital markets.

Chapter 12

The Effects of Monetary and Fiscal Policy: The Role of Financial Markets

Benjamin M. Friedman

Biography

Benjamin M. Friedman is the William Joseph Maier Professor of Political Economy, and former Chairman of the Department of Economics, Harvard University. His primary fields of interest are macroeconomics, and monetary and fiscal policy.

Professor Friedman received the A.B., A.M. and Ph.D. degrees in economics from Harvard University. During his graduate study at Harvard he was a Junior Fellow of the Society of Fellows. In addition, he received the M.Sc. degree in economics and politics from King's College, Cambridge, where he studied as a Marshall Scholar.

Professor Friedman has written extensively on economic policy, and in particular on the role of the financial markets in shaping how monetary and fiscal policies affect overall economic activity. Specific subjects of his work include the effects of government deficits and surpluses on interest rates, exchange rates, and business investment; the effects of electronic financial transactions on the Central Bank's ability to implement monetary policy; and appropriate measures to take in the face of banking and financial system crises.

Professor Friedman's most recent book is *The Moral Consequences of Economic Growth*. His best known previous book is *Day of Reckoning: The Consequences of American Economic Policy Under Reagan and After*, which received the George S. Eccles Prize, awarded annually by Columbia University for excellence in writing about economics. Besides, Professor Friedman has written many other books such as *Economic Stabilization Policy: Methods in Optimization, Does Debt Management Matter? New Challenges to the Role of Profit; The Changing Roles of Debt and Equity in Financing US; Capital Formation; Corporate Capital Structures in the United States; Financing Corporate Capital Formation; Handbook of Monetary Economics*. He is also the author/editor of eleven books aimed primarily at economists and economic policymakers, as well as the author of more than one hundred articles on monetary economics, macroeconomics, and monetary and fiscal policy, published in numerous journals.

Professor Friedman's current professional activities include serving as a director and member of the editorial board of the Encyclopaedia Britannica, a director of the Private Export Funding Corporation, a trustee of the Pioneer Funds, a director of the Council on Economic Education, and an adviser to the Federal Reserve Bank of New York. In addition, he has served as director of financial markets and monetary economics research at the National Bureau of Economic Research, as a member of the National Science Foundation Subcommittee on Economics, as an adviser to the Congressional Budget Office, as a trustee of the College Retirement Equities Fund, and as a director of the American Friends of Cambridge University. He is also a member of the American Academy of Arts and Sciences, the Council on Foreign Relations, and the Brookings Institution's Panel on Economic Activity.

Professor Friedman joined the Harvard faculty in 1972. Before then he worked with Morgan Stanley & Co., investment bankers in New York. He had also worked in consulting or other capacities with the Board of Governors of the Federal Reserve System, the Federal Reserve Bank of New York, and the Federal Reserve Bank of Boston.

Speech

Professor Chen, distinguished guests, ladies and gentlemen, fellow students.

It's a great honor and privilege for me to be here at Renmin University of China and to have the opportunity to deliver one of the Mundell–Huangda lectures. This is a distinguished lecture series and many fine economists over the years, I am sure, will be a part of it. I am proud to be on this growing list.

The topic that I want to address with you this afternoon is the way in which monetary and fiscal policies affect the economy, and in particular the way in which the financial asset markets play a role in shaping these effects, and then thirdly what consequences for the design and implementation of policy follow from what we can say about how the financial markets enter this story. Because our time is short, I am going to restrict my remarks primarily to the field of monetary policy, although when we get to questions and discussion I will be very happy to address matters of fiscal policy as well.

I believe everyone here knows that monetary and fiscal policies are intimately intertwined. The two are not the same, yet they are closely enough related that it is impossible to imagine one occurring in the economy without the other. By fiscal policy, I mean the taxation and spending that the government carries out in the context of its ordinary activity. By monetary policy, I mean the activity of the central bank in providing the medium of exchange used in ordinary transactions in the economy. Why are the two linked? Could one not imagine fiscal policy taking place in an economy with no money? Could one not imagine monetary policy taking place in a world in which the government neither conducted any spending nor levied any taxes? In principle, it might be possible to imagine either of those things, but in fact, in all real economies that we know and all that we have known for at least the past 500 years, the two are linked by virtue of the fact that the form in which monetary policy is carried out is intimately linked to the financing of the government's activities through the issuance of securities. For purposes of this discussion, therefore, I am going to assume that we are talking about a market economy in which the financial markets are freely flexible to establish both the quantities and also the prices of financial assets, and moreover that the central bank carries out its activity by the purchase and sale of securities, mostly government securities. The link between monetary policy and fiscal policy that I have in mind is precisely the fact that it is the outstanding government securities that constitute the market in which monetary actions are executed by the central bank.

The first issue that I then want address with you this afternoon is in what way these monetary policy actions taken by the central bank affect the non-financial economy. After all, when we talk about the central bank's buying or selling securities, that is an activity that takes place in the financial markets. Similarly, when we think of the central bank's establishing regulation or other terms affecting how banks can lend or how other actors in the financial markets carry out their business, that is strictly a financial matter. But the reason we care about monetary policy in the first place, the reason monetary policy is such an important part of any economy, is not just the effect of the central bank's actions in the financial markets, but the effect of those actions on the markets for real goods and services, on the markets for factors of production such as labor, capital and other resources, and in turn the effect of what happens in the markets for goods and services on prices and wages and therefore on inflation in the economy, and finally the effect on the economy's international balance. All of these aspects of real non-financial economic activity are, in one way or the other, affected by what the central bank does, even though the central bank's own actions take place exclusively in the financial markets. As a result, understanding the linkages — what is sometimes called the transmission mechanism — by which these actions of the central bank in the financial markets have an effect in the non-financial economy, is a crucial first step of planning and executing a well-informed monetary policy.

I would like to structure this discussion of how monetary policy influences the non-financial economy by posing two separate lines of argument, and then briefly considering one very specific question. The two main sections of the discussion are, first, how monetary policy affects the demand for goods and services, and then second, how monetary policy affects the supply of goods and services. The question that I will then address before moving on to consider a range of specific policy issues is whether monetary policy is, or even in principle could ever be, neutral in the sense that monetary policy would affect inflation and prices but not the quantities of output produced or employment used, or the flows of goods and services.

Let me first turn to effects on aggregate demand. Here I want consider four separate effects that are familiar in the literature and that are the subject of ongoing attention both in the theoretical literature and also in empirical quantitative research. Those are effects that take place via the interest rate, effects that take place via asset prices, effects that take place in an open economy via exchange rates, and effects that take place through quantitative rationing in the credit market. As I discuss these different effects, I will give some references to the principal works in the literature that constitute the origins of these lines of study.

The most straightforward way in which monetary policy affects the aggregate demand for goods and services in an economy is through interest rates. Economists have known at least since the time of Keynes that investment spending is sensitive to interest rates, for the simple reason that an investment is the creation or purchase of a claim which generates a flow of income over time. Because that claim generates an income flow over time, the interest rate at which the flow from it is discounted back to the present is a crucial part of the consideration in the mind of any firm or any household seeking to undertake any investment expenditure. The lower the interest rate, the greater is the present discounted value of the stream that comes from making the investment, and therefore for a given price of an investment, the more attractive the investment is. As a result, the straightforward implication is that lower interest rates make it more attractive for firms and households to invest. Let me be specific that by referring to investment by both firms and households, I am including not only what the national income accounts of most countries call investment — that is, investment in plant, equipment, factories and machinery — but also investment in the kinds of durable goods that many households buy in order to generate a stream of services that they will consume themselves, like television sets, automobiles, and ordinary household appliances. The analytical understanding of why a refrigerator or a car or a washing machine or a television set is a more attractive investment at a low interest rate than at a high interest rate is analytically identical to why a factory or a machine is a more attractive investment for a firm at a lower interest rate. In each case, the main point is that the discount rate's being lower means that the present discounted value of the steam, either a stream of cash income for a firm or a stream of consumer services for a household, is greater, and therefore the investment is more worth undertaking at a given price.

The central question in research on investment effects of monetary policy that take place via interest rates is how the interest rates that are set by the central bank, which are primarily short-term interest rates, translate into effects on the discount rates that matter for discounting these streams that extend into the more distant future. In most countries, the central bank sets an interest rate that is very short. In my country, for example, the central bank operates in a way such as to set the shortest of all possible interest rates, namely the interest rate on overnight (that is, one-day) loans. But the interest rate on one-day loans obviously has nothing whatever to do in a direct way with discounting the stream of profits that will come from a factory that may be in place for 20 years, or stream of services that comes from owning a car that may be driven for 10 years, or even the stream of consumer services that will come from a television set that someone may watch for 2 or 3 years. As a result, the crucial nexus linking the actions of the central bank in the short-term debt market to the interest rates on longer-term assets, which are what matter for discounting the streams at issue in the effect of monetary policy on the demand for goods and services, is a crucial part of the story. Much of the quantitative research that goes into evaluating the effect of monetary policy, in central banks around the world, bears precisely on this matter of judging how the effects of the central bank in the very short-term interest debt market spill over, through arbitrage and other related transactions, into the longer-term interest rates that matter for discounting those return streams.

Let me now turn to the question of monetary policy operating via the asset markets. Here there are a variety of different channels to be considered. In this case, the analytics of the story differ depending upon whether we are talking about firms or households. To begin with the simplest case, a household's purchases of consumer goods depend not just on its current income but also on its wealth. Under any model of dynamic consumer optimization, whether the familiar

Modigliani life cycle model or a more general model, the amount of wealth in the household's possession is an important determinant of the living standard it will seek to maintain. As a result, anything that either increases or reduces the household's wealth position also has an effect on its consumption.

The interesting issues in this line of research are mostly quantitative: how large an effect on consumer spending comes from any given increase or reduction in consumer wealth. In addition, however, an interesting new line of thought that has come primarily out of the experience of the US in the 1990s focuses on the ways in which different classes of assets that households hold have differing implications for how wealth affects consumer spending. In brief, the issue that gave rise to this line of inquiry is that we had in the US in the 1990s an extraordinary increase in the value of stock market assets, and, as a result, a huge increase in the wealth position of households. The increase in consumer spending, however, was relatively modest during the course of the decade, and certainly much more modest than anyone would have expected by simply applying to the events in the stock market what we thought we knew from estimates of, for example, the Modigliani life cycle model. At the same time, there was also an increase in the value of the houses that people own. At an aggregate level, of course, it is impossible to separate out the value of the houses as it impacts consumer spending versus the value of stock market assets affecting consumer spending, except through having a time series of data in which sometimes house prices rise, sometimes stock market prices rise, and sometimes both or sometimes neither. By contrast, by looking at micro data, it is possible to distinguish the effect of rising house prices from the effect of rising stock market prices, because not everyone's asset holdings are identical. Some people's wealth consists heavily of ownership of a house, while some people's wealth consists heavily of stock market securities, and other people are in between.

One of the interesting things we learned during the decade of the 90s, primarily from observing behavior as reported through these surveys, is that the increase in the value of people's houses apparently had a great deal larger effect on spending behavior than did the comparable increase in the value of people's stock market assets. Why would this be the case? It is not something that would have been predicted from the Modigliani life cycle model, nor would it have been predicted from any simple model of dynamic consumer optimization leading to a focus aggregate on wealth.

The answer leads us in a very interesting direction that is, I think, important for understanding the way in which financial markets more generally affect the linkage between monetary policy and the real economy. What is different about stock market assets compared to ownership of houses is that it is much easier for most people in most countries to borrow against the value of their houses than it is to borrow against the value of their stocks, and in fact most people do borrow against their houses whereas very few people borrow against their stocks. In light of the ease of borrowing on houses, and the fact that most people do borrow on their houses, versus the fact that neither of those is true for stocks, we can understand why the effect of rising house prices on consumer spending is so much greater than the corresponding effect of rising stock market assets. In addition to the ordinary wealth effect that we see in simple consumer optimization models, there is an additional effect of the ability of households to borrow: an easing (a shifting outward) of the credit market constraint that limits how much people can borrow. What we think we have learned, therefore, through observation and research within the last decade, is that one very important way in which rising asset prices have an expansionary effect on the demand for goods and services is by increasing the value of the assets that households can post as collateral behind loans, and as a result shifting outward of the credit constraint that most households face. The direction is the same as what one would find in an ordinary life cycle model, but the story is very distinct and quantitatively it makes a great deal of difference.

Asset prices also, of course, affect investment spending by firms. Here again, there is both a traditional story and a newer story that we understand better as a result of the 1990s. What I mean by the traditional story is the effect on the incentive of firms to undertake investments depending on the value of assets in the investment sphere compared to the cost of financing those assets. James Tobin, another one of the distinguished scholars who contributed to the *Handbook of Monetary Economics*, developed a summary statistic for this effect which he wrote in his original paper as q and that has therefore come to be known as "Tobin's q" — namely, the ratio of what it costs to buy an asset in the market, mostly meaning the stock market, versus what it costs to build a new asset. When Tobin's q is high, in other words when asset values are high relative to the cost of reproducing those assets, the Tobin idea is that this situation gives firms an incentive to build new assets rather than buy existing ones in the market. Conversely, when stock market values are low and a firm can buy a factory from another firm more cheaply than it can build one, then of course the firm has an incentive to do its investing not by building a new factory but simply by buying an existing factory from someone else. All this continues to be true, and the 1990s provided an enormous amount of positive evidence not only supporting the existence of incentive effects along the lines of Tobin's q, but also giving us a greater degree of quantitative confidence in the strength of this effect. The US had a sharp run-up in the stock market in the 1990s, and although consumer spending did not rise, investment spending did. Indeed, just as the Tobin theory would have predicted in the context of a strong stock market, the leading element in the growth boom that we had in our country in the 1990s was business investment.

In addition, however, what we also learned was that the same kind of borrowing story that applies to households' borrowing against the value of their houses also applies for firms' borrowing against their factories and machinery. During the 1990s, as the stock market rose, firms' financing constraints also shifted outward. The higher the stock market valuation rose on factories and machinery, the more firms were able to borrow from banks and in the bond market. As a result, the effect of asset prices on the economy via the effect on firms' investment is greater even than what the Tobin's q effect alone might lead us to believe. There is the Tobin's q effect, which is an incentive effect, and then there is also the relaxation of the borrowing constraints.

Finally, let me remark on an implication of this entire line of thought having to do with borrowing constraints and asset values.

There is a sharp asymmetry in the way in which asset values affect the economy, having to do with the role of the banking sector (for this purpose, by "banking sector" I mean also the purchasers of bonds). One of the important things that happen when asset values rise is that the collateral that has already been posted on loans already in existence increases. But here the asymmetry enters. If a loan is already fully collateralized, by which we mean that the value of the loan is already equal to or greater than the value of the collateral, then when the collateral increases in price nothing particular happens. By contrast, if asset values go down, so that the value of the collateral is now less than the value of the loan, then there will be difficulties in the banking sector. At this point borrowers will have an incentive to default on loans in ways that they would not if loans are fully collateralized. But of course the bank cannot default on its own liabilities without failing. Hence, there is an asymmetric effect, in which rising asset values have little effect on the banking system but falling asset values can have a powerful effect via the risk of bank failure.

We now come to exchange rates. Here too I think we learned something very important in the 1990s. The traditional story of monetary policy in an open economy is that if a country tightens its monetary policy, meaning that the central bank raises interest rates, and this tightening is not matched by countries abroad, then the country's exchange rate will appreciate. The country's own assets become more attractive to hold because the interest rate is higher, capital will flow in the direction of the country with the higher interest rates, and therefore the currency will appreciate. In many countries in the 1990s, however, the effect mostly went in the opposite direction. Here again I am referring especially to the American experience in which, as our interest rates rose compared to European interest rates, the dollar went down rather than up. Then, when we went into a period of several years in which we were pursuing an expansionary monetary policy with lower interest rates while the Europeans were pursuing a tighter monetary policy in line with the more inflation-averse mandate of the new European Central Bank, instead of weakening against the euro, the dollar strengthened. This outcome was very interesting, and to a large extent surprising.

I believe that as a result of this experience, we have now learned more not just about the magnitude but the fundamental analytics of how exchange rates and monetary policy work in the open economy. Think back to the standard Mundell–Fleming story, in which tightening of monetary policy causes the currency to appreciate. The story is based on a two asset model, in which the two assets are the currencies in the two countries and bonds issued in the two countries. Now think how things work, instead, if the two assets are currency and stock market shares. Imagine a two-asset model, as before, but the second asset that's traded in international markets is not a fixed-income security but rather an equity. Now what happens when one country eases its monetary policy? Its economy expands more rapidly, and therefore its companies earn more profits, and therefore its stock market assets become more attractive, and therefore capital will flow into that country rather than out of the country.

Hence the key to understanding both the Mundell–Fleming effect and the contradiction of the Mundell–Fleming effect that we have seen during the last 10 years is to remember that the Mundell–Fleming story is based on a two-asset model in which the non-money asset is a debt security, while what now seems to be happening in international capital markets is the flow of cross-border investment is more in equity securities. Stock market asset flows are sufficiently large to dominate the effect from the fixed income flows, but the stock market implication for exchange rates is exactly the opposite as with fixed income securities. The logic is the same, but the implication for exchange rates is in the opposite direction once the non-money asset flow that dominates is an equity flow as opposed to a bond flow.

All this is even more important because the Mundell–Fleming story, whereby a tightening of monetary policy causes the exchange rate to appreciate, makes the effect of monetary policy on the economy stronger. Tightening of monetary policy in a closed economy means higher interest rates, which for all of the reasons that I mentioned earlier cause the economy to slow. In addition, in an open economy the appreciation of the exchange rate makes it harder for the country to sell its exports and more attractive for both firms and households to import goods as a substitute for domestically produced goods, and we therefore get a further contractionary effect from the tight monetary policy that comes via the exchange rate appreciation. What is interesting and to a certain extent troublesome about this equity market effect is that it goes in the opposite direction. If the economy starts to slow as result of the tightening of monetary policy, and if the dominant non-money asset is an equity security, then the exchange rate, instead of appreciating, will depreciate, which makes the country's exports cheaper as seen from abroad and makes import substitution less attractive, and therefore makes monetary policy less powerful rather than more. This effect operating via the stock market is another example of an aspect of how monetary policy affects the real economy in which we have learned something new. The notion that monetary policy in an open economy works partly through exchange rates is not new, but in this case it is not just the magnitude but even the direction of effect that seems, under some circumstances, in doubt.

Let me finally mention credit rationing effects. I have already referred to those along the way, and so here I can be brief. The main point is that as asset values are increased, for example as the central bank reduces interest rates and people bid up the value of stock market assets, houses, and other assets, to the extent that these assets are used as collateral against loan transactions then the higher asset values cause credit market constraints to shift outward, and therefore we have yet another expansionary effect.

I now turn to effects on aggregate supply. Traditional Keynesian analysis of monetary policy focuses only on aggregate demand, but by now I hope everyone understands that aggregate demand effects are not the entire story of how monetary policy works. There are important effects that work though aggregate supply as well. Two different classes of aggregate supply consequences of monetary policy merit attention. One stems from the need of firms to hold working capital. To the extent that firms have to have working capital, by which I mean a financial base in addition to the physical capital base of production, then even though the capital stock in place at any one time remains unchanged, the higher the interest rate in the economy or the greater the financial constraint on firms' borrowing, the harder it is for firms to acquire working capital and therefore the smaller is the amount of physical production that they are able to do. In essence, there is a third factor of production. Production is a function not only of capital and labor, but also of working capital. If a tightening of monetary policy causes a reduction in working capital, then this also reduces the supply of goods that any given firm, or by aggregating, the entire economy, can produce. Moreover, thinking of a three-factor production model leads, to a certain extent, to an understatement of this effect, because it is difficult to imagine firms substituting working capital for either physical capital or labor. To the extent that firms have to cut back on their working capital, therefore, then they simply have to cut back on production.

The evidence we have is that the more sophisticated and more highly developed a country's financial markets, the smaller the working capital effect is. As a result, the literature of economic development, and of the role of financial markets in development, often emphasizes such working capital effects whereas we speak of them relatively little in countries like the US or those in western Europe. Indeed, there is a particular form of working capital effect in the developing world that merits attention because it has to do with the political economy of undertaking stabilization programs in countries like, for example, Argentina. If there were no effect of monetary policy on aggregate supply, but only on aggregate demand, then the straightforward way in which one would pursue a stabilization program in face of hyperinflation would be through tight monetary policy. Tight monetary policy would reduce aggregate demand, while aggregate supply would remain unchanged, and as a result inflation would come down. By contrast, in many developing countries, where there is also this working capital effect, a tightening of monetary policy will cause not only aggregate demand to become smaller but aggregate supply to contract as well. Consequently, whether inflation goes down or up as a result of tightening monetary policy will depend crucially on whether the effect on aggregate demand or the effect on aggregate supply is quantitatively the larger of the two. Some of the evidence that we have from the Latin American countries suggests that there the effect on aggregate supply can be larger in the short run (to recall, this has to do with the underdeveloped nature of the financial systems in these countries). As a result, when the central bank tightens monetary policy in order to resist inflation, there is a period of time in which even though the central bank is tightening monetary policy, and the economy is shrinking, the inflation is becoming worse. The reason is that the shrinkage of the economy from the supply side is greater than the shrinkage of demand. As a result — and here again I have in mind many Latin American countries — there is a political economy problem in that the central bank must be prepared to face a period of time in which the public believes that its policies are not working, and that all it is doing is shrinking the economy with no visible progress being made on inflation. Hence the central bank will be able to execute a stabilization program successfully only if it has the ability to last through this period, until the effect of its tighter policy on aggregate demand catches up to, and then becomes greater than, the effect on aggregate supply.

Finally, I turn to price misperception models. Beginning with the work of Lucas in the 1970s, and then proceeding through a large literature since then, there is a substantial body of work associated with the idea that firms partly base their supply decisions on the extent to which inflation exceeds or falls short of what they had expected inflation to be. Hence part of the effect of a tighter monetary policy on the economy comes from firms' expecting inflation to be at a certain rate while inflation is actually at some higher or lower rate. Through the process that Lucas laid out, in which firms fail to understand the difference between movements in relative prices and in absolute prices, firms therefore mistakenly believe that what is actually a slowing of general inflation is instead a relative price shift either against them or for them, and they produce either less or more as a consequence.

I do not want to emphasize this effect for two reasons. The literature of monetary economics has, by and large, moved beyond price misperception models, and I think rightly so. First, in the modern world, it is not very credible that firms would make this kind of mistake, failing to understand the difference between a move in the general price level and a move in the relative price of their products.

After all, in most economies the general price level is published on a very frequent basis. The Lucas story is often called the Lucas "islands model" precisely because the assumption made is that these producers are living on islands and have no access to general information. But of course in an actual economy most firms do have this information. The second limitation of the price misperception story is that it crucially assumes that the price firms are observing first, in order for this confusion between absolute and relative price movements to lead them to change their supply in the hypothesized direction, is the price of the goods that they sell. To take a simple example of the Lucas price misperception model, the shoemaker only observes the price of shoes. He sees that shoe prices are higher, he thinks this a relative price shift in his favor, and he is therefore led to produce more shoes. But now suppose that instead of first observing the price of shoes, the shoemaker first observes the price of leather. All he knows is that leather prices are higher. In this case, the Lucas story would then work in the opposite direction. A surprise increase in inflation would lead producers to think there had been a relative price shift against them, in which case instead of increasing their production they would reduce it. A further problem with the Lucas model, therefore, is that it must assume that the price producers observe first is the price of the goods they sell, whereas in the real world many producers observe the prices of the goods they buy — their input goods — either simultaneously with or even before the prices of the goods they are selling.

This discussion of the Lucas story is a useful way to lead into a question that I want to dispense with quickly before going on to address policy issues: namely, is monetary policy neutral in the sense that it affects only the prices of goods and services, without affecting the quantity of goods and services produced and sold? The answer is no. Thinking in terms of a price misperception model leads one in the direction of thinking that monetary policy could be neutral, because we talk in the first instance about monetary policy making inflation greater or less than expected, and then only secondly in that model do we think about the implication for firms to produce more or less. But the question really is, why should sellers of goods and services change the price that they are charging in the first place, and why should the buyers of goods and services be willing to pay a higher price? The only way inflation changes in the first place is by changing the balance between aggregate supply and aggregate demand, and this means that there are effects of marketing policy on real markets if there are to be effects on prices. It is possible to imagine a set of circumstances under which policy would be neutral. Beginning with the classical economists of 19th century, people have gone ever deeper into imagining a such world, but none of the effects we have been describing here would exist in that world. The answer to the question "Is monetary policy neutral?" is no.

I want now to shift from this discussion of how monetary policy affects the financial markets, and through the financial markets affects the markets for goods and services, and through the markets for goods and services affects inflation, to ask what we think we know, as of the beginning of the 21st century, about how to conduct monetary policy. Here there are a series of issues that I want to take up, that I think have been the dominant issues in the discussion of monetary policy at one central bank after another around the world for approximately the last 25 years.

I will begin briefly with the monetary policy instrument problem, an issue on which many of us have worked over the years. If we had been having this meeting 20 years ago, or perhaps even as recently as 10 years ago, the question of which policy instrument the central bank should use to execute its monetary policy actions would have been one of the major topics for discussion. As of 2002, however, this issue seems to have been resolved. Today almost all central banks operating in well-developed financial markets use a short-term interest rate as their operating instrument. The alternative would be to use some quantitative measure of bank reserves, most likely the non-borrowed reserves or the total reserves of the banking system. There is a large literature, to which I and many other people have contributed, on the difference between using a price or a quantity instrument of monetary policy. Years ago, this was an active area of discussion. Some central banks pursued quantitative instruments of monetary policy, while others pursued price (by which I mean interest rate) instruments. But today this matter is largely settled. Central banks operating in well-developed financial systems almost all use some short-term interest rate as their operating instrument.

The question that this situation then immediately poses is whether there is some role for an intermediate target as a focus of monetary policy, instead of the central bank's simply trying to focus directly on the relationship between the short-term interest rate on one side and goods and services demand, prices, employment, output and all of the other aspects of economic activity it is interested in having monetary policy effect on the other. There is also a very long tradition of seeking intermediate targets for monetary policy. The most famous, of course, are targets for money growth. Milton Friedman, for example, advocated the use of a monetary target for monetary policy. By having a monetary target as an intermediate target, I mean in particular that the central bank would conduct policy as if what it was seeking to affect was not output, or employment, or inflation, but rather the quantity of money, or the growth in the quantity of money. We call this an intermediate target because nobody believes that the ultimate purpose of monetary policy is to control the growth of money. Nobody cares about the growth of money per se. What people care about is how well the economy is doing, whether people have jobs, whether firms are making profits, whether people's living standard is increasing, whether there is inflation, whether the economy has a healthy international balance, and the like. All of those important issues are the ultimate goals of monetary policy. But, under some circumstances, the central bank could do the best job of governing those ultimate targets of monetary policy by conducting policy as if it were aiming for a target based on monetary growth instead. There was also a fair amount of work, primarily during the 1970s and the 1980s, to which I and others contributed, having to do not with monetary targets but credit targets for monetary policy. Possible credit targets would be the total loans of the banking system or the total outstanding indebtedness of the nonfinancial economy. A number of central banks around the world also experimented with credit targets.

Today, however, very few central banks use intermediate targets. Again and again, the literature of this line of approach led to the conclusion that whether any given candidate for an intermediate target was helpful or harmful as a way to conduct monetary policy is primarily an empirical question. Consider the example of money growth targets. If there were always a close and reliable relationship between money growth and inflation, and if we observe money growth before we observe inflation, then it might make sense for the central bank to carry out monetary policy as if it were targeting money because, under those empirical conditions, achieving the desired rate of money growth would be equivalent to achieving the desired inflation. As an empirical matter, however, what we have learned within the past 25 years is there are very few economies left in which money growth, or for that matter credit growth, bears this kind of relationship to inflation, or to income, or to employment, or to any of the other goals that monetary policy is seeking to achieve. This is not a theoretical matter. There is no way to know a priori that money has no such relationship to inflation, or to income growth. But the fact is that in one country after another, if there ever was such a relationship to inflation, or to income, it has by now largely broken down.

Most economists in developed countries today therefore advocate neither money growth nor credit growth as intermediate targets. What about asset prices? In many countries, an active suggestion today is that the central bank might target the value of some prominent class of assets. This idea has gained particular currency as a result of the Japanese experience of the late 1980s and then the 1990s. The argument is that if the Japanese central bank had paid more attention to the extraordinary rise of not only stock market shares but also real estate in the 1980s, it would have implemented a tighter monetary policy and thereby prevented at least some part of Japan's "bubble" in asset prices, and therefore some of the explosive growth in the country's financial sector. Conversely, in the 1990s, if the Japanese central bank had paid more attention to the decline in both real estate and stock market values, then it would have executed an easier, more expansionary monetary policy, and done so both faster and more energetically. Although some people refer to this idea as targeting asset prices, it fits less well into the theory of intermediate targets than into what

I and a number of other people have called the "information variable" approach to monetary policy. The way in which we have put it, referring now to work of mine and others going back to the 1980s, is that the question to ask of any particular variable, like money growth or credit growth, or stock market prices or real estate prices, is not whether the central bank would do well to conduct policy as if that it were the target of monetary policy, but whether the particular measure in question contains incremental information about the future path of employment, or output, or inflation, or the international balance, to which monetary policy should respond to as a way of steering those ultimate goal variables in the right direction.

It is obvious from the way in which I have stated the proposition that this too is very much an empirical question. The issue is whether asset prices contain incremental information, meaning information that is not already contained in observed movements of the standard macroeconomic variables describing the path of output, or inflation, or employment, or the international balance, and whether that information bears on the future movements of these and other variables of interest for policy purposes. At one level, the answer would seem to be yes. The simple account of the Japanese economy that I just gave is one illustration. In the 1980s the Japanese economy grew very rapidly, with sharp increases in land values and in the prices of commercial and residential real estate as well as in the stock market. In the 1990s, the opposite was the case. More recent studies, however, even for Japan, seem to cast doubt on this proposition. A recent study by Marvin Goodfriend of the Federal Reserve System, for example, shows that stock market values were informationally redundant in both the 1980s and 1990s in Japan, meaning that there was no information contained in Japanese stock prices that was not already contained in the movement of other standard variables that the Bank of Japan regularly monitors. The parallel question for real estate values is especially interesting. The answer there, Goodfriend shows, is that there was incremental information contained in the movement of land values, but not real estate values more generally. This finding highlights what I think is an extremely important issue in the use of any variable as an information variable, be it asset values or something else. The relevant question is not whether some clever econometrician can come along, after the fact, and by identifying exactly the right variable and running exactly the right regression, show that such and such relationship contained incremental information. The question that matters is whether it's possible, in real time, to identify, in advance, the measures that contain such information. The finding that in Japan one would have to have known that it was the real estate market and not the equity market that contained incremental information, and even within the real estate market that it was land prices and not the broader price of the buildings, casts doubt on whether asset values can be used in this way.

The American example from the 1990s is also instructive. Many people who have been critical of our central bank for not tightening monetary policy sooner during the boom years of the late 1990s, and then for not easing monetary policy more rapidly beginning around the middle of the year 2000, point to the extreme movement of the Nasdaq index of stock prices (primarily those of small, high-technology firms). It is true that during the boom years the Nasdaq had an extremely large run-up, and that since then the Nasdaq has sold off by approximately two-thirds of its peak value. The important point, however, is that not only did the Nasdaq move in a way that was different from how other stock indexes behaved, but also the Nasdaq is a very unrepresentative index of the US stock market — much less representative than, for example, the Standard&Poor's 500 or the Russell 2000, or any of the more broadly-based indexes. Here again, in order to make the claim that the central bank should have pursued a tighter monetary policy when stocks were going up, and should have pursued an easier monetary policy when stocks began to fall, one has to assume that the central bank somehow knew that this particular stock price index as opposed to any other, was the one to which to respond. The tentative conclusion that I believe most economists have reached, from looking carefully at both the Japanese experience and the American experience, is that the central bank should not target asset values. The central bank should use asset values to the extent that they contain incrementally useful information, but it is very doubtful that, in real time, in advance, the central bank can identify which asset price series contain that information.

The next issue I want to discuss, a very broad one, is the question of rules versus discretion. Should the central bank operate according to some fixed rule of conduct? Or should it use discretionary monetary policy? This too is an old issue in central banking, going back well into to the 19th century. For the last 20 years or so, the form in which the rules-versus-discretion debate has taken place has primarily been through the lens of the analytical development called time inconsistency. The idea of time inconsistency, which comes out of game-theoretic notions, is that discretionary monetary policy will lead to undesirable outcomes because in a world of discretionary policy the central bank cannot commit itself to a non-inflationary policy. The public, therefore, will expect that monetary policy will be inflationary in the future. The public will then act in the way that is based on its expectations of higher inflation, and therefore when the future arrives, the central bank will have only two choices: either to be inflationary in the way that the public expects, or to disappoint those expectations and thereby create a recession by having a surprisingly low inflation. The time inconsistency literature first emerged in the late 1970s and early 1980s as a way of trying to understand the high and apparently chronic inflation in just about all countries throughout the industrialized world. The notion of the inability of central banks to commit to low inflation, and therefore their being put in the position in which going ahead and creating inflation, as expected, was the lesser of two bad choices, appeared to be a plausible enough explanation. In the most recent 10 years, however, the industrialized world has not had high and chronic inflation. Moreover, in many countries inflation declined without any change in monetary policy procedures, and in many of the countries that have changed their monetary policy procedures, inflation slowed first and then the new procedures were put in place only after inflation was lower.

As a result, as of 2002 the appeal of the time inconsistency story as an explanation for any problem we observe today is much less.

The rationale for why people pursued this line of argument to begin with has largely gone away. In many countries, therefore, including my own for example, the motivation underlying the push for explicit rules under which the central bank would conduct monetary policy has also diminished. Monetary policy remains mostly discretionary. I predict, however, that this dimension of the monetary economics literature will return, within my professional lifetime, not merely within yours. The rules-versus-discretion debate is fundamental to the question of how to conduct monetary policy. Even though the time inconsistency form of this debate has become less relevant, I believe it is only a matter of time before the rules-versus-discretion issue returns in some other form, which we have not yet observed. Maybe some student in this room today will make the key contribution to introduce the new form in which this very old debate will be revived.

If central banks around the world have changed their way of conducting monetary policy, but have not gone to an operating rule, what is it that they have done? The most prevalent single change that many countries have adopted for their monetary policy — in Sweden, the UK, Canada, and many other countries but importantly not the US — is what has come to be called "inflation targeting." What does inflation targeting mean? Does it mean that the central bank cares only about inflation? The answer to that question is no. As work by Lars Svensson among others has demonstrated, having an inflation target is fully compatible with monetary policy goals for both inflation and real outcomes like output and employment. Why, then, express monetary policy in the form of an inflation target? There are two rationales, which are different yet I think compatible. First, as we learned from the very early work on the fundamental theory of economic policy, as articulated by Tinbergen more than a half century ago, if a policymaker has only a finite number of instruments, then no matter how many targets the policy maker would like to affect, it is possible to summarize the intended trajectory for the economy with a number of targets equal only to the number of instruments. Central banks have only one monetary policy instrument variable. As a result, the Tinbergen insight makes clear that it is possible to express the entire trajectory of the economy intended by monetary policy with only one target variable. But even if so, why choose inflation? Why not have the central bank articulate an intended trajectory for output? Or for employment? One reason here is that even though monetary policy is surely not neutral in the short run, or even in the medium run, monetary policy probably comes close to being neutral in the long run. The further out is the horizon over which we are considering the effects of monetary policy, the more those effects bear only on inflation rather than real outcomes. As a result, to the extent that we want to describe monetary policy in a forward-looking way, it makes more sense to describe it in terms of an inflation target than a real economic target. A second reason is that, for reasons that the time inconsistency argument has highlighted, it is useful, even if the central bank cannot commit itself to a low inflation policy, at least to keep reminding the public that low inflation is an important part of the monetary policy agenda.

For both of these reasons, therefore, a number of central banks around the world have now adopted inflation targeting, by which they mean that they conceive of and articulate the strategy of their monetary policy in terms of a trajectory for inflation. This trajectory typically involves a desired rate of inflation, and in some cases an acceptable band for inflation around that desired rate. Following the work of Svensson, it also typically involves a time path for the return of inflation to the desired rate in the case of any departure. What Svensson's work in particular has shown is there is one-to-one correspondence between the speed with which monetary policy will optimally return inflation to the targeted rate, after any such departure, and the extent to which policy emphasizes real outcomes compared to inflation. The more weight there is on real outcomes, the more slowly inflation will optimally converge back to the desired inflation rate after a departure, either above or below. Conversely, the smaller the weight that the central bank attaches to real outcomes, the faster this convergence will be.

The final issue that I want to address is central bank independence. This may seem more a political economy issue than a matter of the central bank's strategy per se. But after all, "policy" and "political" are ultimately the same word, and so it's never useful to have a discussion of policy without realizing that the political context is relevant. As a matter of political economy, does it matter whether the central bank is independent or not? The idea that having a more independent central bank might be an improvement originally grew not only out of the suspicion that central banks were pursuing inflationary monetary policies as a result of pressure from elected government, but also from observing that countries that with more independent central banks tend on average to have lower inflation rates. In many countries with central banks that were directly under the supervision of the government, therefore, the argument was that the central bank should be made more independent as a way of achieving a lower inflation rate.

Neither the experience nor the research of the last 10 years has been favorable to this line of thought. First, the experience that matters most for this purpose, I believe, is Japan's. Japan in recent years has had a change in its banking laws to make the central bank more independent, but I do not think anybody believes the outcome has been a better monetary policy. To the contrary, many people believe that the Bank of Japan's conduct of monetary policy during the last 10 years represents the second-worst set of monetary policy mistakes of last century (the first-worst, of course, being what my country's central bank did during the great depression of the 1930s). The idea that a more independent central bank will lead to more favorable monetary policy outcomes has been badly undercut by what's happened in Japan. At an analytical level, too, there is also a challenge to the idea that more independent central banks produce lower inflation. A secondary prediction of the model that leads to a lower average inflation rate for a more independent central bank is that a country with a more independent central bank should also enjoy a more favorable output-versus-employment trade-off. In other words, its Phillips curve ought to be steeper. Research by numerous economists, however, has shown that this is not true. There is either no relationship at all between the slope of the Phillips curve trade-off that a country faces and the independence of its central bank, or, if a relationship exists, it goes the wrong way.

Countries where the central bank is more independent actually tend to face less favorable Phillips curve trade-offs than countries where the central bank is less independent. As a result, although this line of argument is familiar in the literature, I think the conclusion we would offer as of 2002 is it that really does not make much difference for monetary policy whether a country's central bank is independent or not. What matters is not the politics of monetary policy but rather the economics.

We still do not know everything we would like to know about conducting monetary policy. There is plenty of work yet to be done. I think a fair conclusion is that in recent years we have learned a great deal. Part of what I have tried to convey in this survey, looking backward, is that if we compare what we know and how we conduct policy today to what was known 25 years ago, or in the case of a few of the topics that I have covered, as recently as 10 years ago, monetary economics and the science of monetary policy is very definitely continuing to evolve. We are learning more all the time. We are learning more not merely as a result of ongoing experience but also because of ongoing research and the way it is pushing forward the frontiers of our science. This is a very encouraging thought for those of us engaged in the field of monetary economics and monetary policy. I hope those students here who are yourselves planning to go into this field will do so in exactly that way, with the spirit that the field is not one in which everything that is to be known is already known. What we will be telling our students, and I hope what you will be telling your students, 10 years or 25 years from now, will presumably be different from the survey of the field that I have given you this afternoon. I certainly plan myself to be a part of the process by which what we know then will come to differ from what we know now. For those of you who go into the field, I hope you will do so with exactly that expectation. Be part of the process, do the research, observe what is happening, help move the frontier of the science forward. That's what we are here for.

Thank you very much.

Review

Qu Qiang

Qu Qiang is Professor in School of Finance in Renmin University, Deputy Director of China Financial Policy Research Center of Renmin University. Professor Qu received his Ph.D. in Economics in Renmin University, China (in a joint Ph.D. program between Renmin University, and Hitotsubashi University, Japan) in 1998. Professor Qu has researched in Germany and Japan. His research interest mainly in monetary theory and policy, financial system stability. His publications includes Development finance in developing countries (2001), The effects of asset prices fluctuation on macroeconomy (2005) and other papers.

Monetary policy is the most important macroeconomic policy in the modern market economy, and the content of monetary policy always changes along with the economic environment, especially the development of financial markets. There is still a long way to go to reach consensus on many relevant issues, whether practically or academically. Head of the Department of Economics, Harvard University, Professor Friedman is one of the main players in this area, who has been very fruitful in the field of monetary economics and monetary policy.

The lecture covered a lot of topics including the objectives, policy rules, effects and transmission mechanism of monetary policy, and gave us a profound analysis of the basic framework and the current major cutting-edge topics of monetary policy from a strategically advantageous position perspective, in a way that is meaningful but easy to understand. After listening to this lecture, I have got some ideas with respect to the transmission mechanism of monetary policy which I would like to share with everybody.

No matter whether the ultimate goal of monetary policy is price stability or economic growth, and no matter whether the central bank executes monetary policy according to some fixed rule or discretionally, a key issue is how the central bank's monetary policy would affect the real economy, which is the so-called "monetary transmission mechanism." However, economists so far hold highly divergent opinions on this important issue. Professor Frederic S. Mishkin hosted a symposium on the monetary transmission mechanism [*The Journal of Economic Perspectives*, 9, (4)], and had invited there representative researchers of this field, that is, J. Taylor (Keynesian View), A. Meltzer (Monetarism View) and B. Bernanke (Credit View). Each of them presented a systematic introduction on their theories respectively. These competing views can be briefly summarized as follows:

(1) The traditional Keynesian View: monetary policy → short-term interest rates → long-term interest rates → investment and consumption → real economy

(2) The Monetarism View: monetary policy → short-term interest rates → corresponding changes in interest rates on a variety of assets → "wealth effect," "Tobin q" → real economy

(3) The so-called "Credit View" (emerged since the 80's): monetary policy → changes in asset prices → changes in the balance sheets of corporate and banks → credit level of the whole society → real economy.

A key point of Professor Friedman's lecture is to integrate the above three theories. He has illustrated how monetary policy can affect long-term interest rates, investment and consumption, and credit scale comprehensively, and also included the problems met when each theory is put into practice. However, the differences among the three types of theories have not been involved, neither the applicability of these theories in China, of course.

In case of China, all of the three theories are inadequate. First of all, from the Keynesian perspective, in order to affect the real economy through long-term interest rates, there must be a prerequisite that investment is highly sensitive to interest rates. However, if $2/3$ of the funds flow into the state-owned sector through the state-owned banks, this prerequisite could hardly be satisfied. Secondly, according to the monetarism view, there must be a highly developed capital markets, and the non-monetary financial assets account for a large proportion of household financial wealth. If not, the wealth effect and "Tobin' q" effect that worked through changes in interest rates and the corresponding adjustments of the returns on assets are not sufficient to affect consumption, investment and other key variables. Finally, although the credit view has been developed rapidly since the mid-80's and can explain the experience of Japan and some other countries well, this theory applies to an economy where there is not only a well-developed capital markets, but also a strong correlation between the capital market and the credit market. However, we are still very cautious about the funds flowing into capital markets from banks, and the listed companies that occupy about $1/10$ of the economy aggregate seldom use stocks as collateral to acquire loans.

Therefore, although Professor Friedman has introduced and analyzed the dominant theories on monetary transmission mechanism, these theories can only be used for reference in China. A key issue is that monetary transmission is related to the relationship between the financial system and the real economy, particularly the institutional arrangements between the two. Whether the real sector borrow or not, how they borrower, whether the financial sector lend or not and what criteria are used, are all decided based on the risk-return trade-off, and such decisions must be based on clear property rights. If most of the lenders and borrowers are state-owned in an economy, and both the borrowing and lending decision-makers do not have to bear the ultimate and potential risk of loss, then monetary transmission may be similar to a water pipe, either too much water or clogged. If banks increase money supply without adequate supervision, there must be a large expansion of credit. On the other hand, if the supervision is too strict and related to the political career of the person concerned, then credit crunch would happen, and a lot of money would be deposited in the banking system. Such extreme situations would do harm to the real economy.

Therefore, an effective monetary policy transmission mechanism must result from the fact that the microeconomic entities can balance risk with return based on their own interest. Only in this way, the financial sector could response to the real economy flexibly. This is self-evident for Professor Friedman, but imperative for us.

Chapter 13

Social Security System and Retirement Behavior: New Perspectives and Evidence

Harvey Rosen

Biography

Harvey S. Rosen is the John L. Weinberg Professor of Economics and Business Policy at Princeton University. He was an undergraduate at the University of Michigan, and received his Ph.D. from Harvard University. Rosen has been a member of Princeton's Department of Economics since 1974. He served as Chairman of the Department from 1993 to 1996, and has been co-director of the Center for Economic Policy Studies since 1993. In 1986; he was elected a Fellow of the Econometric Society.

Professor Rosen has been involved in both the graduate and undergraduate teaching programs at Princeton. In recent years, he has taught undergraduate courses in public finance, taxation, and introductory microeconomics, and graduate courses in public finance. From 1989 to 1991 Rosen's audience changed from Princeton students to federal government policy makers, when he served in the US

Treasury as Deputy Assistant Secretary (Tax Analysis). During a second stint in Washington from 2003 to 2005, he served on the President's Council of Economic Advisers, first as a Member and then as Chairman. In this capacity, he provided advice to the White House on a wide variety of policy issues, including tax reform, social security, health care, energy, the federal budget, and financial market regulation.

Professor Rosen's main field of research is public finance. He has published several dozen articles in scholarly journals on this topic, and authored an under-graduate textbook on it as well. He serves on the editorial boards of several journals dealing with public finance and taxation. In 2007, he received from the National Tax Association its most prestigious award, the Daniel M Holland Medal for distinguished lifetime contributions to the study and practice of public finance.

Speech

My speech is divided into two parts. The first part introduces the basics of social insurance in America, and the problems in the system and potential solutions. The second part discusses mainly from academic perspective some topics in social insurance and retirement, which may benefit students and professors who have a strong interest in economics.

To begin, we should have a general idea of how the social insurance in America Functions.

Social Security is the biggest public welfare program in America. Government spending on this is much larger than any other category, such as defense expenditure. Currently, the spending is about 400 billion dollars. This system looks complicated, but the basic structure is fairly simple. It is financed by a tax on payrolls, which is levied on both employers and employees. When you retire, you are eligible for a benefit. This system originated in the 1930s, during the Great Depression. At the outset, the system was "fully funded," which means that it operated kind of like private insurance. Under such a system, If you contribute a sum of money to an insurance fund, it increases by the rate of interest. Importantly, the money is being used to finance investment When you are old, you can withdraw the funds that have accumulated in the fund. However, the fully-funded form of the program lasted for only four years. In the new program, referred to as "pay-as-you-go," the benefits to current retirees are financed by taxes paid by current workers, not by the money in an accumulated fund. At the beginning, this scheme was very advantageous for retirees, because they could enjoy benefits for many years even though they had contributed for only a few years. For example, the Social Security beneficiary, a woman named Ida Fuller, paid only 24.75 dollars into the system, but received more than 20 thousand dollars of benefits!

In the middle of 1980s, the government realized that the baby boom generation was going to be retiring soon, which would lead to the obligation to make payments that would be greater than revenues. The measure the government took was to increase the social insurance tax rate, so current revenue would exceed current expenditure and the net inflow could be accumulated for the future.

Let me now discuss the benefit structure. In general, your benefit depends on the payroll taxes you paid during your working years as well as other variables. An important aspect of the benefit calculation is that as lifetime earnings rise, benefits increase less than proportionately. Thus, there is a redistributive aspect to the program.

One's family structure also has an impact. Consider a family in which the husband is entitled to 1,000 dollars per month, but his wife never worked in the market. How much benefit should this family get? According to the rules, the wife is entitled to 50% of her husband's benefit, so this family could receive 1500 dollars. Now consider another family in which the husband again is receiving 1000 dollars of benefit, but his wife worked and, on her own, would be entitled to 400 dollars of benefit per month. This family would also receive 1500 dollars of benefit. From this viewpoint, the wife working or not has no effect on the family's benefit. In effect, then, the system redistributes income away from two-earner families.

How the social insurance is financed? The system is financed by taxes levied on workers and employers. For all earnings below a ceiling set by law and which changes every year, the tax rate is 6.2% for you and your employer, or 12.4% in total. Why do employers pay some of the tax. This is because policy maker sthought social insurance is a responsibility of society, and the employers should therefore bear part of the burden. But anyone with economics background should know this makes no sense. The effect of the tax depends on the shapes of the supply and demand curves, and is independent of which side of the market the tax is levied. In fact, it is likely that the entire 12.4 % is paid by workers.

Another interesting question is why this tax is based on salary, not all income? The answer is probably political considerations. Payroll taxation creates an apparent link between payments into the system and benefits, so that the system is not viewed as "welfare," and therefore less susceptible to political pressures to cut it.

To get a better sense of the redistributional effects of Social Security, we need to consider lifetime taxes paid into the system and lifetime benefits received. For example, a low income person who retired in 1995 would receive 125,000 dollars more on a lifetime basis than an individual with average income who retired in that year. A high income individual would receive 370,000 dollars less than an individual with average income. Social Security also redistributes income across generations. For example, if you retired in 1980 at 65, your lifetime benefits exceeded your lifetime taxes by 39,200 dollars. On the other hand, people who retired in 2002 will receive is 36,000 dollars less than what they paid as tax. In short, Social Security redistributes income in a variety of ways, both within and across generations. It is not clear that such redistributions would be politically viable if they were done in a transparent fashion, but since Social Security is so complicated, nobody clearly know what is going on, so it is politically safe.

With an understanding of the benefit structure of Social Security, we can talk about how to reform this system. Currently, Social Security revenues exceed expenditures, a condition that will continue for a decade or so. By about 2030, the Social Security trust fund will be exhausted. While the notion of "bankruptcy" does not really apply to a government program, the situation is certainly problematic.

What are the reasons for this situation? Recall that the system is pay-as-you-go, which means that current retirees' benefits are financed by taxes on current workers. Under this system, the smaller the size of is the workforce, the heavier is the burden per worker. At the moment, one retiree is supported by almost 3.4 workers. But when the baby boomers come to the age of retirement, which is about 2030, one retiree will be supported by only 2 workers. To see the implications of this fact, note that if we need a 12% tax rate to support retirees now, to keep the benefit unchanged, the tax rate would have to be increased to 20% in 2030. This situation exists not only in America, but also Australia, some western Europe countries and Japan.

There are two ways to solve this problem. The first one is to make some small amendments to the program. People who take this view argue that the problem is not really serious. If we increase taxes a little and enlarge the social insurance fund, this system still can work for another 75 years. People who take this view like the current system, and in particular, they approve of the redistributive aspects of the system. Others, though, do not like the current system. They would oppose raising the payroll tax rate because of its effect on incentives, and believe that the redistributions implicit in the system reduce social saving. What many of them want is to privatize the system. Under such a system, everyone have his own account funded by his own contributions. When people retire, they draw down the balances in their own account.

Is privatization a good idea? To think about this, we begin by noting that in every year in the future, society's total consumption equals its production. If we want to ease the burden of providing for the future consumption of retirees today, then the only way we can do so is to increase saving, which will lead to a higher capital stock tomorrow. That is why all sophisticated privatization proposals always include a component whose purpose is to increase the national savings rate.

An important issue is whether individuals can deal with the risk associated with investing in financial markets. One possible solution is to follow the policy in Chile, which promises a basic amount of retirement income to individuals, even if their investments fail to perform well. In any case, proponents of privatization remind us that current programs carry political risk. Governments can and do cut benefits, so there is no certainty about the size of one's retirement income.

We can relate the current status of Social Security to the political situation in the US. The candidate of Democratic Party is probably going to be current vice president Al Gore, and George W Bush for the Republicans. How would each deal with the Social Security problem? Gore wants to maintain the current structure, but to do so, he needs to expand financing. Gore has promised that he will not increase taxes, but without tax increase, where will the money come from? The general approach, as I understand it, is to divert money from general funds to pay for Social Security. But this does nothing to increase national saving, and hence does nothing to ease the burden of providing for the retirements of future generations. Bush's solution is different. He suggests every worker is allowed to put a certain percentage of his social insurance tax into his own account, which he can manage himself. By itself, though, this would not increase the amount of saving either. In effect, during the campaign, neither Gore nor Bush are willing to talk about the difficult choices needed to increase national saving.

Now I would like to discuss some of my own research that relates to this field. The issue is how an increase in income affects people's retirement decisions. How would one design a study to answer this question? One method would be to give different people different amounts of money and observe their behavior. For example, for a group of 62 years old people, we could give some of them 1,000 dollars, some 500 dollars and some 300 dollars. Then we could observe their behaviors after retirement and infer from this experiment whether people with 1,000 dollars are more inclined to retire, or people with 500 dollars less likely to retire. This is a very good method, but it would cost millions of dollars to implement. I do not know who will give me the money to do the research!

I got useful data another, and much cheaper, way. I found these data when I worked in the US Department of Treasury in 1991. The Treasury had assembled a database with information about all kinds of taxpaying behaviors. In particular, the data included estate tax information. The estate tax is levied on the wealth of individuals after they die. Importantly, the data also indicated the identities of the people to whom the deceased individual had bequeathed his money.

My co-authors and I were able to link these data about inheritances with the individual tax returns of the people who received the bequests. We then compared the information on their tax returns before and after they received the bequests. Because the tax return indicates whether or not an individual is working, we could determine whether each individual was working before receiving the legacy, and whether they still worked after their receiving legacy.

I mentioned that I found out about this database when I worked in the Treasury Department. But at that time I was very busy, having no time to do research. So I began to use the data after I left the Treasury and returned to Princeton University. Of course, as a private citizen, I was not allowed access to these data myself. Luckily, one of my friends is still working in the Department of Treasury, and has the right to use these data. So in my research, he is also one of the authors.

What did we find? First we looked at unmarried individuals. We divided the sample into groups on the basis of the size of the legacies they received. We found that the larger the legacy, the less likely they were to be working after receiving the legacy.

Next we looked at families. The situation is more complicated than it is for individuals, because the family can have zero, one or two people in the labor force in each year. The data were consistent with notion of an income effect on family labor supply. In general, the higher a familiy's inheritance, the more likely that the number of workers in the family fell after receiving the inheritance.

As I have described the analysis so far, it has made the implicit assumption that the decision to leave the labor force depends only on one variable, namely whether or not people received a legacy. In reality, a lot of other factors also influence retirement decisions, such as the need to saving for children's education, other source of income (interest income, dividend income etc). A multivariable approach to the problem is needed in order to find out if the size of the inheritance affects retirement decisions, other things being the same. We used standard econometric techniques to address this issue. We found that for individuals, statistically, the legacy they received has little effect on their retirement behavior. And for married people, the legacy has an effect on their future behavior, but it is not significant. We conclude that unless there were a reform that entailed very large changes in income, retirement decisions would not be changed very much through this channel.

Review

Chen Gong

Chen Gong is Professor and doctoral supervisor of the School of Finance, Renmin University of China, senior financial and monetary expert. Currently, he is the Standing Director of the China Association of Taxation Consultancy. He was the former Standing Director of the Chinese Finance Society, Standing Director of the China Taxation Society and the Vice Chairman of the China Association of Taxation Consultancy.

The research fields of Professor Chen Gong are financial theories and policies and his main works are *Analysis of Industrial Business Activities* (1954), *Public Finance* (1964), *Social Financial Issues* (1981), *Course in Finance* (1984), *Fundamentals of Taxation* (1987), *Theoretical Inquiries in Finance* (1993), *Public Finance* (1994, teaching material for core curriculum in the major of finance in colleges and universities), *Securities* (1994), *Financial Theories and Financial Reform* (1995), *Collection of Chinese Regulations on Securities* (1996, 1998), *Public Finance* (1998, the "ninth-five-year-planning" national-level major teaching material for regular higher education, the first prize for national-level excellent teaching materials), *Public Finance* (1999, teaching material for adult education edited by the Department of Higher Education, the Ministry of Education), *Public Finance* (1999, economic and management teaching material for core curriculum of the Ministry of Education facing to the 21st century, the first prize of the State Education Commission for excellent teaching materials), *Public Finance* (2001, teaching material for adult education of the Party School of the Central Committee of CPC) and *Political and Economic Analysis of America's Financial Policies* (2002).

Professor Rosen's speech is like a story from, a great economist a story about old-age insurance. His vivid words and examples show us the basic rationale of social security.

Firstly, Professor Rosen made an introduction to the shaping and changing of America's old-age insurance. The system was founded in 1935 during period of President Roosevelt's New Deal. The system at that time was simple, namely paying when you worked and received when you retired. It was a fully funded scheme like private insurance. But soon people realized that old worker's paying was not enough for the pension fund. So in 1939, "pay-as-you-go" scheme came into being. It was to pay the current retirees' pension by current workers' paying. Another big change happened in 1983, for dealing with old-age boom of the baby boom generation. It was a partial funded scheme: current retirees' pension was paid by current worker's tax, future retirees' pension would be paid by current workers and social security trust fund.

The money of America's pension insurance is basically from tax paid by workers and their employers. There are no government sub-sidies. Tax rate goes up with the increase of welfare expenditure. For now, the tax rate for people with salary below 70,000 dollars and their employers is 6.2%, 12.4% as total, which is 5 times more than the initial rate. Professor Rosen pointed out that the key question of social insurance system is to convert every month's social insurance tax to welfare income per person per month. In general, the welfare income of every one is based on how much tax they and their employers pay, but it is not the same or proportionally equal. There is am income redistribution effect, mainly from people with high income to

people with low income, from the young to the old, between different kind of families. So the social security system functions not only
as security mechanism but also as distribution mechanism. It is stabilizer and adjustor.

Since the social security system is both stabilizer and adjustor, it
has to reform with the change of situation, because part of its structure and mechanism has failed. The current challenge faced by all
countries is the aging of population. It raises a question: how long the
turn-to-go scheme can sustain under the impact of aging society? For
example, now in America, a retiree is supported by almost 3.4 workers. In 2030, a retiree has only 2 workers to support him. Currently,
the revenue of social security is bigger than spending, which situation
can last to 2010. But in 2030, accumulated money will be used up.
Under such circumstance, if social security system has not been
reformed, the tax rate must be doubled. Obviously, it is more than
what workers can afford. America is with a low welfare level among
developed countries. You can imagine how hard it could be in
European high welfare countries. That is why social security system is
a impending global problem. For the potential future crisis, two solutions have been developed. One is to modify little by little, the other
is to make a thorough reform, namely privatization. The so-called
privatization of pension insurance refers to transfer the responsibility
of pension provision from government to workers themselves. The
key measure is to establish account for new workers and let private
fund management companies to manage these accounts. In 1980s,
Latin American countries such as Chile, Peru and Mexico implement
radical privatization reforms; England and Australia do so in a mild
way. These reforms achieve success in some aspects, but there is not
unanimous opinion in economics field. As Professor Rosen said:
"Under privatization, people have to take financial risk, but under
current social insurance system people have to take political risk. It is
unsure which risk is higher." As for the future of America's social
security system, Professor Rosen left us to guess whether it is a small
modification or a thorough reform. Two presidential candidates do
not want to talk much about this problem for the sake of election, as
was said "social security is the third mine field." Fortunately, America's

social insurance system can easily last for another 75 years with some small modifications.

In recent years, many economists paid attention to the negative effects of the social security system on the economy. The debates are focused on its influence on saving behaviors and labor supply decisions. Through econometric analysis, some economists draw the conclusion that the social security system will reduce saving and increase the probability of retirement. But there are other economists who disagree. They thought even the effect exist, it is not significant. And the system can be designed to minimize its negative incentive to saving and labor supply. Professor Rosen made a good use of the data of estate tax to study whether people's tendency to work will be influenced by the money they received on retirement. The result is "unless doing big reform to social insurance, income status has little effect on people's retirement behavior." Because this point of view is different from many other economists, today's speech is titled with "new perspective and evidence."

The topic of Professor Rosen's speech is not big, but it is filled with insight, which we as teachers and researchers can learn a lot from. In the mean time, China's social security system is in the process of establishment and improvement. What Professor Rosen introduced today about America's system and rationale is absolutely useful for us.

Chapter 14

The Challenge to European Financial and Fiscal Policy: Discussion With Formerly Deputy

Caio Koch-Weser

Biography

Caio Koch-Weser, born in 1944 in the Brazilian town of Rolandia, is the German government's Deputy Finance Minister. He studied economics in Germany and joined the World Bank in 1973, where he specialised in aid for developing countries. In 1996, he became the World Bank's Managing Director for operations (a level just below the President) and chaired the World Bank's Policy Committee, with responsibility for a large number of its regional and sectoral programs. Since early 1999 he has been a Deputy German Finance Minister, responsible for international monetary and financial issues such as the reform of the international financial architecture and for European monetary and financial affairs as well as European economic integration. Mr. Koch-Weser is also member of the Advisory Board of the Bertelsmann Foundation and a Trustee of the Institute for International Economics (IIE) in Washington DC. Since 2003, he has been the Chairman of the Economic and Financial Committee of the European Union.

Speech

March 17, 2003, Caio K. Koch-Weser, the temporal Vice Minister of Financial Ministry of Germany, came to Renmin University of China and participated in an academic forum hosted by China financial policy research center (FRC) RUC. After giving a wonderful lecture, he exchanged ideas with experts and scholars on the problems confronted by European economic development and fiscal policies.

Q1: Mr. Minister, after the unification of EU, European economic and fiscal policies have changed so much, so what is the biggest change in your opinion?

After the unification of EU, many aspects of Europe are indeed different with the former. Now, a new and unique culture has been formed in Europe; it is called "peer review system." Originally, we treat each other in a negotiating manner, but now everyone is in a boat. We help each other, to stabilize our currency for a common goal, and to see who contribute more. Now with the common interests, we are not just treating each other politely, but to say what we really want to say. So it does not seem to be so polite when we talk together, and not like the situations in the international occasion, but just like the domestic quarrels and discussions. This reflects the cultural change. I think there is still a considerable distance for Asia to form this kind of culture, but once Asia begins to change, it can be very fast, as well as effective. Japan is in Asia, and there are some other large countries such as China and India, they have negotiations with each other, but far from reaching that step at present. Although there are negotiations now and they will make constant progresses in the future, maybe a formal framework is needed to speed up the unification process.

Next, I want to introduce the G20, a group consisting of the world's 20 largest economies, including several developed countries, several major developing countries and some new market countries. The group hopes itself can exert its influence in the international affairs in the future. For example, it hopes the staffs who take part in the G20 Summit are the finance ministers and central bank governors, and are able to discuss some major issues just as long-term changes in the financial system. It is mainly concerned with two problems. The first one is, how to strengthen each country's domestic and international financial systems. Currently, the crisis all over the world also shows that there are some weaknesses in the current international financial system, so how to overcome the weaknesses and strengthen the current system is a problem to be discussed. The second is, we need to re-examine the roles of international organizations, such as the roles of the IMF and World Bank, about what kind of reform should be taken to ensure their effective function to prevent crisis from happening again. This time I came to China, one purpose is to listen to the Chinese opinions on this issue, the other is to seek for cooperation, and I want to cooperate and communicate with China on these issues. Germany is the next President of the Group of 20, and I really hope China can be the successor after Germany. Then the two countries can cooperate with each other to promote the summit, and play leading roles together. The informal nature is the major character of G20. Just like the discussions made here, finance ministers and central bank governors from different countries sit together and speak out what we want to say freely. But it does not mean that we need to implement the policies we have discussed immediately, so what we have talked about is just like references. G7 is also operated in such a mechanism, it holds a kind of informal discussions, but we cannot say it does not make sense, since discussion will help to communicate, and after reaching agreements, we know what to do next.

I came to your university, with hopes that students here can join in our discussions on how and what should the G20 do in the future. In schools, we are outsiders of this kind of thing, so I think an international economic department can be established in the future. I found a lot of students coming to listen to my lecture, and the students' English is really good. I talked about two problems, the first one is financial and monetary unification and budget problems of EU after the unity of public finance, and the second one is about the active fiscal policies we are implementing.

Q2: Mr. Minister, I have two questions. The first one is how to coordinate the revenues and expenditures between different EU countries, and the second one is about the regulation of some indicators, such as the highest ratio of budget deficit to GDP is 3%, and the ratio of government bonds to GDP is no more than 60%. How is this standard made up? Thanks.

Firstly, let me answer the second question. It is hard to say that there is a scientific method to calculate these figures, but they are the results of long-time discussions. At that time, no agreement has been reached by all countries. For instance, countries with relatively high ratio of budget deficit to GDP thought it was too tight, and it would be very hard to control it within 3%. The ratio in countries such as Germany, England and Italia were all about 6% or 7%, and they thought that such a standard was too strict; while the ratio of several countries was very low, then they thought it should be stricter. Germany has long been in pursuit of stability in its tradition, so the German Bundesbank thought 3% could be appropriate at that time. In fact, we are not pursuing a deficit policy; we are pursuing a balance policy, even with a little surplus. Since there is an obvious aging problem in European countries, and high level of public expenditure can be caused, we hope that certain amount of money can be prepared beforehand. Actually, most countries are in basic balance.

There are manly two aspects about the future development direction of stability and growth in Europe. First, we introduce the concept that structural deficit replace the cyclical deficit, which is a little more difficult to calculate than the nominal deficit; secondly, we will make some simple rules, such as the rules of expenditure ceiling; after the expenditure have reached certain level, it is limited, so the deficit problem can be controlled. In this way, politicians should not break through this ceiling unless you have special demand.

As for the 60%, I think it is reasonable, and in line with the development trend and principles of dynamics of national bond. Just like some new countries like Hungary, Poland and Czech, the ratios are as low as 40%. However, for these countries, it is better to keep in a relatively low level instead of filing the gap. Now the aging problem in

Europe will have great effects on the economic development, so in a long-term perspective, Europe needs a number of immigrants with high intelligence. Young generation in Europe is now facing two problems, one is comparatively high level of public debt; the other is the problem of paying pensions for their parents. They do not want to carry the two burdens at the same time. So we have aims to decrease the level of public debt.

Your first question, something about the EU budget, is interesting. Currently there are two sources of revenue for EU, one source is to put certain percent of several taxes revenue into this budget directly, the other source is from each government's domestic budget. Maybe a special tax called "EU tax" will be levied in the future. It is not easy to begin this tax because the collection should be fair, coordinated, as well as efficient. I also have to persuade the Parliament. In the past, the Parliament governs the expenditure only, now it also evolves in revenue. It should eliminate the flaws of expenditure; otherwise member countries will not turn in money since they think that money are spent unreasonably. At present, Germany is affording most of the expenditure. So in the end, EU tax might be an extra item, since we add such an item into the regular budget sources, and there may be many opposite voices. The proceeding of EU tax mainly depends on our views of Europe's future, our expectation of EU Parliament's function, and how much each government wish to retreat from its power. Except for the European budget and its sources, we have problems on joint tax policy.

About the tax policy, I proposed the rational majority of decision-making mechanism in my lecture, and here it puts forward the problem of tax policy co-ordination. Many enterprises are in business in various parts of Europe, and they demand a unified tax base at least, since if the definition of tax base is non-uniform, it would be hard to handle. The tax rate is not required unified, because different tax rates can generate competition. But different countries can have different views, such as the UK, who strongly oppose on this point. We have to prevent unfair situations, just like that of corporate taxes. For example, we have corporate tax in Ireland, while no such tax in

Estonia, or levied with a low rate, then it will have an impact on company's decision-making and behavior. In this case, a coordination of the minimum level should be required. Another example is resource tax, for the purpose of protecting environment. Now cars produced in Europe are running in various countries, if the energy tax rates differentiate too much among countries, it will have a great impact on the costs. So now we are considering, for instance, whether there can be a minimum resource tax rate, just like the minimum rates for diesel locomotives and trucks. The rate can rise, but we regulate the minimum floor. At the process of European integration, tax is indeed a very difficult problem because of the different historical and cultural tradition, and closely related with everyone's immediate interests.

Last year, the ratio of budget deficit to GDP accounted for 3.7% in Germany, larger than the regulated level of 3%. In accordance with the EU's Growth and Stability Pact, only the economic growth rate is below −2%, can the deficit ratio expand to more than 3%. Therefore, this situation was not permitted by EU. As far as I know, in many countries, like France, the deficit ratios were above the level. Each country has made deposits to EU in advance, so if the ratio is above, the deposits will be kept in EU. Actually EU has delivered ultimatums to these countries, if the ratio is above 3% this year, next year the ratio should be controlled below 3%. Unless members have been suffered from recession, in which case ratio above 3% is allowed, or the ratio should be controlled into allowed range. France is also facing the same excessive problem, the amount of GDP and deficit will be published soon in France, and we will discuss the issue of French at the Group 7 deputy meeting in this week. If the factor "unification of Germany" is excluded, our deficit ratio is 2%, so we can see 1.7% of deficit ratio is caused by East Germany.

Q3: In the past we thought 3% and 60% as security cordons, and considered them as a law, but in late January when I went to France with a delegation of the CPPCC National Committee, we got two messages about the ratios. One is, just like what you

have mentioned, they are the results of compromises. The other is, at least 4 or 5 countries have already exceeded the boundaries, like France, Germany and others. After we brought the information home, politicians as well as scholars were all confused, since in the past we considered these two ratios as the principle and followed it, and it would be safe if we have controlled these ratios to 3% and 60%. Now the problem of China is that the deficit ratio is often above the line, while bonds can be controlled within because we have begun issuing for a short time. From the long-term perspective, can you give us some suggestions? We thought it would be right as long as we control the two ratios, but now we cannot find the indicators for reference.

In order to ensure stability and growth, and to ensure the existence of monetary union, we have made some regulations like simple rules and numbers. The rules are simplified and abstracted, but we will not abandon or change the numbers dramatically. Instead, we are considering how to improve, to make them more complicated, more advanced, more actual-based. This is my first point. As for China, currently, it is in a period of rapid economic development, catching up with other countries, high-growth phase, relatively younger population, and without serious problem of old age. The accumulated amount of debt is not too much right now. If China needs a standard to evaluate the size of deficit, the standard should be set by itself, and I do not think there is a golden rule that fits every country. In Europe, the ministers meet regularly to discuss and determine the standard together, but China cannot just copy the standard mechanically. Meanwhile, I want to know, what is China's financial framework in the future? What is the direction of tax policy reform? How to deal with intergovernmental relations? What is the reform path in the end? How much is the debt share of GDP in local governments? (Local debt not included in 18%). Is there any hidden debts or contingent liabilities in fact?

As for Germany, it is not easy to maintain a steady growth and meet the required standards. That's because Germany is a federal country with many states. The deficit of each state cannot be too high, otherwise deficit of the whole country will exceed the standard. Several countries, like China, the bonds are issued by the central government, and local governments are not allowed to issue, so the total amount of bonds is easy to control. But the control of debt in federal countries is very difficult, like Germany. In fact, there is control mechanism in Germany, called common planning commission, in which finance ministers of each state discuss the expenditure ceiling together. The ceiling is not set by the legal, but by coordination with each other. Federal government of Germany is between the EU and state government, like monkey in the middle. EU's policy is sometimes not easy to be implemented in the states, especially in the states with opposition party in power. In France, it is easy to implement EU's policies since states are controlled together by the central government.

Q4: Minister, when you talk about the macroeconomic, especially in today's lecture, you mention corporate governance. However in China, officials in Finance Ministry hardly mention this kinds of problem, usually the SFC and Economic and Trade Commission will talk about the corporate governance, and SASAC may be the next one. This reflects differences of government function between Chinese financial system and European financial departments. Now we have set up a new institution called State-owned Assets Supervision and Administration Commission, and I guess a new problem will appear from an academic view. On the problem of state capital budget, I want to ask two questions: one is about the management of state-owned equity. As far as I know, in Germany, state-owned enterprises or public enterprises is not so much, but they do exist, so please briefly introduce the situation of state-owned enterprises and how the system of German Finance Ministry operates state-owned equity, specifically, which departments are in charge of those equity.

To be honest, our state-owned enterprises are not so much. After large-scale privatization, indeed, some companies still have some of state-owned equity, and the government will continue to do something to privatize all the enterprises as much as possible.

Just like the large companies Deutsche Telekom and Lufthansa. Therefore, the workload of managing state-owned enterprises is not very heavy in Germany. At present, government does not intervene the daily operation and management of state-owned capital, and it is managers who are responsible for those enterprises. Company's board of directors is made up of people from different walks of the society. From the perspective of Finance Ministry, we do not have the capability and willing to intervene in the daily management and operation.

You have mentioned in the last question, two British ways of enterprise management, which is one of the issues involved in corporate governance. Corporate governance has a very wide meaning, what you focused on is mainly enterprises. Corporations in Germany are now engaged in a two-level system, which is much better than single-level system. America is not engaged in two-level system, which caused many problems. This is my first point. My second point is, for the two-level system which there exist both board of Supervisors and board of Directors in an enterprise, it is better that the former CEO is not entitled board of supervisors after retirement. If not, the independence of the system will be affected. At last, from the future perspective, we can have exchange ideas privately on this issue. For example, in Europe, people concern about this issue, so what are the lessons we can learn from Europe, and how to study together and find out solutions to overcome weaknesses in corporate governance after the Enron case. In this way, enterprises around the world could grow in a common environment.

Review

Zhu Qing

On March 17, 2003, Caio K Koch-Weser, Deputy Minister of German Finance Ministry, came to visit our school. After delivering a wonderful lecture, Mr. Weser, together with some faculties and students of our school, joint in a panel discussion on economic and fiscal policy in European countries. It was my honor to participate in this discussion, and the activity let me know some latest development on government budgets of EU members. Among the issues mentioned by Mr. Koch-Weser, the harmonization of fiscal policies among Euro area members impressed me most.

First, I would like to talk about the warning level of government budget deficit and debt. Nowadays in China, when talking about the warning level, people often use the criteria that the amount of budget deficit should not be more than 3% of GDP, and that of national debt should not exceed 60% of GDP. Many people think that those criteria have been accepted by international society as the generally acknowledged warning levels. However, they do not know how the criteria come out. Mr. Weser told us in his lecture, "these two criteria were not set up by calculation or came from magic; they were the results of long-term discussion." In other words, the criteria were set down through bargains and compromises, according to the situations of the EU countries, not to scientific methods. We all know that, before the naissance of Euro, the Treaty on European Economic and Monetary Union (also known as the Maastricht Treaty) was passed in December 1992. This treaty is affiliated by a file named Protocol on Excessive Deficit Procedure, which requires the countries joining Euro area to obey the fiscal disciplines that budget deficit not exceed 3% of GDP, and amount of government debt lower than 60% of GDP (also called fiscal convergence criteria). The EU was faced with pressures from both sides when making those disciplines: on one side, the scales of governemnt deficit and debt should not be too large, otherwise they would exert negative effects on the economy; on the other side, the two scales were already rather high in some member states (Like in Sweden, Greece, Italy, Britain, Spain, Portugal, France, Austrian and Belgium, the amount of budget deficits were more than 6% of GDP, and in countries such as Belgium, Italy, Greece, Ireland, Denmark, Sweden and Holland, the amount of government debt were more than 70% of GDP). If two criteria were set down at a lower level, some countries would reject to accept those strict regulations. In this dilemma, through fierce discussion, the EU finally established the "3% and 60% criteria." From this process, we know that the "warning level" is made based on the actual condition of the EU member countries. The criteria may not be appropriate for the non-EU countries, nor are they world-wide standards. Therefore, the "3% and 60% criteria" are only reference figures for China, and we should not make decisions just according to these criteria. Like what Mr. Weser said in his lecture: "China should find its own criteria. I do not think there is a rule that fits for every country. Every country needs to make up its own standard."

Next, let's find out why fiscal convergence is necessary for Euro area countries. According to the Maastricht Treaty, after the currency unification, European central bank will issue Euro and implement monetary policy independently, so Euro area countries can only carry out their fiscal policies while losing their own monetary policies. There would be a united monetary policy and different fiscal policies in Euro area countries. Without coordination of fiscal policies, the

254 Realizing Rational Exuberance: An Appreciation

overall fiscal condition in the area may depend on the budget arrangement of each member state. The EU Commission, like a federal government, can only rely on monetary policies to realize macroeconomic control. From the theoretical perspective, federal government should have a good command of both monetary policy and fiscal policy in order to stabilize the economy. The practices of some federal countries like America, Canada, Germany and Australia have all proved this. Therefore, the EU should harmonize their member state's fiscal policies after unifying their currencies. In a short term, the budget scale of the EU Commission itself may not have substantial changes, so the EU need to coordinate the fiscal policy of member states, in order to enhance the control of fiscal policy and prevent the conflicts between monetary policy and fiscal policy. In specific, in the situation that the EU countries have close economic and financial relationship, if the EU does not establish budget disciplines, the following negative results will appear:

(1) If expansionary fiscal policy is implemented in some Euro area countries, the amount of their government deficit and debt will increase. As a possible result, the interest rate in the area will go up and the Euro will appreciate. Therefore, it will slow down the economic growth of other countries in the area and cause tensions in their relationships. It is more obvious when some big countries in Euro area implement such expansionary policy.

(2) At the same time, European central bank will suffer from great pressure of publishing more Euros, or the crowding-out effect on private investment will decrease the long-term growth of the EU countries. To ensure economic development, European central bank has to issue more currency into circulation, which will result in inflation and depreciation of Euro. Therefore, it is considered that implementing a steady fiscal policy is crucial to stabilize the value of Euro.

(3) The Euro area countries may loose self-restraint on their debt scale, since member states in the area may help each other, and which may lead to the further out-of-control of governemnt deficit and debt. It is generally considered that, budgetary

behaviour of the EU countries is affected by the two following changes after unifying currency. On the one hand, the budget deficit of one state can no longer be financed by publishing its own currency, so it must consider the cost of debt service when arranging its budget balance. If too much deficit is arranged, then the interest rate will rise, which will therefore increase the cost of debt servise. This helps to decrease the scale of government debt. On the other hand, governments of the EU countries know that they will help each other when meeting with fiscal difficulties, so they rely on others and loose self-constraints on budget deficit. Besides, in the country's capital market, due to others' help, the risk gap of interest rate wll be lowered, which helps bring down the demand of making tight budget.

Moreover, there were other two considerations for the EU to require fiscal convergence of its member states. First, the EU toke this opportunity to make its members "tying up their own hands," in order to suppress the tendency of deficit climb-up. Actually, the budget deficit of the EU countries was not caused by economic cycle, because even in the period of economic prosperity, the scales of deficit and public debt were increasing. This phenomenon cannot be explained by "tax smoothing" theory, which means, given a certain tax rate, the amount of deficit goes up when in recession and goes down when in prosperity. Actually, budget deficit of the member states was mainly resulted from their domestic political reasons. Deficit problems will not be solved automatically without an external force. Second, population aging is a very common issue in the EU countries, and public pension systems in these countries are "pay-as-you-go" system. In such system, pension contributions paid by young generation are not accumulated as pension funds, but be used as payments to retired people, and in the future, young generation will get pension payment from younger ones. From the perspective of younger generation, they will bear double burden: one is explicit liability (which is caused by budget deficit), and the other is implicit liability (which is caused by pension payment). Since aging problem is severe in the EU countries, the burden of implicit liability is rather heavy. To solve this problem and prevent younger generation from too heavy economic burden, it is necessary that each government makes strict restriction of its budget deficit and public debt amount. Mr. Weser mentioned this consideration. He said that aging problem existed in the EU, and each country should prepare to deal with this problem and reduce high level of public expenditure scale; young generation in Europe were facing with two challenges: public debt and pension payment for the old. That is why we should reduce the amount of public debt.

At last, I will talk about the compliance of the budgetary discipline in Euro area. Euro area countries are all sovereign countries, and they have authority of making their own budget decisions. Then, how can the EU control the deficit scales of member states? To answer this question, let's have a look at the *Stability and Growth Pact*, which includes specific measures of punishment on the countries which have excessive fiscal deficit. According to this pact, when the budget deficit accounts for more than 3% of GDP, the EU Council of Ministers should decide whether the deficit amount is abnormally high based on the opinion of the EU Commission. If the Council of Ministers confirms that excessive deficit exists, a series of measures will be taken, like rectification suggestions, announce suggestions, warnings and sanctions. Sanctions mainly include the following aspects: (a) ask the European Investment Bank to reconsider the credit policies to these member countries; (b) request the countries to deposit certain amount of money, until the Council of Ministers ensures that excessive deficit has been rectified. No interest will be paid for this kind of deposit. The deposit is comprised of two parts: the fixed part of deposit equals 0.2% of GDP, and the variable part equals 10% of the gap between the actual amount of deficit and 3% of GDP. If the countries did not take effective measures to meet the requirement of the Council last year, extra deposit amount is requested. The amount of extra deposit is calculated as the same way as variable deposit, but no more than 0.5% of GDP; (c) fine can be imposed. If excessive deficit does not return back to normal level in two years after deposit is made, the Council of Ministers can turn the deposit into fine. Once the deficit is no longer excessive, all the punishment will be eliminated, however, the fine is not reimbursed. One or several punishments above can be selected by the Council of Ministers according to the actual condition. Besides, if members with excessive deficit accept the suggestion or take measures based on the warning, the procedure above can be suspended.

It should be noted that the EU members will not be bond by the discipline of budget in some special circumstances according to the *Maastricht Treaty* and the *Stability and Growth Pact*. That means, in these cases, even if some countries' deficit amount is beyond 3% of GDP, it is not deemed as excessive, and no excessive procedure is executed. However, the term of special circumstances is rather harsh. They must satisfy the following three conditions:

(1) Contingency: Excessive deficit is caused by uncontrollable events, and these events have seriously affected the countries' fiscal conditions. Or excessive deficit is caused by a severe economic recession, which is, the actual GDP drops by 2% each year, or the decrease rate of GDP is above 0.75%, and the recession can be proved to be sudden.

(2) Temporary: European Commission predicts show that the deficit of one county will drop below the upper limit when contingent event or recession end up. If the Commission's predicts show the opposite result, then the Commission should put this county on the list of counties with excessive deficit in the same year when contingent event happens.

(3) Proximity: This means, the actual deficit of the member state should be proximal to the upper limit, but there are no concrete provisions on this point in any EU document.

Although strict procedures are provided, excessive budget deficits have still been existed in many EU countries for a long time, like Germany and France, which are mentioned in Mr. Weser's lecture. The problem is also serious in Italy. Because of the important status of Germany, France and Italy, it was very difficult for the EU Commission to carry out sanctions or penalties on those countries though it dissatisfied with them. For instance, due to the unification of the east and west region and serious unemployment problem, Germany suffered from high level of budget deficit. In 2002, the deficit reached 3.5% of GDP (the percentage quoted in Mr. Weser's lecture was 3.7%), and from 2003 to 2005, this ratio was 3.9%, 3.25% and 3.3% respectively. The budget deficit had been above the upper limit for more than 4 years without economic recession resons. The EU warned Germany continuously, and required it to take measures and control the budget deficit below 3% of GDP as soon as possible. Just as Mr. Weser said, the EU even gave Germany an ultimatum. On the other side, as the deficit was growing in these big countries, the EU also made some compromises, and even made amendment of the *Stability and Growth Pact*. On March 20, 2005, when 25th Council of Finance Ministers held a special meeting in Brussels. They reached a preliminary agreement on the amendments of the *Stability and Growth Pact* proposed in 2004, and agreed that excessive budget deficit can be allowed in ten special circumstances. Moreover, in a certain period, the deficit in Germany and France can remain more than 3% of GDP. On March 22 of this year, the EU Summit formally approved the protocol. Obviously, it was a compromise to the big powers. At the same time, it showed us how difficult the EU is in the harmonization of fiscal policy of its member states.

Chapter 15

Understanding Modern Economics

Qian Yingyi

Biography

Yingyi Qian, Professor of Economics, Department of Economics, University of California, Berkeley, was born in Beijing and graduated from Tsinghua University in 1981 with a BS in Mathematics. He received his Ph.D. in Economics from Harvard University in 1990, after earning an M.Phil. in Management Science/Operations Research from Yale University and an M.A. in Statistics from Columbia University. Before joining the Berkeley faculty, he taught in the Department of Economics at Stanford University between 1990 and 1999 and in the Department of Economics at the University of Maryland between 1999 and 2001.

He was a National Fellow at the Hoover Institution, Stanford University during the 1994–1995 academic year. He is a Research Fellow of the Centre for Economic Policy Research (CEPR), a Research Fellow of the William Davidson Institute at the University of Michigan Business School, a Fellow of the Chinese Economists Society (USA), and a Non-Resident Senior Research Fellow at the Stanford Center for International Development. He is co-editor of the *Economics of Transition* and on the boards of editors of *China Economic Review* and *China Journal of Economics*. He is an Independent Director of the Boards of Directors of China Netcom Group Corporation (Hong Kong) Limited, Industrial and Commercial Bank of China, and Vimicro International Corporation.

His main research areas include comparative economics, institutional economics, development economics, economics of transition, and the Chinese economy. He has published many papers in top economics journals, and his recent publications include: "The return to capital in China" (with Chong-En Bai and Chang-Tai Hsieh, *Brookings Papers on Economic Activity*, 2006); "Coordination and experimentation in M-form and U-form organizations" (with Gérard Roland and Chenggang Xu, *Journal of Political Economy*, 2006); "Regional decentralization and fiscal incentives: Federalism, Chinese style" (with Hehui Jin and Barry Weingast, *Journal of Public Economics*, 2005); "How Reform Worked in China, (in Dani Rodrik (ed.), *In Search of Prosperity*, 2003); "The Institutional Foundations of China's Market Transition," in Boris Pleskovic and Joseph Stiglitz (eds.), *Annual World Bank Conference on Development Economics*, 2000); "Reform without losers: An interpretation of China's dual-track approach to transition" (with Lawrence Lau and Gérard Roland, *Journal of Political Economy*, 2000); "Federalism and the soft budget constraint" (with Gérard Roland, *American Economic Review*, 1998); "Public vs. private ownership of firms: Evidence from rural China" (with Hehui Jin, *Quarterly Journal of Economics*, 1998); "Insecure property rights and government ownership of firms" (with Jiahua Che, *Quarterly Journal of Economics*, 1998).

Speech

The market-oriented economic reform in China has been underway for over 20 years and a market system is being setting up. Accompanying this process, modern economics and its branches have gradually been introduced to China and even taught in universities and colleges. Now the access to WTO will surely accelerate China's integration with the outside world. This trend calls for a complete and accurate understanding of modern economics.

I.   Analytical Framework in Modern Economics

Economics is a social science studying human economic behaviors and phenomena while modern economics focuses on those behaviors and phenomena in market economy which has been proved to be the only sustainable economic system.[1] Its fundamental principles and analytical approaches are universally applicable and do not differ from country to country. There does not exist Western economics or Oriental economics. By saying so, we are not rejecting its application to particular economic behaviors and phenomena in any given nation at given time. Actually, the consideration of detailed economic, political and social conditions is a necessity.

Modern economics presents a research framework of or analytical approach to economic behaviors and phenomena. As a theoretical framework, it consists of three parts: perspective, reference (benchmark), and analytical tools. They constitute the core for the understanding of modern economics.

First, modern economics provides a practical perspective for analysis which can divert our attention away from meaningless details to significant issues. Generally, economists base their study on three hypotheses: the preference of economic man, the production technique and the institutional restraint, the resources endowment. People, whether they are consumers, producers, workers or farmers, are all interest-motivated when making economic decisions. They intend to reap the maximum gain within the restriction of the present resources, technology and institutions available. From the perspective of modern economics, it is rational that consumers want to buy quality goods with least money and manufacturers aim at profit.[2] Following this logic, economists seek the effects of indirect mechanisms such as price and incentive on the behaviors of economic men, with equilibrium and efficiency as objects in mind. They explore how market participants interact under given conditions and how equilibriums are reached. What is more, they evaluate the possibility of

---

[1]Economics in the paper matches the international definition of economic science, including all of the subjects under theoretical economics and applied economics, viz. macroeconomics, microeconomics, econometrics, finance, public finance, industrial economics labor economics, environmental economics, world economics, development economics, comparative economics, economic history, political economics, etc.
[2]It is worth noting that the self-interested motive does not exclude the possibility of non-self interested motive shown by an economic man since he may take the welfare of another person (say, his child) into his own utility.

improving the welfare of one side without damaging that of other sides i.e., the possibility of Pareto improvement. This approach to economics often gives unexpected yet logical conclusions and has been extended to the study of issues as election, political system, family and marriage in politics and sociology.

Second, modern economics has provided several references or benchmarks which can help us to better understand reality, though they do not describe it precisely. Consider the case with either the Arrow–Debreu theorem (Arrow and Hahn, 1971; Debreu, 1972)[3] concerning general equilibrium or the case with the Coase theorem (Coase 1960) concerning property rights or that with the Modigliani–Miller theorem (Modigliani and Miller 1958) studying company finance. They are all used as benchmarks by economists. Kenneth Arrow, one of the theory founders of general equilibrium once said: There are five basic hypotheses in general equilibrium. Though anyone can mention at least five different reasons going against each hypothesis, it is still one of the most useful economic theories. His implication is that this theory serves as a helpful reference, just like mechanics in frictionless state though frictionlessness does not exist. To define these theorems as references contribute to clarify two common misunderstandings. On the one hand, they are often mistaken as a description of the real world, hence universally applicable. And failure to direct applications leads to the wrong idea of their being useless on the other hand. Actually, these theorems are far from an interpretation of reality. There is gap between reality and theory which differs from case to case.

The establishment of references is essential to the research in any field and economics is no exception. Mr. Martin Weitzman, Professor in Harvard University, who majors in comparative economic systems,

---

[3] Interestingly, in contrast to the fiscal centralization and the steady tax rate increase at present in China, Russia saw a breakthrough in its fiscal reform recently and began to carry out the single income tax system which is even difficult to be put into effect in mature market economies due to political reasons. Has the fiscal centralization in China aggravated the recent slowdown in its economic growth? Has the fiscal reform in Russia contributed to its current economic recovery? Both of the questions are open waiting for further study.

often visited the former USSR. He asked me a question while I was studying for Ph.D.: What is the difference between economists who have received a systematic training in modern economics and who have not? The question was triggered by his frequent contact with the economists in the former socialist country. His answer to this question was that the first type of economists always have some references in mind when they do research so that their analyses are coherent, logical and to point. The benchmark for the study of resource allocation and pricing, for instance, is the general equilibrium theory under full competition and that for property rights and the role of law is the Coase theorem. It is true that some articles written by economic journalists with insight are highly persuasive. However, what makes their papers less worthy is the lack of depth resulting from the absence of benchmarks for their analysis.

Third, modern economics provides us a series of powerful analytic tools which are mostly graphic models and math models. They take advantage of simple graphs and math structure to examine the highly complicated economic activities and phenomena. Here are some examples:

1. Demand-supply curves model with the horizontal and vertical axes standing respectively for quantity and price. It can be applied to analyses of not only the market resources allocation under partial equilibrium but also the policy effect caused by government intervention, market distortion, market failure and welfare issues in income distribution.

2. The overlapping generation model (25) put forward by Paul Samuelson. This model focuses on life limitations and market imperfections existing between overlapping generations, hence a powerful analytic tool for economic growth, fiscal policy and social welfare.

3. The ownership-control model (Sanford and Hart, 1986; Holmstrom, 1999) put forward by Sanford Grossman, Hart and John Moore which is a great help to examine the effect of power allocation on incentives and information availability as well as on corporate governance structure.

4. The non-symmetric information model (Laffont and Tirole, 1986) suggested by Jean-Jacques Laffont and Jean Tirole which is about the trade-offs between distribution efficiency and information rent under the condition of information non-symmetry. It is often applied to examinations concerning conspiracy inside an organization, firm regulation and pros and cons of centralization and decentralization.

5. The bank-running model (Diamond and Dybvig, 1983) that is characterized with multi-equilibriums including good as well as bad ones such as the self-fulfilling prophecy: I run a bank because all other people are running. This prophecy facilitates the analysis of financial crisis and the vulnerability of banking system. The above five models have widely been used as analytic tools and have turned out extremely helpful.

The three parts combined constitute the theoretical framework of modern economics and also the major contents learnt by economic students. The perspectives, references and analytical tools provided have formed a scientific approach to the study of economic life. Modern economics is not a congregation of concepts and definitions. Neither is economists' work to randomly apply them. Rather, what they should do is interpret economic behaviors and phenomena by using the framework implied by these concepts and definitions.

The analytical framework mentioned above has been and will continue to be the only economic paradigm widely accepted by economists around the world. Unlike the case with economics, in some other fields of social sciences such as sociology, there is no leading paradigm. The lack of a consistent analytical framework hinders the development of pluralism. Politics is somewhere between. It is making efforts to follow the example of economics. Scholars belonging to the school of rational choice are exploring political issues with the help of the analytical approaches in economics and their influence is on the increase. However, up to now, rational choice is far from the unique paradigm in politics. Indeed, the convergence to a single paradigm has both weak and strong points. To economics, by far, benefits outweigh losses: Its rapid development and increasing influence relative to sociology and politics has undoubtedly resulted from the use of a widely accepted analytical framework.

II. Mathematics in Modern Economics

One of the major characteristics of modern economics is the increasing use of math (including statistics). It appears in nearly every branch and has almost become a common practice in papers on economic frontiers with no exception. This phenomenon is not difficult to understand. As an analytical framework, modern economics must rely on math to establish benchmarks and to further analytical tools. So in the following part, we are going to probe into the role of math in modern economics from both theoretical and empirical perspectives.

Theoretically, analyses carried on the basis of mathematics models have at least three advantages. One is that math can give a precise description of hypothesis and conditions. The next is that the process of logical reasoning is accurate with no leaks and fallacy. Last but not the least, existing models often help lead to new findings, which are not easy, if not impossible, to be arrived at by tuition. The application of math to economics, therefore, contributes to restricting the research conducted by economists to three aspects: disagree about hypothesis; find out leaks in reasoning; rectify a model to reach different conclusions. This has effectively reduced meaningless arguments and facilitated further research. What is more, it has also made possible the finding of correlations among seemingly irrelevant structures.

Empirically, there are also at least three advantages with the approach of mathematics and statistics. Firstly, econometric models for qualitative and quantitative analyses can be derived from math models. Secondly, data quantification will in turn generalize as well as systemize the empirical study. Thirdly, the use of precise and complicated statistical approach will help economists to draw useful information from the large amount of existing data. Indeed, the mathematical and statistical approaches have added a theoretical element to the empirical study of economics. Quantitative test of hypotheses and rough estimate of parameter values have become possible and contributed to deepen the study by minimizing chance correlations and arriving at quantitative conclusions whose significant levels can be tested.

However, two points need to be clarified concerning the role of math in modern economics. First, there are some really excellent ideas in economics which are hard to be expressed in math language at their initial stage and can only be described in verbal form. Yet it is worth noting that these views should be regarded as "preliminary products." For them to have far-reaching implications, a description in math models and detailed analyses conducted thereafter by subsequent researchers are indispensable. Take two examples. The first one is about the theory of share tenancy. In the 1960s, Steven Cheung tentatively proposed the influence of transaction cost on different contractual forms (Cheung, 1969). Then in 1974, with the help of math model, Stiglitz precisely depicted the effect of incentives and risk sharing on sharecropping (Stiglitz, 1974). Indeed, the view put forward by Steven Cheung was original. Yet without the help of math model, his idea would have been nothing valuable but some shallow analyses on agricultural land issues and transaction cost would have remained a vague concept. It has been the contribution of math abstraction that made possible the spreading of the incentive theory and the contractual theory to other fields. The paper "Theory of the firm: Managerial behavior, agency costs and ownership structure" written by Michael Jensen and William Meckling in 1976, for instance, opened up the study of governance structure of modern firms and thanks to that, researches on incentives concerning company finance took wings thereafter. Superficially, the leasing of land by landlords to peasants has nothing to do with the employment of managers by investors. However, in terms of mathematical model, they both turn out to be about incentive, information and risk sharing in nature. The second example is about the original idea developed by Eugene Fama in the late 1970s, viz. having the competition on manager market as an incentive mechanism. According to Fama, even without the incentives coming from firms, out of career concern, managers are still motivated to work hard due to the pressure from the outside world (Fama, 1980). Later, Bengt Holmstrom (1999) analyzed the incentive impact of career concern with the help of math model and found that Fama was only partially right. This has led the study of managers' career concern and market competition to becoming a hot subject in the field of corporate finance. The two examples mentioned above show that math models are conducive to detailed research and contribute to the convergence of issues, which are similar in nature though superficially different, hence advancing our study up to a further step.

Second, after deriving a theory or a positive result with the mathematical or statistical approach, economists tend to give a description in non-math language. This can be viewed as post products. Policy papers, summary papers and introduction papers belong to this type. Indeed, as to some topics, especially topics concerning policy, if they are not illustrated in non-math language, it will be hard for them to draw common readers and create influence. However, it is worth noting that even if they take the form of non-math language, the perspective, logical inference process as well as the explication of economic phenomena and policy implications involved are all a reflection of the strict training in modern economics esp. in math models. Treatises published in *American Economic Review* are original ones with models while those in *Journal of Economic Literature* and *Journal of Economic Perspectives* are basically about introductions to and summaries of theories. The latter, though expressed non-mathematically, have published papers with math models as their basis and can be stripped down to those models by readers having received a train in modern economics.

Mathematics does play an important role in economics. However, it must be born in mind that economics is not mathematics. On one hand, what matters in papers on economics are the ideas put forward rather than the mathematical and econometric knowledge used in them. It is those ideas that have ultimately contributed to the development of economics. Economists are different from mathematicians just like physicians are different from mathematicians. The task of economists is not and will never be to explore math frontiers. That is what mathematicians are supposed to do. Hence we cannot evaluate an economist by his math level. Likewise, we cannot judge a treatise on economics by the math knowledge used in it either.

On the other hand, economics is a social science studying economic activities and phenomena, indicating not only that all economic theories are subject to the test of realities but also that both the establishment of new theories and the development of existing ones are also closely connected with the real world. Modern economics attaches great importance to positive analyses. Whether they are tests of existing theories or they aim at some empirical data failing to be explained by existing theories, positive analyses are unexceptionally conducted under the guidance of established theories. This distinguishes from the case with other social sciences which are short of consistent theoretical foundations. In the field of modern economics, with the help of statistical regression analysis, economists can focus not only on the correlation between estimate variables and variables, but also on the cause and effect relationship among variables, on the effect of model hypothesis on forecast as well as on economic implications. This is what differentiates economics from statistics.

Economics differs from mathematics in nature. Rather, it carries more similarities to physics. Physics studies the material world while economics studies the economic world. Both are science and their theories are subject to test by empirical data. Yet the case with mathematical theories is not so. Of course, one major difference exists between economics and physics, i.e., in most situations, controllable experiments are not available in economics. Accordingly, unlike the practice in physics, economists rely heavily on hypotheses and mathematical derivation which justifies two characteristics in economic methodology. First, economics attaches great significance to the actuality of its hypotheses. The famous statement by Milton Friedman that hypotheses were less valuable than the accuracy of forecast is wrong because it failed to take into consideration the impossibility of controllable experiment in economics and the limitations of applying empirical data directly to the test of conclusions. Second, abstract mathematical derivations prevail in economics. However, economics is above all a social science and therefore must base its analyses on facts and economic reality.

What we have discussed up to now is the general relationship between economics and math. However, exceptions do exist. Two extreme instances go respectively to Ronald Coase and John Nash, both being Nobel price winners. In the case of one extreme, Coase theorem has not any math models and relies wholly on logical derivation. It sets up a new reference for the analysis of property rights and government intervention and has changed the prevailing analytical perspective. In the case of another extreme, Nash equilibrium is a complete math theorem (Nash, 1950; 1951). Yet both of the two theorems have functioned as the fundamental analytical tools for game study and are widely applied to the study of economic issues. However, it is worth noting that exceptions are exceptions and they are by no means the general situation. This can be proved by the list of bibliography at the end of the paper. Except limited ones, the majority have drawn upon math (or are based on mathematical treatise) and belong to the field of economics rather than mathematics.

III. The Development of Modern Economics

In addition to the complaint of too much math in modern economics, there are two more types of criticism. One is that its research field is narrow. For instance, it is criticized that it just studies market operation while neglecting non-market organizations (firms and government); it pays attention only to resource allocation while excluding political economics; it is interested simply in efficiency while ignoring equality. Consequently it is regarded more appropriate to define modern economics as one branch. Indeed, as a subject originating from classical economics, it is more than logical to have resource allocation as one of its focuses. However, after decades of development, the scope of its study has gone beyond to almost every field of economic issues, which can be suggested by the researches on hot concerns in international economics at present: structure design within an organization; the formation of economic policies and political interest group; economic development and the evolution of political system; the effect of social capital on economic activities; the effect of income distribution on efficiency, to mention just a few. The following are two specific examples.

The first example is about the expansion of corporate finance. For as long as twenty years after the birth of the Modigliani–Miller theorem in the mid 1950s, its main contents — the determinants of corporate financial structure — had been considered dependent on bankrupt cost (including the cost on the edge of bankruptcy) along with the tax rates applied to individuals and firms. It was not until in the mid 1970s when Michael Jensen and William Meckling observed the equity and debt issue from the perspective of managers' incentive did the field of corporate finance begin to embrace breakthroughs. The new approach went beyond the traditional restriction of market in economics by treating firms as non-market organization and has triggered a series of issues such as the agent issue, incentive mechanism, the structure of corporate governance, etc. Then in 1980s, the research conducted by Sanford Grossman, Oliver Hart and John Moore with the aid of the incomplete contract theory brought further development to corporate finance and corporate governance. In empirical term, a study of the relationship among financial structure, management behavior and corporate performance done by Andrei Shleifer and Robert Vishny (1997) has provided much evidence for actual corporate governance. Take an example. Their findings show that the major agent problem does not lie in the relationship between shareholders and managers. Rather it lies in the encroachment on the interests of small shareholders by big shareholders and management staff. At the end of the 1990s, they further probed into the practices in different nations to protect the interests of small shareholders from the perspective of empirically legal framework and thus derived the effect of law on corporate finance (La Porta *et al.*, 2000). During the recent years, their focus has been on a comparative study of the weaknesses and strengths of court judgment and administrative supervision as well as their different roles in maintaining the efficiency of market operation. From the above, it is apparent that corporate finance has been heavily influenced by the development of microeconomics over the latest 20 years and has undergone fundamental changes.

The second example is about the emergence of modern political economics as an independent subject in economics. It is known that the focus of neoclassical economics is on the resource allocation in markets without taking consideration of political factor. However, in the real world, there exist many economic activities and phenomena which can hardly be explained if politics is not taken into consideration. It is well-known that tariff and custom protections reduce efficiency yet they are still common practices in many countries. Inflation may damage the stability of macroeconomics. Yet delays in the adjustment of macroeconomic policies are nothing less than common. Frequent happenings such as purposely slow pace, stagnation and even reversal of economic reforms, market transition and structural readjustment can barely be understood from the perspective of efficiency. To tackle this problem, the political element was thus introduced. However, two points distinguish modern political economics from the traditional subject. First, its starting point is positive instead of normative. Specifically, it is aimed at understanding the effect of politics on economics in the real world, especially the formation and operation of government economic policies. Second, what it uses in analysis is the analytical approach to economics. That is to say, the introduction of political element was accomplished within the analytical framework of modern economics.

Political economics has two major types of analytical tools. One is based on voting, viz. the interest of minority giving way to the interest of majority. In this model, the purpose of politicians is to gain votes and voters vote for their own interest. Economic policies are ultimately decided by the interest of the majority. The other is a framework based on interest group who can influence the decision of economic policies. In this model, interest groups make efforts to lobby, sway and even bribe those politicians who may have a say in decision making. The introduction of political operating mechanism into the framework is for the purpose of delivering a better understanding of economic decisions in different political backgrounds. Early in late 1950s, the median voter theorem put forward by Duncan Black laid a foundation for the voting model (Black, 1958). Then in mid 1960s, the publication of *The Logic of Collective Action* written by Mansur Olson pioneered the interest group approach (Olson, 1965). However, it was not until the 1980s and 1990s that political economics began to see breaking development and gradually became an independent field. The two recent publications, Person (2000) and Grossman and Helpman (2001) are representations of the latest development.

The second criticism of modern economics goes to its hypotheses. Theory needs hypotheses for restrictions. This is the case with both natural science and social science. History shows that the development of any science has come from the criticism of past theories. Yet it also shows that constructive criticisms are most valuable. It is far from enough to just point out the gap between hypotheses and reality. The key is to put forward a new framework on the basis of existent ones which can be closer to reality, hence delivering a more comprehensive explanation of the world. Take physics as an example. The popularity of relative theory by Einstein derived from its better ability to explain more phenomena with mechanics becoming one of its special cases. Over the past 30 years, the analytical framework of modern economics has been undergoing rectification and expansion. By now, it has become much more explanatory. The following are two examples.

The first case is about the rise of information economics in the 1970s. It is well-known that one of the core assumptions in neoclassical economics is the symmetry of information. Yet the introduction of asymmetrical information in the 1970 by Akerlof in his paper "The Market for 'Lemons' brought about the breaking development of information economics". It was ironic that the publication of the paper did not happen until after successive rejections by magazines including the *American Economic Review, Journal of Political Economy* and *Review of Economic Studies. I*ts final publication in *Quarterly journal of Economics* made an immediate stir and has since then become part of mainstream economics. It is worth noting that asymmetric information, though it has corrected many existent conclusions, was developed under the framework of modern economics and does not repel the symmetric case. Instead, it regards the latter as its special situation. What is more, its conclusions can be positively tested. Indeed, on various markets, the difference in the degree of asymmetry has different effect on human behavior. The theories derived from the assumption of symmetrical information are expanded and supplemented rather than abolished. Therefore, the Nobel economy prize in 2001 went naturally to Akerlof, Spence (1973) and

Stiglitz (1974) who made fundamental contributions to information economics.

The second case is the rise of behavioral economics in the 1990s. The findings of empirical psychology have shown that in some cases, there exist a systematic deviance between people's decisions and the rational assumptions in economics. Behavioral economics (including behavioral finance) corrected some of the rational hypotheses by integrating the empirical findings in psychology into economics. It studies market participants' activities under the corrected conditions and is capable of explaining some once puzzling phenomena. This is exactly why behavioral economics can be accepted by the mainstream economics. The traditional assumptions work well in most situations, but in some, the corrected ones work better. The theoretical and empirical achievements of behavioral economics occurred in the 1990s. In terms of behavioral finance, Thaler (1993 1994) and Shleifer (2000) did important work on the effect of limited rational activities upon financial market. And in terms of behavioral economics, Akerlof (1991) made much contribution. Yet among all, the most meaningful event was the bestowment of the Clark Medal on Rabin (1998) who has made great contributions to the basic theory of behavioral economics. Over the past 12 years, it was the first time to bestow this award on an economist concentrating on basic theories, indicating the widespread acceptance of behavioral economics by the economic field. Meanwhile, it also shows that the rise of behavioral economics might be the most significant issue in the development of fundamental economic theories in the 1990s.

IV. Analyze the Economic Reform in China With Modern Economics

China's transition from planned to market economy and its rise is a historical event. However, it is not isolated from the rest of the world. It constitutes part of the universal development and is confronted with similar issues facing other nations in transition. Indeed, the common issues confronted in the process of transformation along with the similar as well as different countermeasures taken by these countries have posed a new challenge for economists around the world. It is evident that not all the established economic theories are applicable in China, though some do. What's more, some common knowledge which makes sense in mature market economies become meaningless or even go against the economic activities and phenomena in transitional economies. Two examples are respectively the recession experienced by the east European countries after market liberalization and the continuous economic growth in China before the clear definition of property rights. Existing theories in modern economics can hardly give an explanation, let alone a satisfactory one of some significant issues that have occurred in the transitional process. This is not strange because on one hand, the focus of modern economics has been on mature economies and on the other hand, the large-scale institutional transformation from planned to market economy is unprecedented in history.

What is the ideal approach to analyzing the economic reform in China? On one hand, a good understanding of China is a necessity. A lack of the related background knowledge concerning its economy, politics as well as the historical and present conditions of its society will undoubtedly bring difficulties to the study. First, it will be extremely hard to distinguish and determine the true cause of the major problems that have occurred in the process of reform. Second, it will be difficult to give assumptions close to the reality. Third, it will be almost impossible to present policy suggestions that are both within the framework of economics and at the same time fit the Chinese conditions. Hence, the understanding of China is a prerequisite for its study. However, on the other hand, just knowing China is far from enough. To study the economic activities and phenomena in transition and to conclude with suitable policy suggestions, a grasp of the basic theories and analytical tools in modern economics is essential. Transition economics presents exactly such an approach to the research on the new phenomena happening in transitional economies including China. A summary of major theoretical and positive achievements in this subject can be found in the book of *Transition and Economics: Politics, Markets and Firms* written by Gerard Roland (2000). In fact, the development of modern economics has always been closely connected with the exploration of new economic frontiers. It has been so with corporate finance, political economics, informational economics and behavioral economics. Now transition economics doesn't make an exception.

Why is it necessary to analyze the economic activities and phenomena happening in the process of our reform with modern economics? The basic cause lies in the fact that China has been reforming its economy with the attempt to establish a market economic system in accordance with that of the international community. Since the core of modern economics is to study the economic operation of modern markets, it will undoubtedly provide us with a useful reference in that aspect, with the help of which we can better our analysis of the numerous issues happening in our transitional process. What is more, it will also help us to distinguish cases specific to China from those general to any economy. With these, we will be able to steer our research in the right direction either in terms of positive analysis or policy suggestions.

The applicability of the analytical approach and theoretical framework of modern economics to the reform in China comes from the following three factors. In the first place, under the restraint of resources, technique and institution, the Chinese consumers, entrepreneurs, managers and government officials are as interest-motivated as their counterparts in other countries. With the perspective provided by modern economics, we can make a consistent and practical assumption about human behavior when analyzing the transitional complexities in China. In the second place, since China's reform is carried in anticipation of bringing itself into the system of internationally prevailing market economy, it is more than suitable and necessary to use the theories in modern economics as references to study the reform issues in China. In the third place, at the initial research stage, the concepts and conclusions in modern economics serve to broaden the thoughts of researchers. Yet the complexities of the reform calls for a systematic, deep and accurate research going beyond the level of definitions. In this case, good analytical tools become indispensable and the various mathematical models developed in modern economics just serve the purpose. Though these models were not invented in accordance with the situation in China, slight modifications in light of the Chinese history and institutional factors will make some of them applicable to the economic activities and phenomena in China.

Let's explore the usefulness and necessity of modern economics in the analysis of the reform in China from three perspectives: market, firms and government. Market, as the mechanism of resource allocation, has always been at the very center of the argument over "plan" versus "market." In modern economics, the general equilibrium theory which is about the role of market price in resource allocation has served as the most fundamental theoretical reference. It tells us why unregulated price can reflect the scarcity of goods and adjust supply and demand. It also tells in what cases self-interested actions of individuals can achieve economic efficiency in markets without government interventions. Indeed, this serves as the theoretical basis in all discussions involving resource allocation, among which including the replacement of plan with market, the evaluation of the reform path in the past, the measures taken at present and new policy suggestions. The failure of the reform experiment carried in the mid 1950s whose focus had been administrative decentralization was actually nothing less than the result of our ignorance of the role of market in resource allocation. Later in the 1980s, the general equilibrium theory was introduced into China. The core role of market price and market mechanism in resource allocation gradually drew and held the attention of the Chinese economists. However, even at present when the orientation of the economic reform has been set, frequently, there are still such practices as price distortion, competition restriction and market depression coming from government. Diagnosis of these practices and suggestions for improvement cannot happen without the general equilibrium theory. This shows that the abstract and seemingly unrealistic references in modern economics are of real value to the research in China.

The second case is about firms, a hot issue in the 1990s. Since the 1970s, especially 80s and 90s, thanks to the development of game theory, information economics and contract theory, modern economics witnessed a breakthrough in the study of property right, ownership and governance structure of firms. With incentive as the starting point, the modern firm theory has conducted an analysis of the interest conflicts among managers, shareholders and other interest-relating groups as well as the adjustment mechanism. The corresponding empirical study has found many rules governing corporate governance structure in reality. The flourishing theoretical achievements of modern economics, their empirical findings together with their analytical approaches were introduced into China around the beginning of the 1990s and have contributed much to the study of the firm reform in China. On the one hand, since the purpose of the reform is to bring the Chinese firms into accordance with the modern corporate pattern, the part in modern economics concerning the study of firms will not only help us to find out problems existing in the reforming process but also be conducive to far-reaching policy suggestions. On the other hand, in light of the great differences between the firms in transitional countries and the firms in mature market economies in terms of their own features and the environment they are in, and further, in light of the difficulty to get rid of these differences in short time, it is obvious that the ready conclusions in modern firm theory cannot be directly applied. In spite of this, however, the analytical tools are still helpful since they have grasped the nature of firms. Slight modifications in light of the Chinese history and institutional factors will enable us to reach meaningful conclusions and deliver reasonable policy suggestions that are in accordance with Chinese reality. This indicates that the research findings of modern economics concerning mature market economies are either directly applicable in China or indirectly with some slight modifications.

As to government, we will discuss the government behaviors in transitional period along with their economic impact. Compared with firms and markets, this is an issue at a deeper level since government behaviors exert strong influence (either positive or negative) on the operation of markets and the vitality of firms. However, relative to the research on resource allocation and firms, the examination of government economic behaviors is rather limited in modern economics. The basic explanation is that developed market economies are legally based and governments must confine their behaviors within the legal framework. Never are they entitled to practice at their own will, say, to encroach on property rights or to place restriction on the free organization and development of firms. The main economic responsibility with government is to provide public goods such as education and health care. Yet the situations in transitional and developing countries are different: It will take years for governments to learn to act within the legal framework. During the transitional period when the legal system is still far from being perfect, the greatest impact of government behavior, especially local government behavior on economy is its attitude to the newly arising non-state-owned enterprises: whether to nourish a suitable environment for them to grow or to overeagerly grab revenue from them thus depressing their growth? This is a position which determines the vitality of local economies. Here comes the question: what are the determinants behind government behavior? As to this, modern economics presents no ready answers. However, it gives us a useful perspective for analysis, i.e., local government officials, like other economic agents, are heavily motivated by incentives. What is more, some analytical tools in modern economics can be borrowed for the examination of local governments. For instance, the model for the study of the weaknesses and strengths of power centralization versus decentralization within an organization can be applied to the analysis of the power-segmentation relationship between central and local governments since they are actually operating within the same governmental organization. And further, it can also be applied to the inspection of the power segmentation influence on the incentives and behaviors of local governments. Accordingly, with the help of the analytical framework provided by modern economics, we can not only evaluate the changes in local governments' behavior but also explain the various economic performances in the transitional period around the country or even around the world.

This approach provides us an insight into the effect of the decentralization and fiscal contract between the central and local governments pursued in the 1980s on local economy. It is well known that, on one hand, fiscal contract intensified local protectionism and reduced the central fiscal revenue. On the other hand, however, it gave local governments a very high marginal fiscal retention rate.

Empirical studies have found that during the period of fiscal contract, the higher the marginal fiscal retention rate, the more fiscally motivated local governments were. And what is more, the more closely interrelated their individual interests were with the prosperity of local economy, the more willing they were to support instead of depressing those vigorous local non-state-owned enterprises, thus resulting in their rapid development. This was a total contrast to the situation in the 1990s in Russia where the fiscal revenue of local governments was hardly pegged to local economy. Understandably, rather than financially motivated to flourish local economy, what local governments did was constant harassment and plundering of those new private firms. This behavior of local governments is believed to have seriously hindered the development of emerging private economy in Russia.

The case illustrates that analytical tools created for the study of issues in capitalism in modern economics can also be applied to the phenomena characterized with the reform in China, which in turn will not only enrich modern economics with significant materials and empirical data but also advance its development. Indeed, government behavior and its effect on economy have been a general problem which has received the most publicity. And during recent years it has become one of the focuses with transitional economics, which has unexpectedly advanced the evolution of other fields of economics. Development economics, for example, has begun to pay attention to the relationship between government behavior and private economy. Other examples include the study of issues that had been almost neglected. Among them are the worldwide comparison of fiscal systems, legal systems and financial supervision systems; their effect on government behavior, corporate finance and overall economic performance. Thus it is easily seen that the research on transitional economy as well as the reform in China has contributed and will surely continue to contribute to the development of modern economics.

References

Akerlof, G (1970) The market for lemons: Quality uncertainty and the market mechanism. *Quarterly Journal of Economics*, 84(3), 488–500.

Akerlof, G (1991) Procrastination and obedience. *American Economic Review Papers and Proceedings*, 81(1), 1–19,

Arrow, K and F Hahn (1971) *General Competitive Analysis*. Amsterdam: North-Holland.

Black, D (1958) *The Theory of Committees and Elections*. Cambridge: Cambridge University Press.

Cheung, Steven NS (1969) *The Theory of Share Tenancy*. Chicago: University of Chicago Press.

Coase, R (1960) The problem of social cost. *Journal of Law and Economics*, 3, 1–44.

Debreu, G (1972) *Theory of Value*. New Haven: Yale University Press.

Diamond, D and P Dybvig (1983) Bank runs, deposit insurance, and liquidity. *Journal of political Economy*, 91(3), 401–419.

Fama, E (1980) Agency problems and the theory of the firm. *Journal of Political Economy*, 88(2), 288–307.

Grossman, G and E Helpman (2001) *Special Interest Politics*. Cambridge, MA: MIT Press.

Grossman, S and O Hart (1986) The costs and benefits of ownership: A theory of vertical and lateral integration. *Journal of Political Economy*, 94(4), 691–719.

Hart, O and J Moore (1990) Property rights and the nature of the firm. *Journal of Political Economy*, 98(6), 1119–1158.

Holmstrom, B (1999) Managerial incentive problems — A dynamic perspective. *Review of Economic Studies*. 66(1), 169–182.

Jensen, M and WH Meckling (1976) Theory of the firm: managerial behavior, agency costs and ownership structure, *Journal of Financial Economics*, 3(4), 305–360.

La Porta, R Florencio lopez-de-Silanes, A Shleifer and R Vishny (2000) Investor protection and corporate governance. *Journal of Financial Economics*, 58(1), 1–25.

Laffont, J-J and J Tirole (1986) Using cost observations to regulate firms. *Journal of Political Economy*, 94(3), 614–641.

Modigliani, F and M Miller (1958) The cost of capital, corporation finance and the theory of investment. *The American Economic Review*, 48(3), 261–297.

Nash, J (1950) The bargaining problem. *Econometrica*, 18(2), 155–162.

Nash, J (1951) Non-cooperative games. *The Annals of Mathematics*, 54(2), 286–295.

Olson, M (1965) *The Logic of Collective Action: Public Goods and the Theory of Groups*. Cambridge, MA: Harvard University Press.

Person, T and G Tabellini (2000) *Political Economics: Explaining Economic Policy*, Cambridge, MA: MIT press.

Rabin, M (1998) Psychology and economics. *Journal of Economics Literature*. 36(1), 11–46.

Roland, G (2000) *Transition and Economics: Politics, Markets and Firms*. Cambridge, MA: MIT Press.

Rothschild, M and J Stiglitz (1976) Equilibrium in competitive insurance markets: An essay on the economics of imperfect information. *Quarterly Journal of Economics*, 90(4), 629–649.

Samuelson, P (1958) An exact consumption-loan model of interest with or without the social contrivance of money. *Journal of Political Economy*, 66(6), 467–482.

Shleifer, A (2000) *Inefficient Markets: An Introduction to Behavioral Finance*, Clarendon Lectures in Economics. New York: Oxford University Press.

Shleifer, A and R Vishny (1997) A survey of corporate governance. *Journal of Finance*. 52(2), 737–783.

Spence, M (1973) Job market signaling. *Quarterly Journal of Economics*, 87(3), 355–374.

Stiglitz, J (1974) Incentives and risk sharing in sharecropping. *Review of Economic Studies*, 41(2), 219–255.

Thaler, R (1993) (editor). *Advances in Behavioral Finance*. New York: Russell Sage Foundation.

Thaler, R (1994) *The Winner's Curse: Paradoxes and Anomalies of Economic Life*. Princeton: Princeton University Press.

Review

Zhang Jie

Zhang Jie, born in 1965 in Gansu province, got his B.A. and Ph.D. respectively in 1984 and 1993 from Shaanxi Institute of Finance and Economics. He did post-doctorate research at Fudan University in Shanghai for over two years. Worked as president of school of finance in Shaanxi Institute of Finance and Economics; head of the center of Financial Institutions and Development in Xi'an Jiaotong University. Now he is vice president of the school of Finance and Economics in Renmin University, tutor of doctorate students, head of China Financial Policy Research Center — one of the top centers in the field of social sciences attached to educational ministry. Besides, he is also a managing director of Chinese Financial Association and member of government decision consultative committee in Shaanxi province.

Professor Zhang Jie has been devoted to the research on Chinese financial institutions and financial development. The majority of his academic papers were published in top issues such as *Social Sciences in China, Economic Research Journal, Management World, Journal of Financial Research*, etc. His major works include *A General Survey of Monetary History in China* (1993), *Structure and Evolution of Chinese financial Institutions* (1998), *Financial Intermediary and State-owned Banks in Economic Change* (2003), *Optional Economics of Financial Institutions in China* (2007), etc. He was winner of the first session prize for college teachers sponsored by the educational ministry (1999), winner of the seventh session prize for teachers sponsored by Huo Yingdong education fund (2000). He also enjoys government special subsidy granted by the State Council.

How to View the Development of Modern Economics in China?

During the recent years, Professor Qian Yingyi has published several papers on modern economics. They are insightful and carry far-reaching significance. Among them all, the one entitled *Understanding Modern Economics* is undoubtedly the masterpiece and has drawn great academic attention. Here, I would like to take advantage of this opportunity to express some of my own views, which can also be seen as comments on this paper.

Indeed, the accuracy and superiority of the analytical approaches and tools provided by modern economics have been more than once proved by economists and their achievements. However, the challenges are unprecedented and beyond expectation when they are applied to China. At the initial stage, while examining the economic phenomena in China with the standard and never-failing economic tools in modern economics, puzzlingly, no ready variables and hypotheses in agreement with the Chinese situation were available. Yet it is well-known that they are indispensable for the construction of strict models. What should we do? Are we to mechanically stick to the beautifully established form of the mainstream economics and simply squeeze our study of the complex and changing reform and development process into it? Or are we to follow the analytical logic and basic conceptions in modern economics so that we can take our time to work out a proper approach which allows us to have a better understanding of the special situation in China?

Comparatively, the first path will be short-run effective. At the initial stage of our reform, the economic situation in China appeared messy and in chaos. To sort out the mess, the only method seemed the standard tools provided by modern economics. Indeed, over a short period of time, the so-called academic papers filled with mainstream economic mathematical symbols and curves emerged in large quantities. In the case of China, which was then at the beginning stage of economic research, this phenomenon was more than normal. However, with the accumulation of such papers and their misleading approach, soon there came into being a wrong illusion in the academic field that this research paradigm would be the only path to take for the poorly technique-equipped Chinese economics to step into the holy temple of modern economics.

Facts have shown that this illusion produced widespread and profound influence. Except a very limited number of researchers, most people wrongly regarded the economic research as a simple technical contest in terms of mathematical models and econometric levels and began to divide literature on economics into grades on that basis. As a result, many outstanding papers with a real focus on Chinese problems were naturally excluded in the list of the so-called standard economic bibliography.

Since the beginning of our reform, Chinese economists had gradually grown out of the Soviet paradigm and came in close contact with modern economics. It can be said we have already been familiar with its basic knowledge system and latest developments. Further, under the influence of those scholars having returned from abroad, their followers who belong to an even younger generation have treated as a fashion the discussion of latest mathematical models and those related econometric models, notions and vocabulary. Undoubtedly, this enthusiasm for modern economics constitutes a prerequisite for the modern development of Chinese economics.

Unfortunately, this passion was accompanied, from the very beginning, by the pursuit of the pure beauty of mathematical models and the practice of indiscriminate econometrical analysis in any situation. This expression does not mean to deny the usefulness of these tools. Yet we are firmly against the practice of doing models for the sake of models. The so-called "standard papers" in the wrap of complicated mathematical symbols actually carry a tone of showing off and public pleasing and will never merge into mainstream. Indeed, what the practice of modeling for the sake of models has reflected is but an impetuous mood under the disguise of the seemingly complex process of derivation.

The development of modern economics in China is thought-provoking. In spite of the early efforts made by our previous generations and their rough experiences, generally speaking, the introduction of economics into China did not happen until the beginning of the open policy. It was since then that most of our economic researchers began to learn the basic notions and analytical tools from various interpreted versions especially from international textbooks. During the process, they gradually mastered the standard frame structure of economic papers. This was in no way a smooth path. Actually, up to now, we are still, in a sense, in the stage of imitation without our own style.

Around the 1980s, the Chinese version of the yearly development reports published by World Bank was first introduced into China. They had an unexpected influence on Chinese economists. Their structure, logic, wording, bibliography and even index showed us a fully fresh, concise as well as practical analytical approach. Thereafter, our economists began to follow suit eagerly. In fact, quite some of our distinguished economists at present experienced that stage of imitation. And to be frank, that imitation process has played a vital role in helping us to go out of the traditional non-standard writing paradigm and to promote our understanding of the true meaning of economic analysis.

After the period of imitation, the question of how to develop modern economics in China naturally surfaced. As to the answers to this question, there are both consensus and divergence. The consensus view is that our study of economic issues must follow the fundamental rules and paradigm in modern economics. We cannot do otherwise. The divergence involves the definition of the development of modern economics in China. Does it just mean to equip our economic researchers with the "technical facilities"? Indeed, such practice is prevailing and can be regarded as the after-effects of the early imitation process. Many people believe that you get a real zebra if you paint black stripes on a white horse. This is a wrong illusion. In a sense, the paradigm of modern economics is like a system which consists of parts that can be imitated and parts that can not. The imitatable part is the economic analysis technique while the non-imitatable are the thoughts in economics. Over a long time, due to our backward analytical technique, many of our economists have developed a sense of inferiority which has nurtured a worshiping psychology toward this technique. This is understandable. However, if we take the application of the analytical technique as the only way to advance the development of modern economics in China, that will be misleading, especially at the present time when there prevails a thirst for technique progress.

Undoubtedly, the divergence will continue to remain. Indeed, its existence is a manifestation of progress itself since consensus comes from divergence. Over time, with the enlargement of the group having mastered the modern economic techniques, the competition in this aspect will reach equilibrium. By then, nobody will have comparative advantage over techniques and the case of gaining "excess academic profit" simply by using models and econometric analysis will eventually vanish. Papers without thoughts will no longer be able to deliver academic return. The evaluation criteria will change as well. That will be an indication that modern economics in China has really grown out of the imitating period and acquired independence.

Our economists have been expecting that maybe one day we can acquire the Nobel Price in the field of economics and some have even begun to predict the candidates. Is there really such a possibility in the near future? Do we have the qualifications? Is it possible for the price to be bestowed on someone for his mechanical application of complicated formula in China or for his bleak conclusions tested by artificial data? Indeed, we are blessed with opportunities. The ongoing economic and financial reform is providing the Chinese economists with a rare chance of theoretical breakthroughs. The question is: can we catch the chance?

To catch the chance means that economic in China must pursue the second development challenging path. As of today, economists with a sense of responsibility should devote themselves to the long-term yet hard exploration of our economic reform so as to find out the true theoretical source for the modernization of economics in China. This searching process will be a tough test of patience, persistence and intelligence for generations since no theorem can come into being overnight. However, as long as our economists take the correct academic attitude, use the standard analytical approach and observe the practical problems in China, then over time, after a period of accumulation, those views and hypotheses which seem immature and even "over-original" at the present time will eventually become the valuable basis for further development of Chinese economics.

Chapter 16

Can State Ownership Really
Promote the Balanced Development?

Chen Zhiwu

Biography

Chen Zhiwu received M.S. in systems engineering from National University of Defense Technology in 1986, and Ph.D. in finance from Yale University. He is the tenured Professor of Finance at Yale School of Management.

Professor Chen's study directions mainly focus on market supervision, management of securities investment, corporation governance, options pricing, and hedging, etc. He is praised by American economy science as one of most creative and active scholars in the domain of finance theory and financial asset pricing topics. Professor Chen wins many major American academic awards, for example, receiving the Merton Miller Research Award for his paper "Baby boom, population aging and capital markets" published in 1994 and the Chicago Board Options Exchange Competitive Research Award for "production-based asset pricing in Japan" in 1995. Professor Chen is the editor or associate editor of some top economics journals, like *American Economic Review, Journal of Financial and Quantitative Analysis, Journal of Economic Theory, Annals of Economics and*

Finance, etc. Besides, Professor Chen is also the founder and second largest shareholder in Valu Engine Company, one of three largest shareholder in Zebra Fund.

In recent years, Professor Chen has been actively doing research on Chinese stock market, corporate governance structure, and securities legislations and litigations of China and America, successively publishing academic papers, such as, Empirical study on auction of legal person share, "The anti-fraud and anti-manipulation part of securities exchange act of USA," "The class action and shareholder protection in security fraud," Discounts for illiquid stocks: evidence from china etc, in which many proposals having great significance for policy guidance and valued by Chinese national leaders.

Speech

During the 27 years' remarkable economic reform, Chinese government has generally made their people's income rise at full speed. But the striking growth of national income could not obscure the fact that the income gap between the rich and the poor is gradually widening. The bare truth is that the fruits of rapid economic growth have not been distributed equally. Thus, a popular belief contends that the economic reform causes the growing income disparities so the government must bring a halt to the market-orientated reform, or gear it down, to stop the income gap in its tracks. According, the government begins to rein in the privatization of state-own enterprises, reinforce macro control, and find new ways to transform the economy. In addition, some extreme economists even argue that only by abandoning the privatization and market-oriented reform on the march could the government solve the problem of widening income gap.

Actually, this appeal is not alien as it sounds. The surging income gap, a side-effect of Industry Revolution during the 17th–18th centuries, left a stain on western societies; but it also infused western scholars with one principle that private ownership and free market spawn income disparity and social instability. In plain language, privatization makes the rich richer, the poor poorer; market economy makes the wealth allocation more uneven. So in order to create a wonderful world of "fairness," the government should take control of all materials for production, strictly regulate the national economy and suppress the functioning of free market.

One doubt, however, is pressing us to be responded to: Does the causal relationship between market-oriented reform and widened income gap truly exist in China? If not, except for the market-orientated reform, are there any other fundamental reasons for the unequal opportunities of the income allocation? Whether the government financial monopoly and economic regulation would lead to the surging income gap? Or would a halt or slowdown of market reform ease the uneven income distribution?

One: Analytical Framework — Four Types of State Systems

First, we classify all the nations in the world according to the two criteria: one criterion is government style, which considers how one government is formed and organized, it more specifically referring to the choices of representative democracy, i.e., whether the administrative power is actually constrained, not based on the separation of powers in particular; the other one is the economic system, which refers to the choices between market economy and planned economy, it more focusing on who directs the allocation of national resources, the government or market (the price system, supply and demand relation, etc.).

Thus, these two parallel criteria naturally divide nations into 4 types: (1) representative democracy plus market economy; (2) representative democracy plus non-market economy; (3) non-representative democracy plus market economy; (4) non-representative democracy plus non-market economy (seeing Table 1).

Type 1 countries include the US, the UK, Canada, and Australia, etc.; today, it's hard to find any pure Type 2 countries. France, Japan, and India may be a few ones close to this state type. The governments in these countries still play an important role in the resource allocation and industry entrance permission. No real countries belong to Type 3, today, after modern democracy systems universally been established, though most countries used to be market-dominated economy without representative government, like China in the early 20th century. In nowadays, there are still several Type 4 countries left,

Table 1. Four Types of State Systems

		Economy systems	
		Market economy	Non-market economy
Government styles	Representative democracy	Type 1 state: Representative democracy plus market economy	Type 2 state: Representative democracy plus non-market economy
	Non-representative democracy	Type 3 state: Non-representative democracy plus market economy	Type 4 state: Non-representative democracy plus non-market economy

Vietnam, for instance. This combination of "non-representative democracy" and "non-market economy" not only empowers the officers to centralize the distribution of the social resources, but also shields them from any restraint.

Here we need underscore one nature of Type 3 countries, which is, that they lie in a more precarious state. A ruler without any constraint to his political power in a Type 3 country would, inevitably, advance the transformation of his country into Type 4, by plundering the nation's wealth to his own purse, despite it initially beyond his reach. But the opposite occurred in China. Appearing in the face of Type 3 country over 2,000 years, China yet could not break the stagnation and move into Type 4. Two reasons might explain this riddle: the first is lack of national transport system; the other fact is in the absence of modern banking system across the country. To elaborate, it is partly because the ancient transport system is not competent for Chinese Emperor to reallocate the resources from the rest of the country to one certain target area in a large-scale. Moreover, it is partly because there is no nationwide financial system to collect the savings of people scattering over the whole country. Hence, under such circumstances, the odds of causing a distorted income distribution by the government are limited, in spite of its centralized power.

However, nowadays, it might be expensive for the society to have a government free from restraints: the centralized power, armed with modern developed traffic tools and nationwide banking system, will build an unprecedented paradise for moral hazard and administrative corruption, which becomes a terrible blow to today's society.

Two: Which Type of State is Better for Balanced Development Among Regions?

Before facing the issue of China, we first cautiously examine the situations in other countries for helpful references, which mean the exploration the potential relationship between the extents of state control over economy and the variations of income gap across regions.

Each country has its own degree of state control and extent of involvement as proprietor or operator in economic affairs. We choose the proportion of one nation's SOEs' productions to its GDP as the measure to evaluate the depth of government control in the field of economy. But this ratio can only partially reflect its government's role in economy life, fails to cover the level of government examination and approval, government supervision of economy, also can not measure the degree of freedom for government to change the market rules. Therefore, here we just adopt this indicator as an approximation to gauge the scope of government's intervention in economy.

In the past two decades, many economists have carefully explored the convergence and divergence principles of regional incomes from the data in different countries. In general, there are two indicators for income inequality: convergence speed and the variance of average income per capita across regions, the former explains how fast the poorer area's income is approaching to the national average income, and the latter refers to the result of the standard deviation of regional average income divided by the national average income.

Figure 1 maps the convergence speed of regional income per capita against the proportion of SOEs in its national economy based on the data from the US, the UK, Spain, Germany, and other countries. As we see here, from 1880 to 1990, the poorer states in the US, annually, shortened 1.7% of its distance to the national average level.

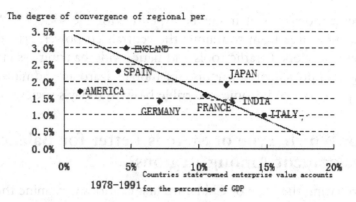

Figure 1. Tighter the Economy Controlled by Government, Harder the Regional Income Gap Narrowed

The poorer ones in the UK needed 23 years for reducing, merely, a half of the gap to their national average income level, although they had the fastest convergence speed — the income gap narrowing at 3% per annum. In contrast, Italy, India and Germanys' regional incomes converged at:

Data sources: the convergent speed of income among regions in India from Cashin and Sahay (1995), that of other country from Table 1 of Sala-I-Martin (1996), each country's proportion of SOEs product to GDP from The World Bank Policy Research Report (1995) the lowest speeds yearly — 1%, 1.4% and 1.4% respectively, inferred from which Italy could cut the margin only in half from 68 years ago. It is obvious in the evidence of these countries: the lower the degree of nationalization in one country, the faster convergence speed of income gap across regions.

Figure 2 points out that, if putting the variance of regional per capita income within one country, at 1990, and the proportion of SOEs' productions in that country's GDP together, we can get an almost perfect match: more the state-owned businesses account for the whole nation economy or tighter the government regulations are in one country, wider its regional income gap is. In Figure 2, the US's and the UK's regional income gap were both 0.14, the lowest ones; India's and Italy's were 0.33 and 0.26 respectively, the highest ones. Meanwhile, American market-oriented economy was the freest one — the rate of SOEs in GDP

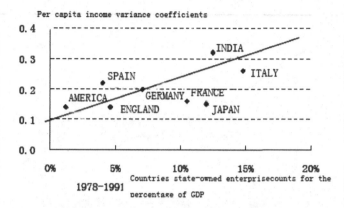

Per capita income variance coefficients

Figure 2. Tighter the Economy Controlled by Government, Harder the Regional Income Gap Narrowed

sources: the convergent speed of income among regions in India from Cashin and Sahay (1995), that of other country from Table 1 of Sala-I-Martin (1996), each country's proportion of SOEs product to GDP from "The World Bank Policy Research Report" (1995).

being 1.2%; India's and Italy's rate hit 12.5% and 14.5% apart. It implies that the lower levels of nationalization in India and Italy could not push these two nations' regional growth toward a more balanced way, the US is, however, experiencing the most even economic development over its 50 states. At 1990, Chinese proportion of SOEs in its GDP was 40%, and the variance of GDP per capita among its 29 provinces and municipalities reached 0.67, the huge regional income disparities surpassing any other countries in Figure 1. Therefore, I decide not to consider China now, or else it will cover up the most part of this chart.

The analysis stated above is merely an overview of the situations in each country at one fixed time, in 1990. We need a further consideration whether the influence of nationalization upon income distribution gap in one country is time-varying. From the time series angle, several countries' historical evolutions, one by one, are to be explored. Let's start with the changes of the US's income gap, among its 50 states, in a time span of 1880–2000.

When the second wave of the industry revolution was taking shaping at 1880, the variance of income per capita of states in the US was close to 0.55, while, by 2000, that figure had fallen down to 0.2.

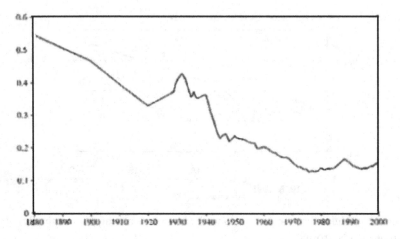

Figure 3.   Variance of Income per Capita Across States in America (1880–2000) *sources:* Barro and Sala-I-Martin (2004).

Yet for American history, in general trend, showing a shrink of income gap, there was still a splashy disparity of regional income in the 1930s and 1940s, just the period clouded by the Depression. To cope with the unprecedented recession, American government launched New Deal to expand the role of federal government in domestic economy, a severe deteriorating income gap among its states emerging at the same time.

A similar story is also told in Japan, as Figure 4 illustrating the tracks of income gap in per capita among more than 30 regions from 1930 to 1990. Forced to confront its economic burdens during World War II, Japanese government intervened zealously in every sector of its economy, and a widening income gap appeared at that time. Until the post-war reconstruction period, the government loosened its economic regulations, subsequently a upturn of regional income disparities emerged.

Next, a group of western European countries are covered in Figure 5 including France, Germany, Italy, Spain and the UK. In general, the regional income gap in a country that traditionally favorable to government control, like Germany, Italy, or Spain, etc., is much wider than that of a country where free economy dominated, such as the UK.

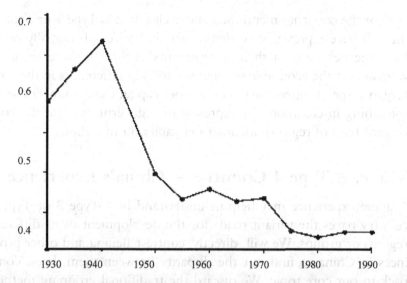

Figure 4. Variance of Income per Capita Across States in Japan (1930–1990)
Sources: Barro and Sala-I-Martin (2004).

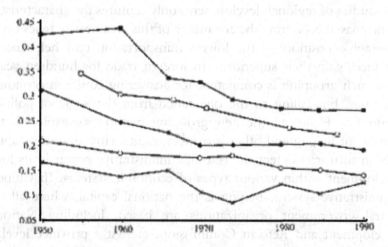

Figure 5. Variances of Income per Capita Across States in Western Europe Countries (1950–1990)
Sources: Barro and Sala-I-Martin (2004).

For the countries mentioned above classified as Type 1 or Type 2, they all have representative democracy and have substantially regulated the behaviors of their governments. Although there are great variations in the economic regulations and big differences in the convergence speeds of regional incomes per capita, these countries share something in common: the representative government and the convergent tend of regional incomes per capita on the whole.

Three: A Type 4 Country — China's Experience

Chinese experience may help us understand how Type 3 or Type 4 country paves the variant roads for the development of its different regions or groups. We will, directly, contrast Beijing and other provinces in China to find out the disparity between them, later, come back to our core topic. We discard the traditional grouping method of the administrative map — divided China into two parts, the coastal and inland, partly because this grouping method, though preferred by past studies of regional development, only captures the characteristics of the coastal economy: the advantage of this area heavily relies on its geographic position — the lowest transportation cost help coastal provinces gain their superiority in foreign trade for hundred years. Thus such grouping is competent for answering common economic questions, but failing to the one raised from the angle of political economics. However, the new grouping method we explored, the contrast of Beijing and other provinces, capital cities and non-capital ones in turn, can detect the role of administrative power in its local development within various types of economic systems. In Chinese administrative system, Beijing is the national capital, where all the central government organizations are based, including National Development and Reform Commission, etc. At a province level, a provincial capital is the city in which the whole province's administrative powers and resources allocation rights are concentrated; in turn, a prefecture city is the power center of its area. What does this power structure of the administration mean to the income opportunities for residents in the different administrative divisions? The answer lies in the government modes and economic forms.

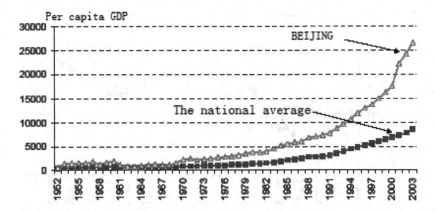

Figure 6.   Comparison of Beijing with Other Provinces in China
sources: China Data Centre in University of Michigan.

Drawing a comparison of Beijing's and the nation's per capita GDP levels (both counted at 1995 constant price) in Figure 6,we find the absolute income gap between them has, writ large, been steadily widening since 1949, so far no signs of slowdown. In 2003, per capita GDP in Beijing reached 32 601RMB, 3.6 times than that in the national average level, 9,073RMB.

In 1952, Beijing was NO.9 in the per capita GDP ranking list of 29 provinces, behind of Shanghai, Heilongjiang, Jilin, Tianjin, Liaonin, Hebei, Zhejiang and Guangdong. In light of this, Beijing was not in the club of richest regions at the very founding of the People's Republic of China. It, however, dramatically climbed to the 5th in 1985, up to the 4th in 1965, reaching the 2nd in 1978 (only after Shanghai). From then on, Beijing remains the 2nd place in midst of 31 provinces and municipalities up to now (excluding Hong Kong, Macau and Taiwan).

Let us look at the variance of per capita GDPs in 27 provinces and municipalities(excluding Sichuan, Chongqin, Hainan, Tibetan, Hong Kong, Macao and Taiwan) as a measure of the dispersion degree of average incomes among these regions: the higher the variance, the more uneven the regional income distribution. So a description for the yearly variance of per capita GDPs over a span of 1952 to 2003 enters into Figure 7.

Figure 7. Why not per Capita GDP Gap Across 27 Provinces and Municipalities in China Shrink?

Sources: China Data Centre in University of Michigan

Based on the retrospect of Chinese economy, New China, roughly, undergoes three stages: the initial planned economy, 1952–1978; the 1st round of economy opening-up and reform, 1978–1989; the 2nd round of economy opening-up and reform, 1992–2003. The contour of variations of regional income gap in these 3 stages is clear in Figure 7. In the planned economy period, the regional income differential was significantly widened; the variance of per capita GDP was 0.79 in 1978, up from 0.58 in 1952. Then, that gap, in the opening-up and reform phrase 1, was straightly narrowed, the variance down to 0.67 in 1989. Since the start of the opening-up and reform phrase 2 (when Deng Xiaoping made his southern tour), the gap among provinces and municipalities bounded back stronger, the variance hitting 0.81 in 2003.

The stories behind this slightly uplifted and zigzag path are as follows: during the period 1955–1960, the nationalization and the Great Chinese Famine happened, the regional gap across provinces and municipalities took a great leap. This severe widening of income gap took place just in the first three years of the 2nd five-year development program, when the Great Leap Forward were carried on — Beijing and few major cities became the areas with intensive investment. In that planned economy era, China was a country in

Type 4, and its state plan, in theory, could facilitate a balanced growth across different regions and sectors, but in reality, Chinese economy was on an unbalanced track and drifted further and further in those days.

The duo of planned economy and state ownership could not just cause a serious waste of resources, but for worse, lead to artificially distort the opportunities of regional development, which would foster the faster divergence of regional income levels. The span of 1962–1978 was regarded as the most sweeping and tightest government control period, as well as a threat to China's regional income distribution — the widest income gap across provinces and municipalities emerged in New China's history, even surpassing the growth of income gap in recent decades (seeing Figure 7).

From 1978 to the late 1980s, the Chinese economic reform was initiated in Chinese rural areas featured by family-based contacted responsibility system and non-state township enterprises. These preliminary market-oriented reforms successfully triggered growth in each province's income, consequently, filled the income gap across provinces.

In 1992, the gap of regional per capita GDP, however, began to pick up, this rally resembling the expansion route of gap in the early planned economy era — by 2002, the gap was back to par with the level in 1978, i.e., the ending of planned economy. Many factors can explain this exacerbated inter-provincial income differentials.

First, Special Economic Zones (SECs) policy strongly supporting the economic development of coastal area could, partly, answer for the income gap hiking up across Chinese provinces. The establishment of SECs, in itself, means an unequal treatment to other provinces. In contrast to the suppressing growth of GDP in the inland since 1990, the coast with the initial SECs and other favorable policies developed vigorously yet steadily, the inland naturally lagging far behind with time.

Second, during the most parts of 1980–1990 period, the reform of SOEs had achieved no obvious progress, in addition, the banking and financial systems were still fully under the government's control. To keep state-owned nature as needed and avoid the appearance of privatization, the government applied the household contracted responsibility system to the SOEs, adopted bonus system and transformed the SOEs into joint-equities enterprises one after another, but these approaches sadly failing to significantly improve the performance of SOEs. Hence, there is little hope for counting on the SOEs to sustain the steady growth of China's GDP.

After 1992, the year when Deng Xiaoping made his famous southern tour, Chinese government began to face the great challenge to reaccelerate economy growth. In light of the limited potential of agriculture and SOEs, Chinese government, again, took more active role in the fields of investment and economic control. It have transferred the savings of the public in the commercial or policy banks, through the bonds issued by state-owned banks or other financial institutions, into the hands of the ministry of finance and other government departments that can make the investment, payment and purchases on behalf of the people and enterprises.

And, since 1992, Chinese government has reinforced its dual identities: the status as an investor and the status as a customer (see Figures 8 and 9).

From 1979 to 1992, the average annual government financial deficit was 9.8 billion RMB, or 0.35% of GDP; however, in the years since 1993, the deficit had increased to 148.2 billion RMB per annum, an average 1.7% of GDP; the figure became 291.6 billion RMB, or 2.5% of GDP in 2002 (seeing Figure 8).

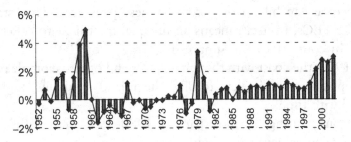

Figure 8.   Ratio of Financial Deficit to GDP

Sources: China Data Centre in University of Michigan.

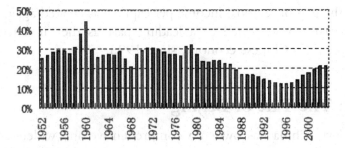

Figure 9. Ratio of Government Expenditure to GDP

Sources: China Data Centre in University of Michigan.

Figure 9 portraits the percentage points of government expenditures accounting for GDP in period of 1952–2003. Surely, the government expenditures excluded those ones from investment programs operated by state-owned units but not belonging to any government agency. These changing rates, by and large, reflected the extent of government's replacement for enterprises and consumers in China's economy. Between 1952 and 1978, the planned economy period, the average annual expenditure-to-GDP ratio of China was 28.7%. Since 1979, the ratio fell gradually from 31.7% down to 14% by 1992. After continuing to decline to 11.6% at the end of following 1993–1995 period, an upturn of the ratio appeared in 1996, when the ratio, boosted by the government broadly intervening the national economy as an "investor" and "customer," began to resilience till taking more than 20% of GDP in 2001. In terms of absolute amount, the government's share in economy also had an overwhelming increase — the government expenditure jumped to 2,460.7 billion by 2003 in a sharp contrast to a historical record of 347.2 billion in 1992 and 128.2 billion in 1979.

Finally, we make a summary of these trends of regional income gaps showing in Figures 6 and 7. First, in the days of planned economy, the inter-regional income disparity, under the full state control, tended to be widened instead of narrowed. Then, the gap had shrunk sharply since 1978, when the market came back to stage with collective enterprises prospering in urban and rural areas and the government, an "investor" and "consumer," took a back seat. But the rapid rise in the gap of regional income per capita was created again just as the government returned to a leading part as the "investor" and "consumer" in Chinese economy since 1993.

Four: The Tale of Beijing

Nowadays, China has owned a comprehensive and widely-covered network of transport system, consisted of railways, high ways, rivers, shipping, and airlift, and a nationwide financial system, in which state government monopolizes the whole nation's financial savings by banning illegal private banks and other private financial institutions. Moreover, the governmental agencies for allocation and utilization of resources are all based in Beijing. Particularly in shortage of administrative regulations, democratic representation and accountability systems, such high centralized power of recourses distribution provides Beijing and other few cities an unprecedented privilege to grow, develop and prosper. This is the simple tale of Beijing.

We randomly choose Henan province, with Beijing, to test this idea. In 1952, Beijing's GDP per capita worthed 1.8 times that of Henan province. Since then this ratio has been climbing steeply, up to 3.6 times in 1977, then reached 4.2 times in 2001.

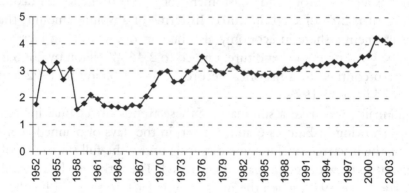

Figure 10. Ratio of GDPs in Beijing to Henan Province

Sources: China Data Centre in University of Michigan.

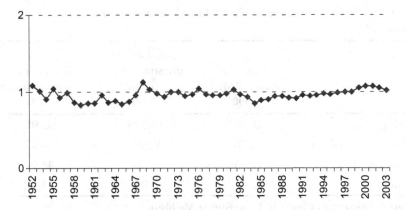

Figure 11. Ratio of GDPs in Hunan to Shanxi Province

Sources: China Data Centre in University of Michigan.

In contrast, far away from the base of central government and lacking of privileges and key support, Hunnan and Shanxi provinces were neck to neck with each other in the GDP race. In 1952, for example, Shanxi's GDP per capita was 1.07 times of Hunan's; in 1978, it was 0.97 times; in 2003, it became 1.01 times.

Being the national capital, Beijing has never been little shortage of investment, as its projects are always top-priority to be supported if needed.

Table 2 shows the statistical figures of GDP in Beijing, provincial capital cities, and non-provincial capital cities and counties. Besides Beijing, the figures of governments at other levels are counted in average according to the grouped data. Due to the difficulty of data collection from the counties, we only give the figures in one year, 2002. In Table 2, the GDP per capita fell with its government's ranking, from 28,499 RMB in Beijing, to 22,655 RMB in a provincial city, to 22,565 RMB in a prefecture city, down to 5,674 RMB in a county. The distribution structure of fixed assets investment per capita followed the similar pyramidal style. Beijing was on the top, 15,905 RMB in 2002, the provincial cities were on the second high stage, 9,233 RMB, the prefecture cities were on the next stage, 5,137 RMB, the counties were on the lowest one, only 590 RMB. The similar story could be told in the distribution of regional ratio of fixed assets investment to

Table 2.   Power Structure From High to Low Determines the Economy Opportunity
From Rich to Poor

	GDP per capita (RMB) (2000)	Fixed assets investment per capita (RMB) (2000)	Ratio of fixed assets investment to GDP
Beijing	28,449	15,905	55.9%
Provincial capital city	22,565	9,223	40.0%
Prefecture city	13,660	5,137	38.9%
County	5,674	590	12.9%

Sources: China Data Centre in University of Michigan.

GDP, which declined from 55.9% in Beijing to 40% in provincial cities, then to 12.9% in counties.

Obviously, the investment distribution plays a central role in boosting the regional income growth.

Table 3 gives the income and investment distribution according to regions classified as the following parties: Three Metropolises (Beijing, Shanghai and Tianjin), coastal areas, northeastern, northeastern, southeastern and the center provinces (excluding Hong Kong, Macao and Taiwan). All data are in average. First, between 1978 and 2003, the net increase of GDP per capita in Three Metropolises was 34,571 RMB, coastal provinces 15,443 RMB, northeastern ones 7,228 RMB, the central ones 7,356 RMB, and southwestern ones 5,374 RMB. Next, in accordance with the descending order of annual fixed assets investment per capita in areas, three Metropolises, with 5 459 RMB, were listed in the first place, the coastal provinces(1,693 RMB) in the second place, the central provinces (750 RMB) in the penultimate one, and southwestern provinces (682 RMB) at the bottom. Last, even ordered by the ratio of fixed assets investment to GDP, the Three Metropolises still had the highest one, 40.53%, northwestern provinces the lower one, 37.1%, coastal provinces the third one, 29.67%, and the central provinces the lowest one, 25.43%. As we have seen, the opportunities of regional economy development were unequally distributed.

Table 3. Difference of Development Opportunities Among Regions in China (Excluding Hong Kong, Macao and Taiwan)

	Increase of GDP per capita (1978–2003)	Fixed assets investment per capita annual (1978–2003)	Rario of fixed assets investment to GDP	Return to the fixed assets investment
National average level	9,351	1,121	30.25%	59.16%
Three Metroplises	34,751	5,459	40.53%	40.54%
The coastal provinces	15,443	1,693	29.67%	65.60%
The northeastern provinces	11,534	1,226	27.17%	55.33%
The northwestern provinces	7,228	1,161	37.10%	47.13%
The central provinces	7,356	750	25.43%	66.32%
The southwestern provinces	5,347	682	27.74%	64.59%

Sources: China Data Centre in University of Michigan.

Five: Which Guides the Investment Allocation: Efficiency, Fairness, or Power?

It is no doubt the "fairness first" principle of resource allocation dominated in pure planned economy, the "efficiency first with due consideration to fairness" was the prevailed guideline in the phase of reform and opening-up, and in today's society where an accelerated polarization between the rich and poor has risen, supposedly, someone will become the advocates of fairness instead of efficiency.

Nevertheless, we may doubt whether the resource allocation was really in according with the "efficiency first with due consideration to fairness" principle during the reform period? The answer to this question hides in the data of fixed assets investment among various areas (see Tables 1 and 2). No matter comparing the investment in Beijing with those of the provincial capitals, non-provincial capitals with counties or among other areas nationwide, we find no proof that the fairness principle was fully respected.

To further elaborate on our view, we use the average regional return rate of fixed assets investment, measured by annual fixed assets investment divided by the increase of GDP in the next year, to roughly count the output of investing, which, in substance, could address our concerns.

From 1978 to 2002, one RMB put in fixed assets could bring, on average, a 0.59 RMB growth of Chinese GDP in the following year, in other words, the national return rate of fixed asset investment is 59.16% approximately. Three Metropolises (Beijing, Shanghai and Tianjin), which had the highest fixed assets investment per capita and investment ratio, were also the places with the poorest efficiency of investment — a return rate of 40.54%, far below the national average level. Among all regions, the central provinces had the highest investment return (66.32%), but the figure in Table 3 tells us these provinces ranked lowest in investment ratios and second-lowest in fixed assets investments per capita. The coastal and the poorest southwestern provinces took the second and third place in the return rate of regional investment respectively, 65.6% and 64.59%,. Thereby, if the efficiency principle was practically adopted, the less investment should have made in Beijing and other metropolises, whereas the more should have been put into the central, coastal and southwestern provinces.

Figure 12 points to a clear negative linear relationship between the ratio of fixed assets investment to GDP and the investment return rate of each province and metropolis. The relatively higher return rates were in Guangxi, Fujian, Jiangxi, Anhui, Hunan and other provinces, however, the lower ratios of investment to GDP were also in these regions. Oppositely, Beijing, Shanghai, Tianjin and Qinghai had the poorest performance of investment but the highest ratios of investment to GDP. Even though the outputs of investment in Yunnan, Guizhou were 50% larger than that of Beijing, these two poorer provinces got far smaller amount of investment than Beijing did. In fact, it is advisable to remove the surplus investment from Beijing, Shanghai and Tianjin and put the additional investment into

Guangxi, Jiangxi, Anhui, Hunan, Yunnan and Guizhou at the sensible consideration of increasing efficiency and improving fairness.

Conclusions

Unfortunately, the recent ignited debate about inequalities in midst of regions, or between rural and urban areas, seems to point to a lop-sided answer, the further the Chinese reform goes in a market-oriented way the larger Chinese growing wealth differential. We have already outlined the most favorable state type for income convergence among regions, based on the analysis of the income convergent speeds in the developed countries, India, China and other countries or areas, is a mixture of the representative government and market economy under constitutionalism. It is not easy to transform a developing country into such a state fairly soon. Otherwise, we can fall back on the alternative ways as follows.

If the government's regulation over economy and the existence of some SOEs are necessary, the developing countries should be transformed from Type 4 to Type 2 and establish the elected representation regime. Type 2 is not an ideal for a country, but in a non-market economy, which has, at least, a system of restriction of government in order to give a more fair recourses allocation. The elected representative regime is a system guarantee for fairness and for decreasing the moral hazard in recourses distribution under government control. India, Italy and Japan have a certain control over their economies, but their regional per capita incomes a basically closing or convergent during the past decades, though they are still slower than those of Type 1 countries. In contrast, the income gap across Chinese provinces is broadening. The key factor brings such difference is that: market economy can correct the national recourses allocation from excessively deviating towards few regions. That is the root reason for Chinese income gap.

Also, China may go further with its market-oriented reform by privatizing the SOEs and reducing the government control over economy in order to turn its Type 4 state system into Type 3. But why Type 3 is more superior to Type 4?

The country in a non-representative democracy, unlike in the representative one, miserably relies on its government for controlling the whole national recourses including banking system, which would create moral hazard. So it makes more sense for the country to move toward the market approach by accepting a private-enterprise plus market-oriented economy which would highly respects efficiency and would provide a fair opportunity for each competitor in the resource allocation race. One fact could vigorously exemplify our argument: the size of income differential across Chinese regions in 1952 is relatively smaller than that in 1978.

The reality in China nowadays is that this nation's recourses allocation and opportunity for income growth are guided neither in efficiency principle nor in fairness concern. A plan to curb the market-oriented reform adds little or nothing to the existing efforts to deal with the income disparity. The democracy and market reform should go hand in hand. Otherwise, according to the past experience of China, the suspension of market reform will only lead to the further and longer income inequality.

Review

Wang Xiaolong

Wang Xiaolong, Professor of Public Finance at School of Finance in Renmin University of China. Professor Wang received B.S. in astrophysics science from Beijing Normal University in 1987, M.S. in economics from Northwest University in 1993, Ph.D. in economics from Northwest University in 2002, and did his post-doctoral research in CCER from July 2002 and July 2004. Professor Wang worked at Shaanxi Observatory of Chinese Academy of Science from July 1987 and September 1990, and at School of Economics and Management in Northwest University between July 1993 and July 2002. Professor Wang visited University van Tilburg in Holland for studying from January 1998 to July 1998, University of Surry in UK as a senior visiting scholar from February 2000 and August 2000, University of California, Berkeley in America as senior visiting scholar from September 2007 to March 2008.

Professor Wang's research mainly covers fiscal decentralization, governance structure of local government and public policy design. Professor Wang has published over 20 papers in economic core periodicals of China, such as, *Economic Research Journal, Quarterly Journal of Economics, Finance and Trade Economics, Journal of Monetary Economics*, etc. Professor Wang's paper, "Governance structure reform of local government in China: An analyses from fiscal angle was carried in Xihua Digest," and the paper, "Employment contract and duteous incentive contract in Chinese public departments — A theoretical model of the principal's moral hazard" won the 2nd Prize of the 7th annual Shaanxi Philosophy and Social Science Publication Awards.

Coping with the problem of contractual governance of public departments in the context of China's transition process, Professor Wang pointed out a series of operable institutional arrangements from a public finance angle.

In general, the mainstream economists position the income disparity as the particularly important phenomenon of inefficient resource allocation, which caused by market failure. They are fond of government-led prescriptions, including policies like nationalizing the enterprises, regulating the economy, or expanding the public finance, attempting to shorten the income distribution gap in midst of social members. The essence of mentioned measures is a phased trade off for fairness at the expense of efficiency and finial balance between each other. To downshift the speed of privatization and reinforce the regulation of economy sound a reasonable way to constrain the mounting wealth gap in Chinese economy transformation reform. However, whether these proposes would be desirably workable or manifestly unworkable is worthy of us to think over. Because if the widened income gap in China is not the result of the marketlization, then we can not see any sense in interrupting our current privatization and marketlization reform for sake of this exacerbated gap.

The lecture given by Professor Chen Zhiwu systematically analyses the relationship between the government regulation and regional income differential, and comprehensively discusses the root reasons for the deepening income gap during the economic transformation of China.

Broadly, the analyses framework is as following. The first is the classification of government and economy systems, the former according to whether the administrative power is constrained by actual regulation and the later according to whether the social resources allocation is dominated by government. When considering these two axes, all nations could be naturally divided into four types, forming our analyses framework for state systems. This framework is not only concise and clear, but also fancy to cover a nation's political system and economy freedom in the analyses of social resource allocation, by which he reaches some fruitful academic conclusions. In his analyses framework, for instance, one illuminating view is that a Type 3 country is in the disequilibrium state, which is constructive to our system reform in the process of economic transformation.

After carving the outline of analyses framework, the relationship between economic regulation and income gap, within representative nations, such as the US, the UK, Spain, Germany, etc., is the first objective. First, there is a negative relationship found between the degree of nationalization and the convergence speed of regional income differential — the lower nationalization, the faster convergence of income — after comparing proportion of SOEs' product in GDP with the convergence speed of per capita GDP gap across regions in each nation. Then, the analyzed relationship between the SOEs' proportion and variance of regional income per capita shows another finding: the income gap across regions scales with the lifted ratio of state-owned part in the economy. Moreover, from the time series view, the historical process of each country's income gap shows a convergent trend, overall, of regional income per capita in any of these countries, but the convergent speed differs from one another, which in line with the tightness of its nation's economy regulation — the income gap of an traditionally regulation-preferred country(like Italy, Spain and German, etc.) is deeper than that of a free market-dominated country, the UK. These studies have somewhat academic values, for it at least demonstrate one truth that lager ratio of SOEs in economy is, bigger regional income per capita is in a country with a representative government. I am, however, reluctant to support the causality relationship between the reinforcement of government control over national economy and enlargement of income gap across regions. Because, besides the increase of the SEOs' proportion, the government could use other measures to control the economy, such as reinforcing the regulations for market economy, adjusting the tax policies, and designing the pubic expenses programs, but the influence of these measures on the regional income gap need a further research.

Following the exemplified analyses in the relationship of one nation's regional income gap and its government control over economy, the second objective is the influential effects of a Type 4 country, China, on its regions' or groups' development opportunities. Starkly contrasting to traditional regional research angles, here a new grouping method is explored: firstly, making Beijing contrast to other provinces, then, the capital cities to non-capital ones respectively, to manifest the influences of administrative power in a Type 4 country on development opportunity among its different regions. The empirical study shows that highly centralized powers of recourses distribution provides Beijing and other few cities an privilege to develop regional economy, meanwhile, the development opportunities among provinces is sharply different. The positions of provincial capital cities, non-capital cities and counties in a pyramid-shaped administrative power structure are lowered accordingly, therefore, the development privileges of theirs descend according to priority, and the development opportunities of theirs, eventually, go downwards one by one.

Finally, the Chinese principle of allocating the social resources is the last objective in his study. If measuring the average return rate of fixed assets investment in region by the increase of GDP in the following year after one RMB invested fixed assets annually, then following the efficiency first rule, according to the data between 1978 and

2002, Beijing and other big cities should have distributed fewer investment, but the central, coastal, and Southwestern provinces should have gotten more investment. Therefore, the method of adding the investment in the central, coastal, and Southwestern provinces and decreasing the investment in Beijing, Shanghai and Tianjin would not only bring more efficiency but also fairness in social resources allocation.

In conclusion, Professor Chen Zhiwu's lecture mainly points to one contrary to a common economic issue, that is if the government, without an accountability mechanism under representative democracy, reinforces its control over the whole economy by nationalization, then the effects of this approach can not bring the social fairness but enlarge the regional income gap. This research carries significant academic and practical values, helping us re-understand the inner relationship between the nation ownership and social fairness on the circumstances of socialist market economy. However, one noticeable thing is that the relationship concerned is the state ownership with income gap across regions, not with the income gap among social members. In the common sense, the fairness of income distribution refers to the equality of social members' income in one nation, and the differential ability, members of society owned, to participate into market economy is the key factor in forming the income gap among them. Thus, I suggest that the economists should go further in thinking and studying one issue, whether the causality between the market-oriented economy reform and the enlarged wealth gap among social members in the process of China's economy transformation exists or not.

Chapter 17

The Flat Tax

Alvin Rabushka

Biography

Alvin Rabushka is the David and Joan Traitel Senior Fellow at the Hoover Institution

He is the author or coauthor of numerous books in the areas of race and ethnicity, aging, taxation, state and local government finances, and economic development. His books include *Politics in Plural Societies* (originally published in 1972 and reissued in 2008 with a foreword and epilogue); *A Theory of Racial Harmony; The Urban Elderly Poor; Old Folks at Home; The Tax Revolt; The Flat Tax; From Adam Smith to the Wealth of America; Hong Kong: A Study in Economic Freedom*; and *The New China*. Rabushka's most recent publication is *Taxation in Colonial America*, which received Special Recognition as a 2009 Fraunces Tavern Museum Book Award.

He has published numerous articles in scholarly journals and in national newspapers. He has consulted for, and testified before, a number of congressional committees. In 1980, he served on President Ronald Reagan's Tax Policy Task Force.

Rabushka's books and articles on the flat tax (with Robert E Hall) provided the intellectual foundation for numerous flat tax bills that were introduced in Congress during the 1980s and 1990s and the proposals of several presidential candidates

313

in 1996 and 2000. He was recognized in Money magazine's twentieth-anniversary issue "*Money Hall of Fame*" for the importance of his flat tax proposal in bringing about passage of the Tax Reform Act of 1986. His pioneering work on the flat tax contributed to the adoption of the flat tax in Jamaica, Estonia, Latvia, Lithuania, Russia, Ukraine, Serbia, Romania, Bulgaria, Slovakia, the Czech Republic, Georgia, Mongolia, Mauritius, Montenegro, Macedonia, Albania, Kyrgyzstan, Kazakhstan, Belarus, Trinidad and Tobago, Pridnestrovie (Transdniestra), several Swiss Cantons, and the Federation of Bosnia and Herzegovina. He has also drafted flat tax plans for Austria, El Salvador, Guatemala, Mexico, Argentina, Chile, Canada, and Slovenia.

Rabushka received his A.B. in Far Eastern studies from Washington University (St. Louis) in 1962, followed by his M.A. and Ph.D. degrees in political science from Washington University in 1966 and 1968. In 2007, he was honored as a distinguished alumnus of the School of Arts and Sciences at Washington University.

Speech

So thank you very much for giving me the honor to be here today to talk to you about my favorite subject: the Flat Tax. I have been working on the flat tax for more than twenty years. To give you some indication of how broad the flat tax is, I have been an advisor to Jury Brown, who was a candidate for president, against Bill Clinton. I have been an advisor to Steve Forbes, who ran against George Bush. Jury Brown is on the far far far left; Steve Forbes, people said, was on the far right. Flat tax is good for the left, is good for the right, is good for the middle.

Let's talk about the flat tax. In my view, when one thing should bear taxes, the purpose of the tax system should be collecting revenue. Now many people think, you should use the tax system to provide incentives to people to behave in one way rather on another. The problem with doing that is that every time you create a special provision in the tax code. To encourage some kind of behavior, or discourage another kind of behavior, you create a distortion. Every distortion cause a huge loss of economic efficiency. The more distortions, the more inefficiency. What you want to have in a tax code is a system to collect revenue, with the least distortion and the greatest efficiency.

I think, if you want to encourage of what I call social manipulation, to get people to, maybe, not drink or not smoke, or to produce certain kind of goods, it's better to do it through the expenditure side of the budget, or through regulatory policy. May I ask do you have your webpage in your system, could you put up my webpage? I wanted to tell everybody that the English version is free on the internet for those of you who know that, and you are welcome to print as many copies as you like. But you must buy the Chinese version.

Anyway, let me go back. So, the primary purpose of a tax system is to collect revenue and wants to try to do it in the most efficiency, least-costly way. The flat tax is designed to accomplish that particular object. Now in order to talk about any tax system, one must have some criteria for evaluating a tax system. And in public finance, there are some standard criteria. Scholars may disagree about precisely the best way to achieve these criteria. But we have general agreement about what these criteria are. The first one is efficiency. You want to maximize economic growth. Because more growth, more output, higher living standards. The second principle is neutrality. Generally speaking, you want resources to flow to their most highly-evaluated use, which means you do not want to restore flow of resources, you want to have a complete neutral tax system with respect of the use of the resources. Third is equality, the fairness. And it is this subject, I think, produce the most controversy in tax policy. Many people criticize one rate, by saying it's not fair, because rich people should pay more than poor people. Rich people do pay more than poor people. The question is, how much more should they pay. So some people like the concept of vertical equality, graduated rates. Some people prefer the concept of horizontal equality, I do. All people should be treated exactly the same with respect of tax code. If I earn ten times as many as you, I pay ten times as much tax as you. No twenty times, not thirty times, not fifty times. Only a ten times. And them finally, in some ways, I think the most important criteria of all, is simplicity. If you have a complicated tax code, it means that very smart people think long and hard of how to get special advantages for themselves. In the US, in Washington DC, we have a street, we call it K-street, after the letter K. There is eight block section from fourteen street to twenty-second street. There are seventy thousand voyeurs on that eight blocks who do not practice wall. They lobby the government for a preferential tax treatment of their industry, their business, their hobby, their sector. That is what happens when you have a complicated code. The US tax code takes thirty-three feet of library space. To understand.the reason one person in the entire world who understand the US tax code. And that's because over the years, we have abandoned the principle of simplicity.

Now what is the basic structure of the flat tax? When Professor Haul and I sat together, we decided, instead of reforming the income tax, we would throw it away. Start over again. And it is possible in our book to write the entire income tax code of the US in four pages. Four is about number, but it only takes four pages. Not hundreds of pages, not thousands of pages, but four pages. It is all it takes to write the tax code of the US. What are the principles? Tax all income once. Only once, no more than once, no double taxation, very easy principle. Number two, tax all income at the same low rate. Because if tax the income at the same low rate, it is not matter whether you are an employee, a soap provider, a partnership, a small business, a median business, or a multinational corporation. Every form of business is taxed at the same low rate. In my opinion, the third principle is, to ensure maximum economic growth, one should provide an exemption of industment. I prefer one-hundred percent first-year ride off of all industment, what we call the expensing of industment. When you remove endorsement from the tax base, what is left? Consumption. You tax consumption through the income tax, providing the incentive for endorsement, which provides the incentive to increase capital stock, which makes labor more efficient.

Now, let me go through what I see to be the advantages of the flat tax. Tomorrow I am participating a seminar here, at Guest House with the Ministry of Finance in the International Monetary Fund on reforming the personal income tax. And I am going to make the two of the following basic points, about why I think the flat tax is good for China. In the US, when you try to explain to somebody what is the purpose of flat tax, usually in the television interview, you get ten or fifteen seconds. So how you can explain the flat tax in ten or fifteen seconds? I have developed six words: remove tax code from the economy. What the flat tax does, it to vow all the businesses and individuals, to concentrate on the economic decision, not the tax consequences of what they are doing. In most of the American businesses, half of their planning is economic, and half of the planning is tax. Tax planning is as important as economic planning. So if you have a similar, low, flat, simple rate, every single economic dollar earns the same rate of return. You no longer have to engage in tax planning, the tax system is fix, and constant. Second advantage, the flat tax is productive of industment. It encourages firms and individuals and others to make investments in their business activity. In this sense, what you do with the flat tax is try to stimulate the maximum of amount of economic growth. A third principle, you know, in every country, discrimination is wrong. We try not to discriminate on the basis of race, sex, religion, gender, handicap, color. But what does tax code do? It discriminates against everybody, because a complicated tax code treats everybody differently. A simple tax code treats everybody the same. So the attraction of flat tax is to eliminate the discrimination against businesses and individuals. Based upon what kind of businesses they are, or what kind of individual they are, in emphasis the principle of absolute equality treatment in the tax system. A forth principle, the flat taxed are simple.

Now what I wanted to do is to explain to you how the tax code works. (Could I ask you the other figure? Figure 3.2) Now the nice thing about the flat tax, is not only it is simple, but the little forms themselves, provide all the information you need to know about how to comply about tax code. First of all, what's the tax base of the flat tax? It is the growth domestic product. We start with the entire cash flow of the economy. And if you look on the business tax, we treat, say, an enterprise. In the book we have examples of major corporations of solo proprietors of the partnerships. On the first line, you put growth revenues from sales. That's very simply the income of a business. On the second line, you deduct all of your allowable cost. What are the allowable cost? The first one is the purchase of all goods, services, and materials that you use in your businesses. Then why do you deduct those? Because the people who sell you those have already pay tax on their business cash flow. Also you subtract obviously the cost of production from your output. The second line is wages, salaries, and pensions. Now it is not really necessary to do that. We could simply have the enterprise withhold the tax on individuals and file on behave of individuals. In the Russian flat tax, most of taxes on workers and employees is collected and paid by the enterprises. But I will explain it to you in a few minute why I prefer to do that separately. The third thing is the purchases of capital equipment. This is the one-hundred percent depreciation, expensing provision. Now another attraction of expensing is you don't have to make a decision about what is the capital asset and what is a tool. A factory, or a screw driver, each of them can be written off. So every businesses growth revenues from sales might see allowable cost, you have your total income. When we first wrote our book, first wrote our article in 1981, we decided that what we would to do was to make the revenue in a neutral tax system. Now there is a debate of how big the government should be. Bigger government, higher rate; smaller government, lower rate. We have an expression in the US. Members of congress cannot walk in chew gum at the same time. We do not want to debate on how big government should be. We decided that we would replace the revenue of US income tax, and the proper rate was 90%. Some countries have lower rates, some countries have higher rates. My opinion is, the rich be less that 20%. Because over 20%, you have tax evasion, you have tax avoidance. Under 20%, most people will pay the tax, because you keep 80 cent of every additional dollar earned. We also believe that if you have a previously carry-forward, you should collect interest on that. Then, you pay a tax due if you have a positive number. So if you are a new and growing and standing business, and in fact, you are losing money, you will have a tax loss so you can carry forward into future years until you become profitable at which point you use that up.

Ok, now, if we can go back to the other form, please, the individual form, as I said before, it's really not necessary to have an individual form that we decided we wanted to have the individual form for one very important reason: we think every citizen who pays income tax should do a tax accounting with the government very year. That is to say, when a year is over, you know, that was my income, this is my tax. Did I get back from the government efficient services? So in order to have a consciousness in the taxpayer, I think it is very useful for each taxpayer, once a year, to go through a tax form and see exactly how much money that individual actually pays in taxes. Now in every personal income tax, every in the world, we allow an exemption or a standard deduction. And the idea is, not the tax the basic necessities in life, or for very very poor people, below a the very low poverty line, they should pay no income tax. Each country should decide differently what their level should be. What we did when we design our tax system, was to simply use the same numbers that the current US income tax use. So for 1995, we had an allowance for American couples of 16,500 dollars in jointly. For each child, each dependant, we had another 4,500 dollars. Single head of household had a different allowance. So a family of four would not pay any tax until their income was well over 20,000 dollars. As I said, that number is different for every country. Well, scribe the number multiply by 90%, and that's the tax due, most businesses will withhold the tax, so there should be no extra tax. Now, you are asking where is dividends? No tax on dividends. Where's capital gains? No tax on capital gains. Why not? The reason is, that you want to avoid double tax. Once the business pays the tax on its profits, it can retain them for future industment, it can distribute them as dividend. If they distribute them as dividend, the money has already been taxed, and they should not be tax again. Why no capital gains? What is a capital gain on a financial asset? A capital gain on financial asset is basically the gain and the value of the asset due to the expected future earnings of the asset. If you retain the profit and reinvest it, and the business grows, the future profit will grow. The taxes on the future profits will grow. If you tax again, the underlying capital appreciation of the financial asset that will be a double tax on that single stream of business cash flow. So no tax on capital gains, no tax on dividends. In our system we change the tax treatment of interest, we do not have business deduction for interest, so individuals pay no tax on interest received. We could do it the other way, but this was the simplest and easy way to do it. We also have no estate tax, no gift tax, why not? Because all money you have you give to your children, is after-tax income. It's already been taxed. So if you follow the rule taxing income only once, you can make for a very very simple system.

Now to go on to the advantages of it, you see, I have now explain to you in about seven minutes on how the flat tax worth in practice. If I try to explain to you how the Chinese tax code works, how the American tax code works, I would need three months. At least three months. To go through every single detail, I needed five minutes. That's the advantage of simplicity, you understand it? The form is self-explanatory. You do not need a big, thick book of regulations to understand it. It gives you very strong incentives to work save and indust. And it collects the same amount of money. In fact, it collects more, because you reduce tax evasion, you reduce tax avoidance, you eliminate tax planning. We have in the US 500,000 people, who do nothing but for plan the taxes for everybody else. And if China is in careful, it would have 5,000,000 people, who do the planning for everybody else.

The way this flat tax is designed, it achieves full integration, across individuals, and business central prises. So it does not matter what you tax of the enterprise level, or if the individual level, it's exactly the same. Now, one more reason why the single rate is very important. If you have two, three, or four rates, every individual and every business will do this: take a deduction at the highest rate, and declare the income at the lowest rate. But if there is one rate, it makes a difference. Every deduction is valued exactly the same, or income is valued exactly the same. So the benefit of one rate is that you evaluate the opportunities of arbitrage, and think about how they manipulate the tax system for your own purpose.

Now, how about the history of flat tax? It is very interesting history. The first two countries to actually adopt the simple flat tax system are the little islands of Jersey and Guernsey, off the coast of France, the channel islands in 1940. So why does not everybody not know about the channel islands? Because we know about the Jersey cows, and we know about Guernsey cows, these are little tiny islands that nobody ever heard of, the tax havens. So nobody can use that as an example. It is the posted-stamp country. It is not a real country. In the US, we have a lot of discussions about the flat tax. So when

President Reagan took office at top rate of 70%, then it fell to 50%, then it fell to 28%, two rates 15, 28 by 1986. But then it went back up to 31%, under the first President Bush. Then it went back up to 39.6% under President Clinton. So the problem with two rates is that it is not stable. You need one rate to have a stable system. Since then, the countries that have adopted flat tax, or all the newly independent countries of the post-Soviet block, the first country is Estonia. It adopted the flat tax in 1994, it has also accomplished four integration with the corporation income tax. So if you go on to a website, and have a look at the Estonian income tax, it is the country that has really copied the system Professor Haul and I recommended twenty years ago. The next year, the neighbor of Estonia, Latvia also adopted the flat tax. Now the rate was very high, the rate was 25%, too high. But those countries have constitutions that require a balance budget. You may not have deficits in the constitutions of Estonia and Latvia, and so the rate that was necessary was 25%. The most important country to adopt flat tax, by far, is Russia. Russia adopted the flat tax on January 1, 2001. On my webpage, I have written a detailed description of the Russian flat tax. In the three years, almost three years, the Russia flat tax has been in the effect. Real government revenue adjusted for inflation from the income tax is 80%, even though the top rate came from 30% to 13%, I want to tell you a story, very often the economic policy is an accident, just good luck. One day, my colleague, who knew a young gentleman named Andrea, invited him to Stanford. I met him; I gave him a copy of my book. The next thing I know, Boris Yeltsin stepped down, Vladimir Putin becomes president. He appointed the young man as the presidential economic advisor. The next thing I know, Russia adopted flat tax. So by the accident, I just gave a person a book. You can change a country's economic policy. That is a true story. Starting next January, Ukraine will follow Russia with the 13% flat tax. Now for the past 16 months, I have been going back and forth in Email with government officials in Slovakia. About one month ago, the government of Slovakia adopted 19% flat tax. The beauty of internet is that it is not necessary to get on an airplane now to convey your ideas. It is very easy to communicate on the internet. And in may ways, I have found that one have more influence by not getting on an airplane. Because in Russia, they thought it was their idea, not my idea. As a result, it is very easy sometimes for people to develop their own ideas instead of thinking they simply follow the ideas the before. Now China is different, I think they need my help.

In other countries, they are considering the flat tax. One of the political parties in Poland has introduced flat tax; the opposition party in Czech Republic has proposed a 50% flat tax. They are interested in the South Republic of Korean. No western country in Western Europe has talked about the flat tax. Only all of the new countries moving from central plan to market economics, why is that? When you start from the beginning, you do not have to clear away all of the underbrush, you do not have to cut it out. You have a clean open field, and you can put in place a well-designed system. But when you have a fifteen years of politics, and interest groups, and special provisions, and you have deductions, exemptions, credits, allowances, hundreds and hundreds of them. The politics of reform is almost impossible. That is why when you try to make a reform, you should make a comprehensive reform and go for a system. Because if you just changed around the edge a little bit, you cut off the branch, two more will grow back, and will become even more complicated.

Why should China adopt the flat tax? I think a flat tax make sense for China. Simply because if you look on the future, and you want a tax system that provides investment, opportunity, growth, that rewards hard work and production and industment. This is what I think will help China to achieve the economic objectives, raise living standards for as many people as possible. If you choose a complicated system, I think it will go down the road of American and Western Europe. It is very difficult in the future to reform such a system.

Secondly, the flat tax, will as China growth, generate sufficient revenue, I think, to contribute to its budget. You all know what elasticity means. The flat tax is very highly elastic with respective to income. Because as small enterprises become bigger, as start-ups become profitable, and as more and more people earn higher salaries and they can push into the tax next. The growth of revenue will be faster than the growth of GDP without disincentive effect, a punishing high marginal tax rate. I think one must look into the future.

We Americans have a very short history; China has a very long history. You have the patience to think about what kind of tax system you would like to have in 10 years, 15 years, or 20 years? What do you want your tax system to look like? Think about that. Do that kind of tax system today. Do not make a change, a change and a change, then it would be impossible to change. So if I may, I would be happy to take any and every question, and try to give you my possible answer. Thank you for listening to my talk.

Review

Guo Qingwang

Robert Hall and Alvin Rabushka, two scholars at Harvard University, brought forward the idea of flat tax in 1981, and published a book named "flat tax" in 1985, which introduced the framework of flat tax. They published the second edition in 1995 based on further development. In 2003, China financial and economic publishing house published its Chinese edition. This paper is exactly the speech that Rabushka gave at "Huang Da-Mundell Lectures on Economics" and publication ceremony.

"Flat tax" is translated as "single tax" now in China, which might be very easy to lead to confusion that all the tax system only has one or several taxes. Actually, the innovation idea of "flat tax" is for income tax system, and the word "flat" means "no level" (taxable income) or "not progressive" (tax rate). So "flat" is closer to "Bian ping hua" in business management theory. Therefore, "flat tax" should be translated as "Bian ping hua", which used to be translated as "consolidated tax".

Since most of us take "flat tax" as "单一税", I will also use it. The reason is that I believe only the idea that matters, not the name. So what is the central idea of flat tax? I think that there are mainly 3 important characteristics: flat tax, consumption tax base and clean tax base.

Flat tax. The most attractive characteristic of flat tax is single tax rate. All countries are using progressive income tax rate now, but if they turn to flat tax, they have to abandon current tax system and use single tax rate. Although real flat tax is for all tax base (from the first 1 yuan to the last one), every flat tax plan have a certain exemption no matter tax base is income or consumption. That is, zero tax rate will be applied to the tax base lower than limit, and single tax rate for all tax base higher than limit. That is why the plat tax actually has the progressive nature: average tax rate is increased with the increase of tax base. The progressive level depends on exemption and tax rate.

Then, why should we use flat tax? There are a lot reasons listed: flat tax could lead to economic growth; neutral effect on income distribution and easy to administrate. However, the most controversial issue of flat tax is whether it is neutral to income.

Consumption tax base. There seems no linkage between consumption tax base and the "flat" of flat tax. But for economist, the "flat" in consumption tax base means to tax consumption now and in the future, but it makes the consumption in the future more expensive because the interest of saving is also taxed.

Why should we tax consumption? There are a lot of reasons, mainly in 3 catalogs: (1) taxing consumption will encourage saving, investment and working. The tax base of current income tax system includes saving interest, investment revenue and labor, so it will have negative effect on saving, investment and working but consumption tax will not.

(2) Consumption tax is fairer than income tax. Consumption tax seems to be regressive which will make the tax burden of the poor heavier. But it might not be the case because the income in a certain year is not the best standard for welfare, the ratios of consumption to income of different persons varies a lot. It is obviously wrong to draw a conclusion that person with lower income has a higher consumption-income ratio or person with high income has a lower consumption-income ratio. Plus, in a life time, the present value of consumption must be equal to the present value of labor income and inherited fortune. So there actually is no big difference between consumption tax base and income tax base.

(3) It is much easier to calculate taxable income using consumption tax base than current income tax system, because it is not involved with capital income and much easier to execute consumption tax.

Clean tax base. The third characteristic of flat tax is clean tax base. The nature is to cancel all or most part of the intensive for certain consumption and investment. The aim is to widen the tax base, "clean the competition field," to neutralize the tax system, to make clean the tax base.

In current income tax, there are two reasons for messy tax base: the first one is uniqueness of capital income tax (for instant, it should not double tax capital income tax); the second is the tax intensive for certain expenditure and activity. These happen to be inefficient, unfair and complicated.

Base on the three characteristics above and Rabushka's speech of flat tax, it seems that we could find the conclusion: this plan is the fairest, most efficient, simplest and executable one among all public plans. There are countries try this new tax system since it is so good. Rabushka presented that Estonia, Latvija, Russia and Slovakia have already tried flat tax, and he suggested China to take flat tax sincerely. There also some people insist that China should try flat tax. I have several issues to talk about.

First, Hall and Rabushka analyzed the American tax system and brought forward tax innovation plan for the problems existed in it.

But after 20 years discussion in the US (not only academic, but business and in congress), there is still no decision to put it into practice. Why? And why all the countries taking flat tax are economic transform countries.

Second, the flat tax plan of Hall and Rabushka is for American federal tax system, and federal tax system only includes several taxes, most of which are income tax. But our tax system is an "all together" one, a unified tax system. If we take flat tax, should we apply it to only income tax or all taxes, only central taxes or both central and local taxes?

Third, Rabushka emphasized on "positive effect on investment" when he talked about "why should China take flat tax." However, in Chinese macro economy, government is always worried about efficient control of investment, especially when China plans to change economy growth style now, which depends too much on investment. How to solve this problem?

Forth, in the past 50 decades, tax is always the economy adjustment tool of government. Once we take flat tax system, how could we make the function of tax still work?

There might be more such problems. Obviously, flat tax system has both very good and bad sides. This is exactly why the flat tax idea gives us a great space of thinking.

Chapter 18

The US's Experience in Venture Capita

Mario W. Cardullo

Biography

Mario W. Cardullo is Counselor for Technology and Entrepreneurism, Office of the Under Secretary, International Trade Administration. US Department of Commerce. His experience as engineering and management professional specializing in technology management is considerable. Marlo Cardullo was chosen as one of the 100 technology leaders in the Commonwealth of Virginia (1997–1998). Mr. Cardullo is widely published (130 papers, books and articles) in the fields of management of technology (MOT), energy, and systems engineering. Mr. Cardullo serves as the Counselor, Technology and Entrepreneurism, to the Under Secretary of the Department of Commerce for the International Trade Administration. Mr. Cardullo has served as Senior Research Associate and Adjunct Professor of the Virginia Polytechnic Institute and State University in the Department of Industrial and Systems Engineering at the Northern Virginia Center and in the Pamplin College of Business for eleven years. At the Virginia Tech, he teaches the capstone course in the Master of Engineering Administration Program, developed, and teaches the Management of Technology course for the University and has taught the capstone in the MBA program, Strategic Management. Mr. Cardullo was a Visiting Fellow at the Economic Strategy Institute in Washington, DC where he completed a study of the impact of the internet on the automotive value chain entitled "From Push to Pull: Impact of the Internet on the Automobile Industry." This study covers from B2B through B2V (Internet vehicles). Mr. Cardullo held the position of Visiting Professor at the Polytechnic Institute of Dubai, UAE for three years and has been a guest Professor at Master of Science Finance Program at George Washington University. Mr. Cardullo has also been a Visiting Professor of the University of Texas at Austin IC2 Institute and where he taught Financing of New Ventures. Mario Cardullo is a Visiting Faculty at the RH Smith Business School of the University of Maryland where he teaches Globalization of Knowledge Management in the MBA program. Mr. Cardullo has also served as the Chairman of the Board of Advisors for PriceDrive, Inc, Champions (CSBR), and for VSE Corporation (VSEC).

Mr. Cardullo has been the founder or principal in a number of technology companies. Mr. Cardullo was instrumental in developing and merging SciCentral. com the premiere science and technology news site where he served as COO/CFO. The company was merged into to SciQuest.com, Inc. in February 2000 for public stock.

Mario Cardullo has also served as a technology advisor to the State Science and Technology Commission of the PRC through a contract with the US Department of Energy. He has served as consultant to information technology companies including technology strategy for BTG, the American Red Cross, the Japanese utility industry, US Department of Energy, Italian natural gas industry, International Energy Agency, and other major technology enterprises. He has served as the Vice President of the Energy Division of PCI, a consulting company, where he provided senior level support to the Office of Assistant Secretary for Fossil Energy of the US Department of Energy and other PCI clients. Before this position, Mr. Cardullo was a Director of TMS, Inc., another energy consulting firm. These positions required a detail understanding of the various energy systems under development and international economics. He planned and directed studies of the feasibility of transferring the technologies developed in the various fossil energy research and development programs to developing countries. He also directed and performed detailed analytical studies of technologies to determine the feasibility of using them to reduce the reliance of foreign petroleum imports during any potential disruption.

Before joining TMS, Mr. Cardullo was the President and Chief Executive of YND, Inc. a vertically integrated company that was funded to develop and market technological advanced products in the food service industry. Prior to forming and financing YND, Mr. Cardullo had spent twelve years with the US Department of Energy, where he had held senior positions in energy transportation, coal exports and had been the first director and organizer of the National Energy Information Center (NEIC).

Before joining DOE, Mr. Cardullo had been the President and Chief Executive of two high technology companies specializing in medical electronics, computer processing, technological development and venture capital. Mr. Cardullo also served as the president of Venture Management, Inc, a venture capital firm in joint venture with the Mexican Government in the industrial development area. As the Chief Executive Officer of Communication Services Corporation, Mr. Cardullo developed in 1970 one of the first digital systems for the use of standard telecommunication system for the acquisition and the computer processing of medical data. Mr. Cardullo is the inventor of one of the basic patents for the "RFID-TAG" devices (E-Zpass, Fast Toll, etc.). The "RFID-TAG" transponder invented by Mr. Cardullo was developed and built as an electronic license toll system in 1970. Prior to forming these companies, Mr. Cardullo was the first Planning Officer of the Communications Satellite Corporation (COMSAT), where one of his achievements was the conception of the Maritime and Mobile Communications Satellite Program (IMARSAT) and the highly successful Rescue Satellite System. The eight years prior to joining COMSAT, Mr. Cardullo was involved in liquid rocket propulsion R&D including the development of the variable thrust concept used by the Lunar Lander (LEM) and the variable thrust plug engine for the Lance missile system. Mr. Cardullo also served in the Apollo Program as the Senior Propulsion System Engineer for all aspects of liquid rocket propulsion from R&D to program management.

Mr. Cardullo holds BME, MME and MEA degrees and has done considerable doctoral studies at Polytechnic University (Brooklyn, NY), Steven's Institute of Technology (Hoboken, NJ), and MIT. He is a Registered Professional Engineer. He is an Associate Fellow of the AIAA, life senior member of the IEEE and holds patents in electronics and mechanical devices and systems. Mr. Cardullo during his career has published over 130 articles and papers in professional and technical journals. He is the author of the *Introduction to Managing Technology, Research Studies Press/John Wiley and Sons, ISBN 0 471 96787 4*, (1996). *Mr. Cardullo is the author of Technological Entrepreneurism: Enterprise Formation, Financing and Growth, Research Studies Press/Taylor & Francis, ISBN 0-86380-223-0* that was published in June 1999. He is a contributor to the IEEE/CRC *Handbook on Technology Management.* Mr. Cardullo was awarded the Bronze Medal for Outstanding Service from the US Department of Energy.

Speech

Today we are going to talk about Venture Capital in the US. You will see in the beginning. You have FFF and angels. What does that mean? FFF is founder, family and friend. Sometimes you also call it family, friends and fools. And then those are the money for starting a company in the US, coming from individual entrepreneurs. They take out their wallets, they take their credit cards and they get as much money from their credit cards as possible. They go and mortgage their house. Sometimes that ends up you are getting a divorce. But there were some risk and that is the C capital. And you notice when we are dealing with it here, debt. Most companies take 3 to 5 years to basically break even. Somebody has to give them money. And what happens is the money that the entrepreneurs originally invest is quickly used up.

The next important pieces are angels. Now angels are wealthy individuals, who are willing to invest money. Now, in many cultures, that investment cycle, they are angels who want to have control. That does not work. The angels should provide help money and help. It should be smart money, as we call it in business. Usually, ethically break-even but not always the case is when venture capital has entered the cycle. And it happens to have different stages, A, B, C or 1, 2, 3, investment just prior to merger and acquisition, or before IPO. And I will show you later most companies do not go IPO. Then you get the banks in. Banks are not a big player in the growth of companies because banks require collateral and there's nothing hypothetic or lend against. So, you know, an idea, who's going to give you money for an idea? So, that is the cycle I want you to keep in mind as we talk tonight.

Now, those of you who have probably taken Professor Liu's class know that asset classes that are used in portfolio theories. There is another one as we need that, would be art as new asset class. So I had the ability to invest in all of these and approved investor and institution investor would do all of these, to maximize return, minimize risk, using portfolio theory.

Now when we have been looking at this and I cheer for the US side working groups with the governments of the EU, with your own government which we had our first meeting today, with Australia, and we had one with her majesty's treasury in England. These are different definitions. And this is the real problem, because not everybody will say venture and really mean private equity buy-out. In the US, you see they have a different definition. And they do not consider venture capital as part of private equity cycle. Every academic I know, every European, mostly Asian, consider part of venture capital as a piece of the private equity market. Put in retrospect, for every dollar in venture worldwide, nine dollars are in buy-out and M&A deals and hedge funds. So, venture is really a small portion of the entire world market, but it has high leverage effect, but this is even further when you look at how the different groups look at it. Now what is happening is that the European venture capital association has started codifying the definition with the Asian venture capital association and more of the European subgroup within it, including the British BCA and the Australia. Only the US is out of the other step. Sorry to say, but that will change because of the developing company evaluation concept. We have talked about that further on. But I want you to understand that it has been different things to different people. And the SI is the strategic investors. Companies like Intel, Hp, and Microsoft invest also. They invest latest stage usually. Then you have IB and finally you find banks. There is something. So this is the complexity of it.

Now everybody thinks venture companies are big business, right? No. They are SMEs — small medium enterprises. And I will show you. This is a chart from 2002. This is the graph that shows the break-up. You noticed the majority of the companies are below 250 million dollars. You think it is a lot of money, but it is not. Remember, that is the money on the management. Companies work on somewhere between 175 and 250 basis points. Now let's say 250 bps. That means companies that are managing 100 million dollars only have how much revenue a year? Two million dollars! That is a mall business, isn't it? Banks manage billions because they are usually on 175 bps or less. And I will show you there are very few of there that are successful. They are only successful for the management of the venture capital companies, not for the investors or the companies they judge. And I now have data.

332 Realizing Rational Exuberance: An Appreciation

I will show you. There are only 74 companies that manage more than 1 billion dollars. Very small number of companies that are large, the majority and the large, they are not terribly large, maybe the large is only 355 people. It is a small business. And I will show you even further. I went back looked in for data for since 1980s and computed it the staff size of those companies. I just took the number of national BC association gives. Look at that. The average size of VC firms in US is 14 people. 14! No matter where you are, that is SME, that's a small medium enterprise. Now, that raised numbers of problems. Remember I said the corporation needs smart money. They need help and the money is part of it. Without the help, it is useless. And this amazes me, the absolute average size. And there is a reason for that. We will talk about it. And then I will show you the impact.

If you go back historically and look at how the revenue of the industry is, it is made of two portions: management fee and carried interests, which is a profit. Normally, a VC firm charges, let's say, 2 bps for managing. Secondly, they split the profit on 80 to 20. Basically what they do is they first return the capital at the end of the fund, then say hurdle rate of usually 8% by the average and they split it, 80% to the limited partners and 20% to general partners. If you compute this, for all these years, the big year with the bubble and the whole industry did less than Walt Disney did in 2002. WD is not doing well then. This shows that the industry is not at big as you think it is. And this is the US, which is the largest in the world. And I know it is hard for you to think. This is for all of us, who are students and I still think of myself as a student, even I did not teach in 15 years.

The fact is that we must be honest with ourselves. This shows what is happening in the industry. You can see the bubble in the growth of these companies. Remember I said it is unregulated. So it is easy to start a VC if you have people to give you money. But look at the average size. The average size starts to increase. And the number of companies is dropping. So the company is going to an average size of 1 billion dollars probably by 2010, which means bigger companies, which we say is consolidation of industry. For those of you who have studied industries that have grown and developed, road lines, banks, there is always a consolidation because there is not enough food in it. And this is what venture industry in US is.

60% of the people in a firm are principals or bosses, 40% are the workers or apprentices. Not everybody can be a boss, right? It just does not work. But this has an impact. We went back and we did a time survey of the companies and this is just average numbers. The principals spend 50% of the time looking for new money for the next fund. They spend 15% reviewing business plans, and smaller or larger amount managing their companies and working with assisting the portfolios. This has an impact. We went back and say, ok, how many business plans do you need per investment? It ranges between 300 and 500. And if you go back from 1980 to 2000, look at the range you get. That means for every business plan they get, they are spending an average of lees than a minute to a minute a quarter fro a business plan. That is real. Those are their numbers. I did not make them up. I calculate the numbers they gave me. It is something interesting. The venture capitalists, if you talk to a number of them, will say, oh, we do not really look at in great deal business plans that are coming over the transit. Business plans are sent in but do not waste our time. We look at business plans that basically come from people we trust, lawyers, other venture capitalists, our accountants. So how many good ideas must be omitted because there are not enough people to read their business plans? This is just simple mathematics. If we look at 200 bps, these are the IRRs (Internal Rate of Return), Right Here is what venture capital gets at 80–20 split. So actually they have to make more than 24% to double their fees. Look at what happens to the limited partners: This is Nasdaq 12 year's average. The venture capitalists are only working for fees. They are not working for the profit. And now they are starting to increase their fees for start-ups. Ladies and gentlemen, it is a very nice business, very happy to take 100 billion from everybody here or all of you, lock it up for 10 years, take 2% fee for 10 years. I end up with the money. I am not sure what you end up with.

So this is the Wilshire Consulting. This is what they showed us: Less venture capital, fewer firms, fewer sources of capital, increasing globalization, etc. This is a very important part. Now, one of my working groups, about 2 groups that collect data, and they went back, they went through the US for every new investment, at least new investment for 12 years, and they gave us quantitive data.

Summarize is this: This is the percentage close, the vintage year when the funds were put in; this is the percentage that went M&A; this is the percentage that went IPO. And that was left. And we call this the walking dead, the walking wounded. They are still in business. They have not got an exit. These are the successes. These are the, you know, you are happy to get rid of, the dwarfs. That is what we call it in business. This business has its own way of speaking. This is interesting, as many of you know that, by 5 years, 50% of the companies are gone. That has not changed. Look at the bubble. The bubble does affect that chart. Or all it did was to affect the number that died. If you did not have the bubble, they would just have gone M&A and it takes us almost 5 years to go to IPO. So when we went back on this, the bubble had little effect on industry efficiency: slightly change in companies closing. It is an inefficient industry by the way. Based on the estimates, the total performance is hilarious: cash-on-cash of between 0.85 and 1.34 for 10 years period. If you put some number to this and I have done this a couple of ways, the IRR is between losing 1.7% and gaining only 3%. The system is not efficient as it apparently structured in US. I am going to give an answer to how we make it efficient. And this is what I have been talking to your government about.

Now, here is the real numbers: between 1992 and 2004, 270 billion dollars have been invested in start-ups in US; 17,608 companies have received investment; 935 went IPOs, which is 8%; 36 billion dollars were invested or an average of 38.5 per company. So you have a lot of money if it goes IPOs. M&A went or sold 20 million dollars. The existing companies, for some reasons, 2500 companies was closed, 48 billion dollars was lost. Look at this. That is lost, ladies and gentlemen. And that is what really concerns the US government. 49 billion investments lost, half of them are from our pension funds. And half of that are from public pension funds. In the US, we guarantee the pension funds. The US government, as unregulated industry, yet pension funds' money is being lost. That is lot of money. And every country I have talked to who has followed our steps has lost billions of dollars: the Japanese over 10 billion; the French has lost almost 2 billion; the British have lost billions; the Chinese RMB, you lose many billions.

Now let's say this, the venture capital is against releasing their information. They do not like transparency. There is a very good reason. Now they are forced because we have a freedom of information acts in US that a company can sue a public company and say you have to release that information. So they put on their silence and I have all the data for every single fund and then I analyzed it: 19 billion was committed; 12.9 billion was put in; 8.2 billion was taken out. The remaining value which I doubt is true is 16 billion. Well, if we look at these numbers, this is an IRR of 4.4%. This is what actually comes out. If you weight it by the amount of each of the fund, the IRR is 2.43%. My initial analysis was 3%. This is one of the most well-knowledgeable investment groups that private equity that invests in venture and buy-out and all they did was 2.43%? I mean, if you put your money at a bank, you can make more thank this. So what is the US venture capital industry? It is fragment. There's no market share leader as I showed you. Companies that need to go to venture capitals in relation are SME. It is a gild. Returns may not match risks. We are going to talk more as we go through here.

So what are the other economies? Well, here is Europe. You see the bubble here too. It is small. They probably have less than 100 billion dollars under management. And by the way, because of the definition, most of this is not venture capital; they are mostly the buy-out funds, which they also call venture capital. And you can see this interesting data. In Europe, the institutional investors that invest the biggest chunk is banks; pension funds are in smaller portion, 16% and then you have everybody else, including government agencies. I questions for governments to do regulated investments. In the US, look at this, 58% are corporations. So it is a different mix. In Japan, it's mostly banks. Size of venture capital companies in Japan, remember this is in yen, is really tiny. No wonder they lost 10 billions dollars. We work also with Japan on this. They are great at technology but they are not so good in venture. Entrepreneurs, in a word, they do not understand. What start us on looking at this is data from US Venture Capital Association and European Venture Capital Association.

This is the US venture capital industry. Thank you.

Review

Liu Manhong

In his excellent presentation, Professor Mario Cardullo introduced the US's experiences in venture capital industry: from venture capital's deals screening, investing, exiting, to its key factors to secure a successful investment. He also explained venture capital operational mechanism in the US, and predicted the future trend of the industry. As Professor Martin Haemmig said, US venture capital runs "under the most desirable economy and the most desirable environment." It gave us some useful and valuable insights on how to develop China's venture capital in the future. I think Professor Cardullo's presentation has at least the following meaningful implications.

Firstly, at the early stage, especially the seed stage, enterprises usually seeking financing from their families, friends and "fools" (or founders themselves); this is also called the 3Fs (family, friends and fools), in addition, it also depends on angel financing. At this stage, venture capital seldom get in. For startup companies, including technological startup companies, 3Fs are still the most popular source of funding. This is a common phenomenon, not only applied to the US, but also to China.

Secondly, it is very important for us to study private equity, including venture capital as sources of entrepreneurial financing. Learning from the experiences of US's venture capital industry, we acknowledge that an active private equity industry plays an important role in promoting entrepreneurship, in addition to the strong R&D investment by big corporations and by government agencies. China's domestic venture capital industry has been basically led by the government and they were not very active in the past. However, it has become stronger and stronger in recent years due to the domestic stock market's recovery. In the past, because of the under developed regulations and the under performed domestic stock market, China's venture capital industry experienced a "two ends outside" situation: fund-raising and exiting are outside of China while investing and post-investment monitoring inside China. And this may be one of the reasons of relatively poor performance of the Chinese domestic venture capital industry. To further promote domestic venture capital industry, we should expand funding sources: allowing certain foreign financial institutions to enter the Chinese venture capital industry; developing an active domestic market; and strengthening the governance of venture capital and private equity management.

Thirdly, we should help the establishment and development of the venture capital institutions. Venture capital institutions are managers of venture capital financing; they are the intermediaries between venture capital investors and the startup companies. We need to actively support the development of venture capital institutions. In addition to government supported venture capital institutions, we also need to promote private venture capital firms and private venture capital market. At the same time, we should collaborate closely with foreign venture capital institutions; try to learn managerial skills and investment strategies from them. Meanwhile, if possible, we should also try to recruiter seasoned venture capital fund managers from foreign venture capital firms.

Fourthly, venture capital company's internal structure and mechanism are very unique. They tend to adopt a flat-management model as compared with the corporation type of management model. That is: in venture capital limited partnership firms, the number or partners is almost the same as their assistants. This structure provides some special services for venture capital investment; it may also present some problems. Under a typical corporation structure, company's board, CEO and other managers often appear to be in a pyramid-shape form. In contrast, venture capital limited partnership is usually different. It is may be because of the need of a practical, accurate and timely investment decision needed for the venture capital companies.

Lastly, venture capital funds are relatively small compared to that of the private equity and other types of capital. However, venture capital is crucial in promoting a country's hi-tech industry and therefore is very important to its economic development. From our country's national economic development perspective, we must learn from the US venture capital experiences as well as their lessons to promote the Chinese domestic venture capital market. At the same time, we need to construct a right venture capital infrastructure. We need also to recognize international trend of venture capital industry. Currently, venture capital goes global. Monetary capital, technology, human resources are all flowing between countries, and exiting through overseas market has become a norm in venture capital. The trend of globalization is becoming more obvious than ever. Therefore, we need to recognize the international venture capital trend and construct a health domestic venture capital industry accordingly.

This comment should be regarded as my personal point of view, hope it can stir further interests in this topic.

Chapter 19

The Issues on Corporate Governance Structure of Chinese Listed Firms

Bei Duoguang

Biography

Bei Duoguang is the Managing Director of China International Financial Corporation Limited and the Vice Chairman of the Investment Banking Committee of China Securities Industry Association. He is also the part-time Professor at Renmin University of China, Shanghai University of Finance and Economics and Dalian Institute of Advanced Executives. Mr. Bei got his B.A. degree in Economics in 1982 and Master's degree in Economics in 1985 from Shanghai University of Finance and Economics. In 1988, he received his Ph.D. degree in Economics from Renmin University of China.

Mr. Bei's academic field involves financial theory and policy, capital market and macroeconomics etc.. His representative academic papers include "Deposit structure, investment structure and financial structure" (*Economic Research Journal*, 10), "On the general balance of social capital flow" (*Economic Research Journal*, 9), "Social Capital Flow and development of capital market" (*Economic Research Journal*, 4), "An analysis of a new monetary phenomenon: The coexistence of external appreciation and domestic depreciation of RMB" (*Economic Research Journal*, 9) etc.. Due to his achievements he won the Sun Yefang Prize for Economics Paper in 1990.

Speech

I would like to give a speech on corporate governance structure of Chinese listed firms in the perspective of an observer in the (capital) market. Controversies have long been existing among governments, markets and intermediaries in terms of corporate governance structure, although it is a rather novel topic in China. Ten years ago, I was working at China Securities Regulatory Commission, when (CSRC) World Bank delegated me to investigate the development of China's capital market. In a meeting, an expert from World Bank asked me about my viewpoint on corporate governance of Chinese listed companies. I was stunned, since it was my first time to hear about corporate governance. Delightfully, in the past five or six years, corporate governance has received great concerns among Chinese scholars, practitioners and regulators. Besides piles of papers attributed by researchers, CSRC held a high-level, large-scale national conference discussing corporate governance of Chinese listed companies.

I learn that both scholars and practitioners show their interests in this issue in our country, and many listed companies have begun to transfer their focus to how to improve corporate governance structure. In my opinion, the corporate governance structure means how to realize the mutual balance among shareholders, directors and managers, given the conflicts of interest among them. On the one hand, a common and unified framework of supervision system should be established. On the other hand, investors and management should play different roles through executing their rights, fulfilling responsibilities and sharing profits, which will eventually form a healthy and harmonious institutional arrangement. Their common objective is to improve the core competitiveness of enterprises. I do not think there will be huge divergences about this understanding. The principle should be the same either in western countries where the issue is raised or in the countries that are in the transition from a planned economy to market economy.

For the same principle, however, the implementation is entirely different between the East and West, even within the Western countries. Compared with economics, the history of the introduction of this concept into China is rather short. Given this fact, we have to accept that there will be a long process through which such a principle becomes practicable and even longer to implement. Even in the UK and the US where corporate governance is frequently taken into consideration, their institutional arrangements are quite different. For example, in the UK, the chairman of the board and the CEO are two independent individuals, while in the US they are usually held by one person. We can argue about which paradigm is better, but from this we can see that the institutional arrangement can be greatly divergent in the guidance of a universally acknowledged theory. The arrangement seems even more unique in China. According to the corporate law of China, the chairman of the board is the so-called legal representative and CEO is the executive of business who take charge of the day-to-day operation. The requirements asked Chinese listed companies to separate the positions of chairman of the board and CEO, but this arrangement is rather superficial. All stated-owned enterprises in China have a (Chinese Communist) Party Committee by which all decisions are made and checked, thus making it even more difficult to reach a balance. This mechanism cannot be reformed in a short term. It is hard to imagine that the concepts and approaches from the western country such as the UK and the US could bring about the expected effects in China.

In the past, we were happy to see the reformation of state-owned enterprises by involving them in the capital markets. However, in a rather long period of time, even till today, the state-owned shares are still dominant among others. Consequently, the reformation did not change the situation that controlling shareholders expropriated the benefits of minority shareholders and the management expropriated those of stock shareholders. To make improvement, the independent directors were introduced, though accompanied with controversy on its effectiveness. CSRC insisted Chinese listed firms having at least two or three independent directors. According to the updated requirements, at least one-third of the board should be comprised of independent directors. The introduction of independent directors appears to be a great progress in corporate governance in China and a good signal to capital markets. But if we review its practical effects as an important institutional arrangement, I wonder whether it actually represents the interests of minority shareholders as we expected. It is well-known that in China, the management holds the power to appoint independent directors, so the independent directors only care about whether they will be re-nominated rather than whether they have effectively monitored the management. Will the independent directors actually represent the interests of minority shareholders? As a matter of fact, the independent director system does not work perfectly in other countries as well. Some literature shows that there are many problems unresolved as to the source of independent directors in the US firms, and it has always been a shortage of the qualified independent director supply. Let me give a simple case to show how the independent director system works in China. One financial institution is now being asked to elect independent directors to meet the one-third-of-board requirement. The management will appoint independent directors who are in favor of them in case that the management has great divergence with shareholders in decision making. They can deny any proposal or decision made by the shareholders even with the presence of independent directors who account for one-third of the board. This is very paradoxical. So it is still a challenge how to improve the independent director system in today's China and it is of course not overcome in a short term.

The third point is related to the so-called shareholder interests *vis-a-vis* stakeholder interests. About five or six years ago, the CSRC called a meeting on corporate governance and intended to improve corporate governance of Chinese listed firms. On that meeting, the CSRC required firms to maintain the objective of "maximizing shareholders' value." But in practice it is far from simple as we imagined. The stated-owned enterprises follow the principle of "maximizing the shareholder's value" and leave aside nonperforming assets and others in order to go public overseas. And among those that have been left aside are a great number of jobless employees. In the Annual Conference of the National People's Congress of China, Premier Wen

Jiabao particularly emphasized that the government should take into account the employees' interests in the reformation of state-owned enterprises. How to protect their interests is a serious issue.

In addition, enterprises are always facing serious environmental problems in daily operation. The so-called "externalities" are now becoming a big challenge to economic development in China. In fact, environmental problems are related to how to protect public interests during the growth of enterprises. It is a critical problem that whether public interests are satisfied while shareholder's interests are met. Here I can give you a concrete case to illustrate this dilemma. There is a state-owned enterprise called Huayuan Group which expanded very fast in the beginning but is now at the edge of bankruptcy and insolvency. Ironically, its shareholders said they did not worry about its bankruptcy and they felt satisfied with its performance. Through further investigation, you'll find that the dividends distributed to shareholders are borrowed from banks with a high interest rate. Although the company will go bankruptcy, its shareholders can still get a dividend of 15% annually. Shareholder's interests were satisfied but creditors' interests are trampled. It can be seen from the above case that to simply emphasize shareholders' interests is not enough. About five or six years ago, China followed American to lay our focus on "maximizing stakeholders' value," which has actually come into being for a long time. From my point of view, in China's economic and social circumstances, it's important to consider the balance of interest among all parties, such as environment, employees and creditors. These are connected with society, economy and culture in this or that way and cannot be improved in a short term. Accordingly, the establishment of credit culture, the concept of protecting employees' interests and the further recognition of environmental problems are all long-term phenomena in China.

Of course a more serious problem about corporate governance is that it is closely related to and actually restrained by social governance. In other words, the paradigms of social governance will determine the corporate governance. The issue has been already raised by many scholars and I will not discuss it here in specific. A report from the Asian Corporate Governance Association shows that corporate governance of Indonesia and China are the worst two in 2004. The issues about China's corporate governance are worth thinking about carefully. It reminds us that these problems cannot be resolved in a short time and we have to undergo a gradual, long and historical process.

We are talking about corporate governance issue here since it is one of the key factors in determining the development of capital markets. In fact, if we look back, we will find that this issue is not raised from the perspective of the growth of enterprise but from the development of capital markets. Some Chinese listed firms did not perform well in capital markets because of their poor corporate governance. That's why corporate governance issues are raised. Given the improvement of corporate governance is a long process; we should understand better how capital markets developed. Let us review the history of those developed markets. The US capital market in the 1970s is similar to China's capital market nowadays. That is, the New York Stock Exchange, established in 1792, has been developing for 180 years to reach the level of ours today. The US capital market is not the only one that lacks risk control of investment banks and security companies, and there was no efficient corporate governance system in the early stage to restrain listed companies from rampant insider trading. Insider trading is rampant in Belgium even in 1990s and its laws did not put many restrictions on insider trading. There are a lot of irregularities in 1990s and the maturity of the capital market would be a long process. I think the following six aspects are critical if we hope to make our capital markets mature.

Firstly, a mature capital market must have an effective judicial system without which capital markets would seem to have been established on the sands. An effective judicial system will make different decisions to different companies based on specific cases. In China, a typical situation is that the government require all companies, either well-performed or bad-performed, to give social investors certain compensation to make up for the loss due to the market fluctuation in the past. In a mature market with an effective judicial system, bad companies deserve punishment while good companies should get rewarded. In the United States the investors could protect themselves from being expropriated by the insider mainly through class action. If some companies in the United States are in troubles, such as Worldcom, Enron etc., their minority shareholders can join together to get back their compensation through effective justice.

Secondly, the maturity of capital markets depends on the open media and free press. Without them, capital markets cannot be well supervised. The supervisory job to the capital market in China is now only taken by regulation authorities. However, effective supervision should be social supervision which is implemented mainly by the media (for example, following Berne Convention in America). The function of media is not just to praise promising firms but to discover problems and disclose the dark side of Chinese listed companies. Only through powerful press supervision can the market correct its errors. We still have a long way to go in this aspect.

As for regulation, we need to pay special attention to law enforcement in Chinese capital market. Recently the supervision authorities of China put forward a slogan, that is, "to pursue development through establishment of standards and to pursue establishment of standards through development." What on earth are we striving for? Development or establishment of standards? We are not taken by surprise that more violation cases are discovered in a bull market and less are disclosed in a bear market. As a matter of fact, while the market is inactive, a large number of insiders trading are taking place. This reflects that the targets of the regulatory policy of the government are uncertain and swinging between development and establishment of standards. I do not think this is solely caused by the nonfeasance of the supervision authorities themselves. In fact, its occurrence is related with the social circumstances which cannot be changed overnight.

Forthly, the market maturity relies on the presence of a large number of professional intermediaries. Frankly speaking, the professional accomplishment of intermediaries in China such as lawyers, accountants, investment banks and rating agencies are of low quality in comparison with those in the developed countries.

The maturity of market also needs mature investors. The power of institutional investors is relatively weak in China, but the numerous retail investors believe that the risks they face will eventually been undertaken by institutions, companies or even the government. This subconsciousness would accordingly make retail investors' moral hazard problem more serious. We would never expect that the market would be very mature unless investors also become mature.

Finally, as mentioned above, the most important thing is to have healthy corporate governance for Chinese listed firms.

To conclude, we need to emphasize both corporate governance and the development of capital markets. However, we should not expect that the market could become mature overnight, since this process needs efforts of one generation after another. When we have established long-term, historical notion and strategies, our policies and actions will be more appropriate. Therefore we need a road map to achieve the goal, avoiding "rash advance" and impetuous mistakes.

Review

Zheng Zhigang

Zheng Zhigang is Associate Professor in Finance at School of Finance, Renmin University of China since 2006. He received his Ph.D. in Economics from Guanghua School of Management, Peking University in 2003. His dissertation "The Conflict of Interests among Investors and the Integration of Corporation Governance Mechanisms" gained the second annual Mundell–Huang Prize in Economics, which is nominated by 1999 Nobel Laureate Robert Mundell and Chinese famous economist Huang Da and granted as the Best Ph.D. Thesis, Peking University. He did research as a visiting scholar at UCLA Economics Department from April 2007 to April 2008.

Dr. Zheng's research interests involve corporate governance, the theory of the firm, corporate finance and financial development. Up to now, he has published dozens of academic articles in the top Chinese journals such as *Economic Research Journal and China Economic Quarterly*. He also serves as academic referee to *Economic Research Journal, China Economic Quarterly*, and *Quarterly Journal of Finance*.

Corporate governance is originally supposed to address the conflicts of interest between investors and the management in modern corporations. An important theme of corporate governance is to ensure the accountability of investors in modern corporations through mechanisms that try to reduce or eliminate the principal-agent problem. Although it has been of concern as early as ninety thirtieth, for example, Berle and Means (1932), not until recent twenty years has corporate governance become an independent branch of finance. Especially after the frauds at Enron, Worldcom and Global Crossing, corporate governance began to attract the world's attention. According to Rajan and Zingales (2003), "the recent scandals show that even in the most developed market economy, there is still a long way to go to improve the corporate governance of its firms."

Except for this, the huge economic and social costs resulting from unsatisfactory corporate governance of emerging markets arouse the special interest of theorists over the world. La Porta, Lopez de Silanes, and Shleifer (1999) and Johnson *et al.* (2000) find that, in emerging markets with less efficient legal investor protection, controlling shareholders expropriate dispersed investors by tunneling through pyramidal corporation groups. In some markets, the agency problem between controlling and dispersed shareholders is more serious than that between investors and management, which is traditionally regarded as the principle conflict in corporations. Claessens, Djankov and Lang (2000) particularly emphasize that, with highly dispersed ownership structure, it is rather rare for US firms to face interest conflicts among investors; consequently, academics need to collect evidence from countries and areas outside the US to study the agency problem among shareholders rather and its resolving approaches.

It was not very long before the concept and practice of corporate governance was introduced into China. On the one hand, the subject of corporate governance is comparatively novel to both international and domestic academics; on the other, the practice of which keeps putting forward topics in need of further study. Such reasons make corporate governance one of the most active field in corporate finance and microeconomics.

In his speech, Professor Bei discussed corporate governance in five aspects based on the reality of China's capital market, which propose significant and fundamental suggestions to the governance improvement of Chinese listed firms.

First, Professor Bei pointed out that "mature capital markets must have an effective judicial system, without which capital markets would seem to have been established on the sands." This is in accordance with the findings of "law and finance" literature developed in 1990s (see Zheng, 2007a, for a simple literature review). According to LLSV (1998, 2000), better investor protection results in financial development, such as broader and more valuable capital markets, faster speed of going public, and a more dispersed ownership structure. A country's legal origin is an important determinant among others on protecting outside investors from being expropriated by insiders. To be specific, the common law countries are generally superior in protecting dispersed shareholders than civil law countries. In the world of civil law, countries with German legal origin do better than those with the French legal origin and the Nordic legal origin. Demetriades (2004) further documents that only if financial system takes root in a sound institutional framework can financial development greatly promote economic growth. The sound framework includes the respect for property rights, transparent accounting and information disclosure system where contracts can be enforced at a low cost, and the regulation system that protects consumers' interest and encourage competition. Claessens and Laeven (2001) find that the differences between legal frameworks not only affect the amount of available external financing but also the proportion allocated to different nature of assets. In countries with inadequate protective provisions for property rights and weak law enforcement, the scale of capital market is small, and the proportion invested in intangible assets is negligible in comparison to that of its counterpart — fixed assets.

Second, Bei's view of "the maturity of capital markets relies on the open media and free press system, without which capital markets cannot be well supervised" is in line with the recent propositions which emphasize the role of extra-legal institutions in corporate governance, such as media (see Zheng, 2007b for a simple literature review). According to Dyck and Zingales (2004), the mechanism through which media affects corporate governance is to affect the reputation of board directors and politicians (thereby make amendment or promote enforcement of the Company Law). They further (2004) indicate that among various extra-law institutions (competition, average newspaper circulation, tax compliance, social norms, etc.), the effect of public opinion pressure is significant. Countries with high newspaper circulation usually have a low private benefit of control. Based on Russia's data, Dyck, Volchkova and Zingales (2008) empirically shows that increasing media coverage will reduce violations in corporate governance.

Third, the size, composition and function of the board will affect the effectiveness of corporate governance. Theoretically, the board is a platform for outside investors to monitor and restrain the management, which is even considered as the core of modern corporate governance mechanism by Hermalin and Weisbach (1998). In search of an optimized "core," Jensen (1993) suggests a small-sized board mainly consisting of outside directors with CEO, the only internal director. However, as is mentioned by Professor Bei in his speech, there is a huge gap between the theoretical and practical image. In practice, the board independence is promoted by China Securities Regulatory Commission as one of the key measures to estimate the quality of corporate governance of China's listed companies. While theoretically, a number of empirical studies find this relationship statistically insignificant. Many cross-country empirical studies provide the similar evidence.

The reason of this huge gap is now a hotspot to academics in corporate governance. Here are some arguments among others. Some scholars believe it is the institutional defects of the director's election procedure that prevent theoretical suggestions into practice. For example, in some countries, CEO plays an important role in renominating and reappointing a director. The desires for good compensation, reputation and social communication, which is accompanied with renomination in the next board election, drive directors cater to the CEO instead of supervising him or her. Ironically, a director with a "reputation" of "enjoy challenging CEO" will have to face an embarrassing situation of being unwelcome to every company. Thus, supervising becomes an ambiguous obligation of board members, and they are inclined to compromise with the management. As is pointed out by Bebchuk and Fried (2003), although the board is regarded as a potential instrument to resolve the agency problems, it becomes a part of the agency problem itself. Moreover, some scholars believe that having independent directors is originally meant to send positive signals of corporate governance to the capital market; however, it will eventually lead to signal convergence and lose the signaling function of the board independence originally supposed as today's by law coerces all corporations into conforming this policy.

We are really confused by the current governance system that some board directors will be appointed to replace the manager who is involved in scandals in Chinese listed companies, instead of taking responsibility for their supervisory negligence. Consequently, board directors prefer to monitor the management after violating regulations rather than setting precautions to them. We have to say that this is attributed to the institutional defects of the non-market-election procedure of directors under the current paradigm of state-held and state-owned assets management.

Forth, Professor Bei laid stress on the importance of professional intermediaries in improving corporate governance. In particular, we emphasize the important role of institutional investors. It is widely accepted that the introduction of strategic investors would reform the current corporate governance system of Chinese listed firms in that, unlike dispersed shareholders who often take free ride with rational ignorance, as active major shareholders, strategic investors have greater incentive to supervise the management and prevent controlling shareholders from expropriating shareholders' interest via related transactions. As a result, it protects minority shareholders' interest. In particular, the shared-control theory developed by Bolton and Thadden (1998), Pagano and Roell (1998), documents that the introduction of active major shareholder will facilitate resolving the agency problem both between managers and investors and among investors themselves. This theory has important policy implications for China in terms of resolving the unique-major-shareholder problem, and the interest conflicts among investors.

Finally, as to the stakeholders, Professor Bei indicates that an efficient corporate governance system should take into consideration the interest of stakeholder, including creditors and employees. In his speech, he particularly cited a case to illustrate that a mechanism that only satisfy shareholders does not mean the improvement of corporate governance. From the case, however, we can learn that this is a typical fraud in which the management violates the fundamental principle of information disclosure, rather than the conflict of interests among shareholders, creditors and employees. When the dividend goes to as high as 15%, which is obviously unsustainable and eventually did their wealth a lot of harm in the long run, a rational shareholder will either sell off the shares in capital market as so-called "voting by foot," or replace the manager by calling an extraordinary shareholder meeting, in accordance with the Company Law or corporate charters. In this sense, the above stakeholders have the interest in common.

Why do we here put stress on shareholders' value orientation in corporate governance instead of the stakeholders' value orientation? Just because the mechanism to protect the right of creditors and employees is significantly different from that of investors. Creditors and employees will obtain the contract revenue in the distribution of enterprise residue, and they can ensure their basic rights by defining them in the contract (for example, there will be some provisions in the contracts that creditors can claim a compensation for certain possible changes of government's regulation policy; or the labor union in western countries will play a key role in striving for contracts in favor of employees). However, investors own residual claim based on limited liability; that is, they get the surplus (loss) after having distributed the contract revenue. As a consequence, without effective corporate governance, investors will face the risk of losing their investment, for they cannot ask for a fixed return through contracts or collateralize certain assets beforehand as creditors did.

If we follow the principle of stakeholder's value orientation rather than shareholder's in corporate governance practice (for instance, firms have managers to be responsible for all stakeholders and stakeholders share corporate control), the management will be confused by conflicts of interest among stakeholders, thereby making less efficient decisions. Moreover, it will be difficult to restrain managers from harming the interest of some stakeholders in the name of protecting others' (for instance, enterprises may increase the price in the name of protecting the interest of employees, and eventually harm others' interest such as consumers). Therefore, either managerial agency or controlling shareholder's tunneling, the logical starting point of corporate governance is to protect the interest of minority shareholders. In some sense, we should not accuse the companies (as micro-agents) as well as their corporate governance of ignoring the protection of employee's interest in case of high unemployment rate or human resource allocation inefficiency brought about by the labor unions.

In current corporate governance practice of Chinese listed companies, an inevitable problem that Professor Bei did not mention in his speech is how to improve the market which makes takeover a powerful threat to ineffectively governed corporations. This problem has become even more urgent after the shareholding-split reform of Chinese listed companies. Some papers show that the agency cost will be greatly mitigated through integration of external governance mechanisms (such as the takeover market and product market competition etc.) and internal corporate governance mechanisms (such as the introduction of institutional investor etc.). This will facilitate achieving the objective of corporate governance; that is, suppliers of the capital market could assure themselves of getting back their investment as well as a reasonable return on time.

References

Berle, AA and GC Means (1932) *The Modern Corporation and Private Property.* London: Macmillan.

Bebchuk, LA and JM Fried (2003) Executive compensation as an agency problem. *Journal of Economic Perspectives*, 17, 71–92.

Bolton, P and Thadden Ernst-ludwig Von (1998) Blocks, liquidity, and corporate control. *The Journal of Finance*, 1–25.

Claessens, S, S Djankov and L Lang (2000) The separation of ownership and control in east asian corporations. *Journal of Financial Economics*, 58 (6), 81–112.

Dyck, A and L Zingales (2002) The corporate governance role of the media. NBER Working Paper.

Dyck, A and L Zingales (2004) Private benefits of control: An international comparison. *The Journal of Finance*, 2, 537–600.

Dyck, A, N Volchkova and L Zingales (2006) The corporate governance role of the media: Evidence from Russia. NBER Working Paper.

Jensen, MC (1993) The modern industrial revolution, exit, and the failure of internal control systems. *The Journal of Finance*, 831–880.

Johnson, S, R La Porta, Florencio Lopez-de-silanes and A Shleifer (2000) Tunneling. *American Economic Review*, 90(2), 22–27.

Hermalin, BE and MS Weisbach (1998) Endogenously chosen boards of directors and their monitoring of the CEO. *American Economic Review*, 88, 96–118.

La Porta, R Lopez-de-silanes, Florencio S Andrei and V Robert (1998) Law and finance. *Journal of Political Economy*, 106, 1113–1155.

La Porta, R Lopez-de-silanes, Florencio and S Andrei (1999) Corporate ownership around the world. *Journal of Finance*, 54(2), 471–517.

La Porta, R Lopez-de-silanes, Florencio S Andrei and V Robert (2000) Investor protection and corporate governance. *Journal of Financial Economics*, 58, 3–27.

Pagano, M and R Ailsa (1998) The choice of stock ownership structure: Agency costs, monitoring, and the decision to go public. *Quarterly Journal of Economics*, 187–225.

Rajan, RG and L Zingales (2003) *Saving Capitalism From the Capitalists: Unleashing the Power of Financial Markets to Create Wealth and Spread Opportunity.* Crown Business, Random House.

Shleifer, A and RW Vishny (1997) A survey of corporate governance. *Journal of Finance*, 737–783.

Zheng Z (2007a) The determinants of financial development — A literature review. *Management World*, 3.

Zheng Z (2007b) The corporate governance role of extra-legal institutions — A literature review. *Management World*, 9.

Chapter 20

Thinking of the Management Strategy of the Financial Holding Company

Xie Jianping

Biography

Xie Jianping graduated from Kent State University and obtained a Ph.D. in Finance. He taught in Cleveland State University and now he is Professor of Finance in National Chengchi University In Taiwan. Professor Xie Jianping is accomplished in modern financial theory, with over 30 academic papers and popular finance textbooks. Besides, Professor Xie Jianping actively participated in financial practices. He was a member of renovation group of Ministry of Finance in Taiwan, general manager in Chung Hsing Securities Company, and now he is executive vice president of the biggest financial holding company in Taiwan, the Mega Holdings.

Speech

- The trend of financial mixed operation
- Financial environment and challenges in the future

- Strategy choice according to financial industry's possible future
- Reasoning and case study of value creation in financial holding companies

It is my honor to give a lecture in Renmin University of China. I will try to combine my lecture with my experience in Mega Holdings. I am working in Mega Holdings in Taiwan, which is a pretty big financial holding company with subsidiaries including banks, insurance companies and security companies, and we have a great track record so far.

About 200 years ago, there were not many financial practitioners and most of them were Jews. That is because the Jews only believed in the Old Testament while the others believed in the New Testament which denies debt and credit. However finance has become one of the most important industries nowadays. The appearance of financial holding companies is a new characteristic of financial development.

In a broad sense, financial industry includes commercial banks, investment banks, bill finance, insurance, etc. For quite a long time, the US insisted the firewall concept, or the divided operation, because during the financial storm from 1929 to 1933, stock operations in banks brought great risk to the whole banking industry. However, mixed operation in banks became legal again in the US in 1998, largely due to the fierce competition in financial industry. In Europe, universal banks are allowed and that means they can do all business. In face of the fierce competition in so huge a market in Europe, the US resorted to the mixed operation again.

Taiwan faces the same situation. When I was a member of financial renovation group in Taiwan, we discussed three possible development reform modes. The first is financial holding, which means a holding company can have subsidiary companies operating different business and offering clients total solution to satisfy client companies' different needs in its birth, growth, financing, company separation, merger, etc. The first mode is generally a US mode. The second is investment shifting, which is now in practice in Taiwan and Korea. Investment shifting means financial institutions can invest in other business without establishing a holding company. The third is generally a European mode, or universal bank mode, which means banks can do all kinds of business. Taiwan chose the first mode because it meets Chinese tradition better. With the holing company established, subsidiary companies joining in can keep their former chairmen or general managers, maintaining the original personnel. However, the financial holing company mode may bring risk control problems and without proper supervision it may cast great impact on the financial system. Cross-subsidy is one of the operations which may produce risk. Cross-subsidy means the holding company sacrifices some of its subsidiary companies to benefit some other subsidiaries. For example, if a security company of Mega Holdings bids for a client's stock underwriting, the holding company may force one of its subsidiary banks to provide large loans or low-interest loans to the client in exchange, which may negatively influence the subsidiary bank's profit. Besides, too many loans to a single client company can greatly raise the bank's risk level. Ministry of Finance in Taiwan takes the supervision of financial holding companies quite seriously and a new Financial Supervisory Commission will be founded in June (2004), with different departments responsible for bank, security and insurance supervision.

Now I would like to talk about the trend of mixed operation of the financial industry. We can take the Citigroup as an example. All the subsidiary companies of Citigroup are listed together and this is an outstanding example of financial holding companies. The Citigroup's product line mainly includes the following parts. The first part is global consumer banking, which includes private banking, credit card, mortgage loan, etc. Consumer banking was not valued highly enough, but it has expanded greatly. Another part of the product line is called asset management, which means banks operate clients' asset according to clients' requirements or attitude toward risk. And corporate banking is also part of the core business of banks. Corporate banking involves huge loan scale but it also means lower interest rate. Corporate banking includes giving loans or services to help client companies get listed, issue corporate bonds, etc. The ability to create derivative financial products such as forward, swap, and inverse floaters is crucial for corporate banking. In 2002, consumer banking took 60% of Citigroup's core income, and the percentages for corporate banking, asset management and insurance are 22%, 18%, and 6% respectively. The percentage of consumer banking has become a measurement for financial holding companies because the consumer banking business has bigger interest spread, lower risk than other business, which makes its income sound and stable. Wealth management is a very promising part of consumer banking. Banks provide asset management and financial advisory to clients and earn the wealth management fee.

It is very lucky of you to be finance major because the financial industry is a promising industry. However, you need always to be modest and maintain your investment idea and attitude.

If the bad debt is well under control, we can believe that a financial holding company with higher percentage of consumer banking and more fee income has a higher value. Shinsei Bank was the 7th biggest bank in Japan. After Shinsei Bank claimed bankruptcy, the Japanese government handled the bad debt and sold the bank to foreigners, forming a new bank with 60% shares held by foreign investors. I want to introduce this bank to you because the bank shifted its main business to consumer banking and turned out to be quite successful. In Japan, banks have become a close part of everyday life.

In the future big financial institutions may probably become bigger and provide more business services while small institutions become more focused on what they are good at. The expansion of big financial institutions can bring lower cost, and shifting of small institutions can help them find their own way to survive fierce competition.

Standards used to measure an international financial institution includes bad debt ratio, transparency, financial strength, credit, scale, risk control, etc.

The shift from an old financial institution to a new one means the change in operating strategy. Old financial institutions mainly focus on deposit and loans to expand business scale while new financial institutions focus on how to provide better and more services to clients. Capital structure should be changed. According to the New

Basel Agreement, the scale of a bank's business should be limited by its capital. Besides, operating mode, credit technology and marketing also need to be improved to face the new challenges.

There is a principle called 8–2 principle in finance, contending that 20% of all the clients bring 80% of profit, so more services should be provided to the 20% of clients who bring 80% of our profit. Hence, product line familiarity and client analysis can help maximize shareholder value.

For the time being, venture capital, retail asset management, retail brokerage, institutional retail brokerage, corporate banking, offshore banking, private banking are some of the most attracting and promising product lines. Some of the product lines gain poor profit because of over entrance and fierce competition. According to specific customer needs, the banking service can be divided into liability management service and asset management service.

Now let us have a brief view at the value generation model of financial holding companies. Financial holding companies have higher value firstly because the holding company can unite subsidiary companies so as to reduce cost and reach economy of scale. Secondly, skill transfer and skill building can improve all the subsidiary companies' business skills and experience. Besides, with the holding company established, financing ability of subsidiary companies gets improved. All the aspects add to the value of holding company.

In face of the future financial environment and challenges, we should be aware that foreign institutions will come to domestic financial market competition sooner or later. This is true for both Taiwan and Mainland China. Domestic financial institutions have their own advantages such as capital, scale, etc. Competition will surely bring some impact to the domestic financial institutions but only with completion can the financial industry develop healthily.

Another trend of future financial industry is that private assets will gradually turn to funds or annuity products, and asset portfolio will become more international, bringing new opportunities to financial industry. As domestic financial business gets more globalized, the competition will become fiercer. The domestic financial market should aim at raising strength from personnel, resource and business level as well as reducing financial risk through internal risk control.

Generally speaking, I think financial holding company is only a transition from traditional bank to universal bank. We should create a mechanism to retain talents, improve management skills and increase product selling opportunities. In other words, gaining comprehensive strength is the only way to face future challenges and competition.

Review

Qu Qiang

In the recent years, the obvious trend of getting more integrated is gradually formed in the financial industry and financial holding company is a typical example. Taiwan joined in the trend since the year 2000 and Mainland China should take some of the experiences and lessons. We are honored having Mr. Xie Jianping give us a lecture on this topic. Mr. Xie Jianping studied and taught in the US in his early years and then he returned to Taiwan to teach and do business. Now he is executive vice president of the biggest financial holding company in Taiwan, the Mega Holdings. He has deep understanding of financial theory and practical experience; moreover, he also took part in the financial reform of Taiwan. Due to limited time, the lecture is not fully unfolded. However, the specific operating strategy of mixed operation and the analysis of future trend have left us deep impression. I hereby add a brief introduction to the background of international financial industry integration, in order to remind everybody that different nations have their own standpoint though mixed operation does exist in international financial industry.

Theoretically speaking, mixed operation in financial market has its intrinsic motivation. For example, it can reduce cost, realize economy of scale and economy of scope, raise industry entry threshold, prevent potential competition, etc. Besides, in the 1990s, external conditions such as IT technology revolution, loosened government regulation and international economy and finance integration stimulated the intrinsic motivations into practice.

The trend of financial integration originated in the UK and the US, and spread to other nations in Europe and Asia. Because of the influence of historical politics and the overreacting of the government after the Great Depression, the American banking system is made up of large number of small size banks, which is not an ideal banking industry organizational structure. The American banking system keeps reforming. In 1986, the limit to open new subsidiary banks was released; in 1994, the the limit for banks to operate across states was relaxed and henceforth brought large number of bank industry mergers and acquisitions with the start of Citi Corp. and Travelers Group merger in 1998; in 1999, Gramm–Leach–Bliley Financial Services Modernization Act was enacted. The American financial industry integration is profit and market oriented, and it is similar for Europe. In face of the capital market impact, the traditional bank based financial system strengthened the universal banking system by all means. It was more complicated in Asia. For example, in 1998 a financial reform called "Tokyo Big Bang" created four big financial groups (including Mizuho, Sumitomo Mitsui,

UFJ and Tokyo-Mitsubishi) in Japan. However this was not actually an active motion to meet the international integration trend but a government-lead bank restructure after the double impact of Japanese asset bubble and 1997 Asia financial crisis. The banks hoped to help each other within one group but their performance was not satisfactory even after the restructure. Taiwan's situation is more or less between the US and Japan because there is both internal needs and external pressure. In the 1990s, Taiwan applied financial deregulation policy by loosening the restriction on the foundation of new banks and new branch banks, but it lead to rapid increase in bank numbers, malicious competition and cumulated system risk. So, the Financial Holding Company Act enacted in 2001 is the requirement of both international trend and internal financial system restructure.

So, we should realize the intrinsic motivation of financial holding companies because it is the future trend. At the same time, we should study the specific background of the reforming nations and analyze the risk and return before we learn from them because this determines the time and mode of China's financial reform.

Index